COMMAND INFLUENCE

COMMAND INFLUENCE

A story of Korea and
the politics of injustice

Robert A. Shaines

Outskirts Press, Inc.
Denver, Colorado

ACKNOWLEDGEMENTS

Thanks to the following:

To my loving wife, Denise, who proofed, advised, and encouraged me to complete this book and told me when I should make the story more interesting.

To my daughter, Pamela Ikegami, for proofreading and helping me to lay out my story.

To my buddy, Larry P. McManus, for his encouragement and advice and his positive critical reviews.

To my assistant, Eileen Fraser, for helping me to organize this book for publication and coming through with help at every phase of production of the manuscript.

To Pat Lynch for her encouragement and suggestions.

To all of those brave men who gave their all in the "Korean Police Action;" and to those

Graybeards who carry memories within their hearts today; and

In memory of Lieutenant George C. Schreiber, may he rest in peace.

Foreword

BY ADMIRAL GEORGE E.R.KINNEAR II

THIS COMPELLING STORY of Lt. George C. Schreiber's encounter with the military legal system during the Korean War provides a penetrating look into a lamentable time when politics, bias and personal opinion combined in the form of command influence to subvert justice.

Schreiber, by all accounts a fine young man and an exemplary officer, was caught in a web when he was charged with the premeditated murder of a Korean civilian and found guilty by court martial. Robert Shaines, then a relatively inexperienced young Air Force JAG officer, was unable, despite his best efforts, to prevent his client from being victimized, leaving his life in ruins.

Now, more than 50 years later, after long reflection and with the experience, knowledge and maturity gained through a distinguished career as a practicing attorney, Shaines recounts the entire episode with clarity, insight and objectivity.

Shaines' meticulously researched, thoroughly documented firsthand account provides a eye-opening look into the wholesale problems that permeated the military justice system at that time, and even exposes senior officers who, sometimes as a result of incompetence and often for purposes of personal gain, allowed them to go unchecked.

It's a fascinating story long overdue in the telling, and richly rewarding to any reader who values the truth…however painful or damning it might be.

Dr. George E.R. Kinnear II is a retired Admiral of the US Navy, He served as the Chairman of the Retired Officer's Association (now MOAA); Interim President of the University of New Hampshire; and Corporate Senior Vice President of Grumman Aerospace Corporation. Dr. Kinnear served on various boards, including Compaq Computer Corporation, the Aerospace Corporation and Precision Standard Corporation. Dr. Kinnear received his Ph.D. (Engineering Management) and MS (Industrial Engineering) from Stanford University. He is one of the four members of the Kindal Associates of Portsmouth New Hampshire.

Admiral Kinnear commanded the Naval Air Force U.S. Atlantic Fleet and served as the U.S. member of the NATO Military Committee in Brussels. He has personally flown aircraft ranging from yesteryear's propeller-driven biplanes to today's F-18 fighter jet. He has the distinction of flying four different jet aircraft in combat during Vietnam and the propeller driven AD during the Korean War. He has logged more than 5,000 pilot flying hours and more than 950 carrier landings.

Author's Comments

The Schreiber, Toth, and Kinder murder charges were initiated under the 1951 version of the Uniform Code of Military Justice. The American Articles of War and the Articles for the Government of the Navy predated the Constitution and the Declaration of Independence. These Articles were based on the 1774 British Articles of War. They remained essentially unchanged through the First World War. Up until World War I, the United States maintained a small standing army and navy, so there was no call to change the long-standing system of military justice in the United States. Those entering the armed forces as volunteers understood that they would live under a different standard of justice than the civilian population.

In World War II, there were more than sixteen million citizens serving in the armed forces, most of whom were not volunteers but were drafted as citizen-soldiers. In World War II, there were approximately two million courts-martial during the war years. There were more than sixty general courts-martial convictions for each day until the peace treaties were signed. There were eighty thousand felony convictions during the war by military courts. Many of those convicted of offenses by courts-martial were citizen-soldiers and sailors who resented the way that military and naval courts were controlled by the commanders, often allowing command influence to run rampant in such proceedings. Almost every safeguard of the Constitution was eviscerated in the armed forces. After the end of the war, several organizations concerned about justice for our military personnel lobbied Congress to make improvements to the system. Congressional hearings were held and led by the American Legion and the American Bar Association. The Uniform Code of Military Justice (UCMJ) became the military's criminal code, effective in 1951. The Manual for Courts-Martial (MCM), 1951, was published and distributed throughout the armed forces as an executive order. The Code has been amended several times since then, and there have been several versions of the MCM published, the latest being in 2008. There have also been significant changes, such as the establishment of an independent judiciary of military judges, the use of the Federal Rules of Evidence, the establishment of military judges and the establishment of the Court of Appeals for the Armed Forces with civilian appellate judges. There will soon be the right to appeal to the U.S. Supreme Court from the military courts. While this now exists only when the Court of Appeals for the Armed Forces refers such a case, it will exist as of right within the next year.

The Uniform Code of Military Justice (UCMJ is implemented through Executive Orders of the President, pursuant to his authority under Article 36 of the UCMJ, 10 U.S. Code Section 836. These Executive Orders form the Manual for Courts-Martial. Each branch of the armed forces has established voluminous regulations under the Secretaries of the various military services further implementing the Executive Orders, such as Air Force Instruction 51-201, Administration of Military Justice.

While I have been harsh and critical of the administration of military justice in the Air Force in 1952 and 1953, I am aware that Congress and the military judge advocates themselves were aware of the shortcomings of the new Code of Military Justice and its implementation, coupled with the evils of command influence over the system of courts-martial. Commencing in the early 1960s, Congress was lobbied by The American Legion, the American Bar Association and the Judge Advocates of the armed forces to make improvements to the system, and amendments to both the UCMJ and the Manual for Courts-Martial were promulgated in 1963 and periodically thereafter. Today UCMJ and the Manual for Courts-Martial are works in progress, allowing military law today to be as fair and Constitutional as is feasible when put against the precept of maintaining good order and discipline.

The preamble to the Manual for Courts-Martial reads:

"The purpose of military law is to promote justice, to assist in maintaining good order and discipline in the armed forces, to promote efficiency and effectiveness in the military establishment, and thereby to strengthen the national security of the United States."

On November 22, 2000, the United States Congress enacted the Military Extraterritorial Jurisdiction Act of 2000. because of the constitutional constraints identified by the Supreme Court. That Act provides for jurisdiction over civilians employed by or accompanying the armed forces overseas and over former members of the armed services who were separated from active duty and who attained civilian status without being prosecuted for offenses committed while on active duty and subject to court-martial. The Act is limited to offenses punishable by imprisonment for more than one year.

Table of Contents

Daffodils of the Sea

I am an ever tragic bird.

I am wandering in a dark cave and a deep valley.

Hit by a wave, my soul cannot fly.

The sky is torn and the earth is divided.

My soul has been wandering for half a century.

My wounds have not yet healed over the many years.

Time has passed, but nothing seems resolved.

I wish I could see eternity.

I hope our dearest wish can move the heavens,

And the heavens send us fresh spring water and peaceful doves.

—Seo Young-sun, a bereaved family member of Ganghwa Massacre victims Truth and Reconciliation Commission (South Korea). This poem was released by The Truth and Reconciliation Commission.

Korean Papa-san, man of wisdom, 1953

PROLOGUE
Reflections

HOW DID GEORGE C. Schreiber, a twenty-five--year-old second lieutenant, get caught up in a series of events that would ultimately involve the governor of the state of Illinois, the attorney general of the state of Illinois, the president of the United States, the judge advocate general of the Air Force, the chief of staff of the Air Force, the Supreme Court of the United States, U.S. senators and congressmen, major newspapers, and thousands of people in his home state of Illinois? This same young officer had been a fifth- and sixth-grade teacher and a village recreational director employed by the Board of Education, District 95 in Brookfield, Illinois, until June of 1951, when he enlisted in the United States Air Force as a staff sergeant assigned to Officer Candidate School at Lackland Air Force Base, Texas. Upon graduation and receipt of his commission as a second lieutenant, he was assigned to Air Police School at Tyndall Air Force Base, Florida, from which he graduated in March of 1952. In August, he was sent to Korea to be the officer in charge of an Air Police guard unit at the 543rd Ammunition Supply Squadron located near Pusan, South Korea. Within a year, he was to stand convicted by a general court-martial of premeditated murder.

It all made no sense to me then, and now, almost 57 years later, it begins to become clear. Both Schreiber and I were really pawns in a power game among ambitious and vindictive men, eager to please those whom they felt could advance their military careers. The alleged murder by Schreiber was, in my opinion, the result of a young airman's indifferent and poorly conceived action. This action resulted in the death of a man who no one knew and who ultimately would be described as an Oriental male with no known name and no family to ever come forward and claim his remains – a man who some clever assistant staff judge advocate would, for the purposes of the military justice system, call "Bang Soon Kil."

When Airman Thomas Kinder came home to the United States, he had pangs of conscience that he had taken the life of an unknown Oriental man in the course of his service as an Air Police guard in South Korea. He confided his troubles in his mother, who in turn communicated her son's story to the Office of the Chief of Staff of the United States Air Force. The result was a reopened investigation into the events leading up to the killing by Kinder and his conviction by a military court for the murder, as well as the arrest and trial of Lieutenant George C. Schreiber and the attempted arrest and prosecution of former Airman First Class Robert W. Toth.

The distance of time, experience, and a studied revisit of the facts and events lead me to see more clearly what was not visible or otherwise discernable to me as a twenty-three-year-old Air Force lawyer in South Korea in 1953. This story has haunted my thoughts ever since, and this effort to revisit and tell the story is a vindication of conscience on my part – the result of a late-life effort to understand what happened that year in the war-ravaged country of South Korea.

Some of the events, which I now better understand, have become clarified by the tempering of my understanding of human nature after almost sixty years of being a lawyer and by the process of maturation. These are the stories of several good and patriotic men who felt they were doing their respective duties to God and country. The victims were a couple of otherwise dedicated but naive and trusting young men who happened to be fellow officers at a time and place that shaped their characters and lives. George Schreiber was one, and I was the other. We were both victims in our own ways.

CHAPTER 1
Arriving in Korea

IT WAS ABOUT as cold as it gets. I was raised in New Hampshire, so sub-zero temperatures were not strange or difficult for me. In fact, I was fond of cold weather, as opposed to hot and sultry weather. But there was something uncommonly cold about being in the steel innards of an old landing craft, called an "LST," off the South Korean coast in the middle of a war as midnight approached. Maybe it was the sense of peril. Maybe it was the dampness and cold in the empty, steel-hulled vessel or the below-zero temperature mixed with the darkness, dampness, and apprehension of danger awaiting us. Was it the loneliness, the feeling of fear, the sense that we were not in control of our destiny and safety? Or was it that, in regard to both clothing and arms, we were poorly equipped to enter a war zone?

There were twelve hundred men on that vessel, and the silence was so overbearing that if someone coughed, everyone jumped. Our private thoughts overwhelmed our bodies and nervous systems. The ceaseless "chug a chug" of the diesel engines drummed away in our ears like a form of water torture accompanying the numbing cold, the diesel fumes, the fear, and the exhaustion. Sleep would have been welcome, but there was only the cavernous, empty steel deck, which radiated the damp cold, and it would have been miserable to lie upon.

We had left the warm, benign weather of South Texas four weeks ago. We were equipped with only summer uniforms, as the new Air Force was not immune to the well-founded stories of military bureaucratic foul-ups. The wing had been destined to go to a base in the south of France. But our orders and mission had been changed at the last possible minute. Our wing, the 75th Air Depot Wing, was rerouted to the Korean War Zone thanks to a change in orders in late November of 1952. The war in Korea had not eased, and the thought of an early armistice appeared misguided. The powers that guided us in Washington had different plans for us.

Our ordeal lasted through the day and into the night. We had just taken a two-day leave in Japan after our ship docked at Yokohama. We all knew that our brief time of rest and revelry would be our last for a while. But after the relative comfort of the troop ship with regular meals and a lot of time for rest, we were not ready to experience more than twenty-four hours with no food, little water, no rest, and an abundance of discomfort, hunger, and thirst.

Finally, just after midnight on New Year's Eve 1952, we arrived at Chinhae, South Korea. Hungry, lonely, numbed by the cold, and almost dispirited, we arrived at K-10, which was to be the headquarters of the 75th Air Depot Wing. It was a bleak place, with water on two sides, a plain on one side, and mountains a few miles distant. Those mountains would prove to be deadly to some pilots who failed to heed the warnings of our base operations officer. We soon learned that every air base in South Korea was designated with the letter "K" followed by a number. Some of us, over the course of our stay in this country, would become very familiar with most of them. Others would know only the place where they disembarked and nowhere else, ever after.

I will tell this story, which may read like fiction, from my perspective as a twenty-three-year-old first lieutenant in the United States Air Force Judge Advocate General's Corps. Lest you confuse that with the Adjutant General. I will quickly point out that there is a definite distinction between the two. The JAG, as the Judge Advocate General's

Corp is known in military parlance, is the legal branch of the Air Force; the Adjutants were, in essence, the administrative folks who did most of the work relating to human relations (called "personnel office" in the service), accounting, payroll, and other tasks of that nature.

This is a story of politics, intrigue, mystery, and skullduggery worthy of the best works of fiction. It is the story of the vanity of a few, the dedication of some, and the indifference of most others. In other words, it is a story of modern civilization set in a place of horror and deprivation, which is how I remember war-ravaged South Korea in 1953.

After we disembarked on that New Year's Eve, sloshed through a four-foot depth of freezing surf, and waded ashore, we began to set up our base. The place had served as a prisoner of war camp for Allied prisoners of the Japanese Army during World War II. Many of the guards who had served in the Japanese Army here were cruel Koreans. The base was the recent home of a South African Air Force Squadron of P-51 fighter planes, which were part of the United Nations Air Forces during the early part of the Korean war effort by the UN. On the one hand, the South Africans were glad to see us. But they were also very glad to be out of that rat-infested piece of turf that had served as a landing strip and place to sleep for them.

My best pal was Warren Mengis, a former Marine corporal from Opelousas, Louisiana, who was smart enough to go to Tulane Law School on the GI bill, but unlucky enough to enlist in the Air Force Reserve and get himself activated to serve in Korea. My boss, Major Charlie Weir, was from Oklahoma, but had migrated to Texas after World War II. He had decided on an Air Force career as a military lawyer. Together, we were to be the lawyers for almost four thousand men.

The 75th Air Depot Wing, in running the Air Force supply and materials facility in Korea, was responsible for equipping the entire 5th Air Force, which was the combat Air Force in Korea for the United

States' version of the United Nations forces. It took a lot of manpower to handle the guns, bombs, and ammunition. In fact, in order to obtain volunteers to man the ammunition-supply depots in Korea, the Air Force made a deal with its stateside offenders serving time in military prisons and stockades. If they would volunteer for such duty, their sentences would be remitted. And if they served honorably in Korea, their sentences in most instances would be commuted upon return to the States. That's the military equivalent of a pardon. So, at that time, it was, "Let's clean out the stockades and ship the poor bastards to Korea. And if they survive, then we'll let them serve out their time and give them an honorable or a general discharge. If they don't make it, at least it won't be a good guy who 'got it.'" In other words, "the brass" thought of these men as expendable.

Nobody ever said war was easy, but this wasn't even designated as a war – even though we, as a nation, lost about thirty-eight thousand souls killed in action and innumerable wounded and MIA. It was as deadly as the "war" in Vietnam. Perhaps because it came so close on the heels of the Second World War and because there was a prevailing thought that the war in Europe and the Far East had been the war to end all wars, our war was termed a "police action" in support of a United Nations resolution. But hour by hour and day by day, it was deadlier to our troops than each of the Second World War and Vietnam. A lot more were killed and wounded in Korea in far fewer years than in the war in Vietnam.

During the Korean War, formerly known as the "Korean police action," an interesting and unusual event occurred, presaging the type of international and interservice cooperation that was to become routine years later. In 1951, 1952, and 1953, it just wasn't fashionable for one branch of the armed forces to cooperate with another. In those days, interservice rivalry was the norm.

At that time, I was a young lieutenant in the United States Air Force. I had recently graduated from law school and was that rarest of law-school students – an ROTC-distinguished military cadet. That designation entitled me to a commission as a regular Air Force officer as opposed to a reserve commission. However, being a law-school graduate and also having passed the Massachusetts bar examination while I was still in school entitled me to apply for a commission as a first lieutenant in the Judge Advocate General's Corps of the Air Force instead of going on active duty as a second lieutenant. In those days, the Massachusetts Board of Bar Overseers permitted certain second-year law students to take the bar examination as a practice exercise. But if you passed, they continued to process the successful applicants for admission to practice law. I passed.

I then set out to secure an assignment with the Air Force JAG Corps. How I got the job is another story. I was accepted and assigned to the JAG Staff Officer Course, which was a part of the Air Command and Staff School at the Air University at Maxwell Air Force Base in Montgomery, Alabama. As an adventurous young man, I felt that the switch from deployment in France to Korea was a great opportunity for adventure.

My friend Warren Mengis kept telling me that I must have had a mental defect of some kind to be quite so cheerful about our assignment. Warren rarely used profanity and was an avid reader of Shakespeare. As a result, he had a knack for being derogatory and insulting in the kindest, yet most forceful way that I had ever experienced. Usually, this was accompanied by some reference to the fact that I was a "Yankee," said in a smooth, educated kind of Southern drawl. He left off the term "damned" when using that epithet. Since the 75th ADW was comprised of men from Texas, Louisiana, and Oklahoma along with a few of us "carpetbaggers" from the North, I soon learned that most Southerners regarded the term "Yankee" as derogatory. These guys regarded themselves as Southerners, rebels to the core. Before this, I thought that being a "Yankee" was a complimentary term.

Warren was also my mentor when it came to things military. Even though I was a distinguished ROTC cadet at both the University of New Hampshire and Boston University School of Law, I soon came to believe that an ex-Marine was the best expert on things involving the military. It was on this basis that I readily accepted Warren's version of truth on all sorts of subjects, whether the lack of adequate clothing, food, or shelter, or the fact that we had to equip the wing law office with furniture made of empty packing crates. "Quit your bitching. This is a war," became his routine words to me.

While he wasn't my bunkmate, hut mate, or tent mate, Warren became my mentor, my opponent in numerous courts-martial, and my friend. Warren was a tall, lanky Louisiana lad who had grown up in what he called "hard-shell Baptist country." Much to the chagrin of his family, he had thrown off the image to become a free thinker of sorts and a devout Catholic. He was a rebel in the South at a time when it wasn't fashionable to be one. He was that rarest of all Southerners of the time – a liberal without any pretense of racist thoughts. He valued every man, whether black or white and from whatever ethnic or religious background. That wasn't really surprising to me since, at the time, I was not really acquainted with the typical Southern mentality. I would soon become much more educated in that regard thanks to my friend. Later on, Warren represented the Catholic bishop of Baton Rouge in the integration of the parochial schools of the diocese long before such integration became fashionable. I well remember a visit in New Hampshire from him years after Korea, with his admonition after expressing his thoughts on integration, "If I talked this way back home, they would hang me from the nearest tree." He was a role model for me.

Having been an Eagle Scout, I had no trouble foraging for a cot and a place to sleep soon after coming ashore. While it was bitter cold, windy, and damned inhospitable, I saw that if I picked up a cot and a sleeping bag and selected a hut with a stove, I could spend a comfortable night. So, with the expert guidance of my friend Warren, my own eagerness, winter camping experience, and sheer exhaustion, a well-earned night's sleep was available.

In the morning, I awoke to the sounds of sobbing and cursing. The medical people had been drafted directly from civilian life and had been given an extremely abbreviated version of basic training. This did little more than teach them how to salute – not even who or when to salute. My awakening had come courtesy of two of these doctors who had been sitting on a crate and huddled against the cold all night, unable to adapt or set up a place to sleep. They had stayed awake all night gently sobbing. At dawn, one was actually wailing, "I am going to call my congressman. This is cruel and inhumane. We are doctors and officers here against our will, and we demand that we be treated as such." There was to be no comfort for them, as they would learn since it was a war zone and things were not meant to be nice and comfortable. There were no servants for the doctors. They had to take care of themselves, like the rest of us. Warren's only comment was, "I hate people who start bitching before they have had a good cup of coffee." He carried with him some good old Louisiana chicory coffee.

Of course, the weather that day was bad for flying, and the only food in the mess hall was powdered eggs, pork stew in a can, and canned hamburger meat, probably left over from the Second World War. I actually was quite fond of powdered eggs, and my food preferences became the subject of much good-natured ribbing. I also liked the C-rations – those packages of canned food that you could throw into boiling water or put on or into a fire before opening with a knife, a screwdriver, or a little can opener that was provided with each packet of food and which was destined to cut open each hand before the contents were accessed. You ate this stuff right out of the can, and it could be anything from beef stew to spaghetti to peaches or plums. In any event, I thrived on such stuff, much to the amazement of my more seasoned fellow officers. At least it provided them with some opportunity for a joke in an otherwise not-so-funny place. With all that said, my solution for the ailing doctors was to bring them each a slice of bread with peanut butter and jelly that I had scrounged from the mess sergeant. I then invited them to join us for some of the chicory coffee that Warren carried with him. All in all, I think this was probably one of the first real breakthroughs in interdisciplinary cooperation between the medical and legal professions.

After a few days elapsed, things sort of settled down. Quarters were found for everybody. The mess halls were functioning. The sun came out, and the booze supply for the officers' club arrived. We had a lousy selection of food, but a great selection of liquor. In my naivety, I happened to express that opinion in the club bar one night and damned near started a riot. Most of the officers in the wing headquarters had served in the "big war," and their priorities were well established. It was better to be well watered than well fed in the 75th. After an absence of alcohol on the ship one officer committed suicide and another tried it after a going on a drunken binge after arriving in Korea. I had no real experience with alcoholics and drinking up to that time and was soon educated as to how big a part alcohol was in some people's lives.

This takes me back to another episode in my worldly and my military education. We boarded a ship, the USMS *General Gordon*, at Corpus Christi, Texas, for our trip to Korea. USMS stood for United States Maritime Service. The USS *General Gordon* was a former Presidential Lines cruise ship that had been federalized by the U.S. Navy for use as a troop carrier in the Korean "police action." It was manned by a Navy crew. As you may know, unlike the British Navy or any other civilized navy, the United States Navy has a rule banning alcoholic beverages of any kind aboard a naval vessel, the only exception being for medicinal purposes. Not having had any history with alcohol, this meant little to me. However, this was not the case with most of the senior officers of the wing. Bear in mind that the cadre of the 75th included members of the Texas Air Force Reserve Wing that had been called to active duty. The Texans were a proud and hard-drinking lot. They even bragged about it. This was especially true of our most-senior officers, who could not let a day go by without the imbibing of alcoholic spirits.

When we boarded the *General Gordon*, we were assigned bunks according to rank. It went like this – there were about forty-five hundred enlisted men and officers, maybe two hundred fifty of these officers and the remainder enlisted men. The ship was divided in half. The lower half of the ship was for the enlisted men. This consisted of the holds, where bunks were set up five on top of each other, and a portion of the lower deck so that the lower ranks could get some fresh air on what was to be a one-month sea journey. I was to later joke with some Navy friends that I had more sea duty than they did. The officers had the staterooms, with varying degrees of population density. The second lieutenants, of which there were few, bunked about fourteen to a room. The first lieutenants, among whom I fit in, had twelve to a room. Compared with the enlisted men's quarters, this was downright luxurious. The holds smelled of urine, sweat, feces, and diesel fumes all of the time.

We were assigned a locker apiece in our quarters, which is where we stored our gear. One in our midst was the son-in-law of one of the senior officers, a man of intelligence with a dire need for booze. This lieutenant colonel, being an officer of considerable experience and wit, had brought aboard a case of White Horse Scotch whiskey. Not wanting to offend our Navy hosts and also not wanting to be denied the cocktail hour with his peers, he arranged with his son-in-law, a first lieutenant, to stash the booze in our stateroom. The son-in-law, being of junior rank and wishing to accommodate his father-in-law, stashed at least one bottle of Scotch whiskey in every locker in our stateroom. Of course, old dad paid a daily visit to see how the boys were doing and to resupply what came to be known as "the senior officers' cocktail hour." This included officers of the rank of major and above. These "troops" all had above-deck staterooms. Majors shared quarters with one other major, and lieutenant colonels and higher ranks had private quarters. All in all, the ship was arranged very democratically, following the old military adage —"RHIP", or "rank has its privilege."

As luck would have it, one of the sailors on board smelled alcohol on the breath of one of the senior officers. He then reported that the medical personnel – meaning the Air Force doctors, who had their own staterooms – were into the booze. The medical officers were billeted right next to the first lieutenants' quarters. Well, the inevitable happened. There was a shakedown inspection to search for contraband, otherwise known as booze. The searchers were a Navy chief petty officer, two sailors, and none other than the colonel in command of the headquarters group, who had buried some of his own whiskey in our stateroom. I'll never forget the look on the face of the young sailor when he pulled the first white container of White Horse Scotch out of the first locker and then, one by one, assembled several such containers on the deck, as the floor of the stateroom was called. There was a lot of coughing and backing away as each locker was searched. The colonel demanded to know in each instance, "Whose locker is this?" I stood there, gently shaking my head to signal to my confederates in this wretched scheme to say nothing. Being a bright bunch of young men, they got my message very quickly. As the only lawyer in the stateroom, I became of elevated in stature among my peers. We all remained silent throughout the search and, afterward, during the "investigation."

Warren was seasick for most of the sea voyage, and he was in a different stateroom from me. Every officer had taken at least one course on the Uniform Code of Military Justice and was, or should have been, aware of the fact that no one needed to say or admit anything so as not to incriminate oneself. Adhering to the premise that we could be of greater service to God and country if we weren't convicted of a military offense at sea, we agreed to be of one mind – and that was to keep our mouths shut, say nothing, and admit nothing.

After repeated attempts at intimidation by the good Colonel McShane, the Air Base Group commander, I spoke up and reminded him that he would blow whatever case he thought he had if he persisted in badgering us to speak, because we all had a right to keep silent and not incriminate ourselves. With a scowl and a muttered statement that I was too damned smart for my own good, he ordered the assemblage to stand at attention. He then wheeled about, told us that we were confined to our quarters, and left with the sailors carrying the evidence trailing him. Figuring that we didn't need to stand at attention any longer and peeking to see if he was out of earshot, the room exploded with laughter, recriminations, curses, and questions.

When things died down, I advised the group on our legal rights. The first of these was the reminder against the need to incriminate oneself, and the second was the right to counsel of their choice. I became the choice of the group as legal defense counsel, then advised the group that I believed that it was okay to go to the head, which is what the Navy called its toilets. That being done, we refused entry to our quarters to the assembling curiosity-seekers and well-wishers hovering at our door. I told them that we were conducting consultations with legal counsel, which indeed we were. One of the first inquirers was the father-in-law of the guy who planted the booze in all of our lockers, namely the lieutenant colonel who carried the stuff aboard the ship with his son-in-law. He was concerned that, "The bastards got it all, huh?" Of course, the colonel was also one of his nightly drinking buddies, and we knew it. The wing commander was also a confirmed alcoholic and was dead drunk much of the time.

I guess the senior officers missed their cocktail party that night. In fact, it got so bad that one of the poor guys shot himself after a few days without a drink available to him. He was buried at sea. Booze, or the lack of it, does that to some people. At mess time, we all appeared in the wardroom for dinner, and no one said a word despite our having been confined to quarters. I guess they figured that no one was going anywhere since we were two thousand miles at sea in the middle of the Pacific Ocean.

That evening, my boss, Charlie Weir, showed up and asked to talk to me. He had moist eyes and said, "Bob, just tell me you are innocent, and I'll move heaven and hell for you," or words to that effect. So I looked him straight in the eye and said, "Charlie, I'm innocent. Just ask that bastard Colonel Miller, the father-in-law." Later that night, my boss returned to advise that the wing commander, after meeting with the ship's captain, had preferred charges against all twelve of us and that an investigating officer would be appointed to carry out an Article 32 investigation. In every serious case in the military, there must be such an inquiry by an impartial officer. This officer replaces the civilian grand jury that determines if there is sufficient evidence to warrant a trial when one is accused of a crime. Since all of the accused, as we were called, were officers, the commanding officer of the wing said we would have to be tried by general court-martial and that such a trial would take place at sea aboard the ship. This was good news to me, since I knew damned well that he was an alcoholic and one of the nightly party participants. I then passed the word that we wanted the investigating officer to take sworn statements from every senior Air Force officer on board the ship as to who owned the whiskey, who brought it aboard, etc. Charlie, who was my boss and the senior legal officer of the wing, was my means of delivering this information to the higher authorities. We all agreed that we would remain silent since we could not be compelled to say anything. Thus, there was a dilemma for the senior officers. They must decide whether to lose face with the Navy, commit perjury, or admit that they had blown it and that we were not guilty of any provable offense.

The investigation took place the next day. We were called in, one by one, by the investigating officer and asked if we wanted to make a statement. We all said "no," relying on our rights against self-incrimination. In addition, everyone said that they appointed me as their legal counsel. I said I wanted Charlie as mine, knowing full well that he could not be. Warren was the only other lawyer on board, and he was so seasick the entire time that he was medically not available for duty.

The investigating officer, in addition to being Charlie's best friend, was a very astute fellow and told the senior officers that if things progressed any further, we intended to prefer charges against most of them, including the wing commander, the air base group commander, and the father-in-law, Lieutenant Colonel Miller. In the military, anyone on active duty has the right to be the accuser against any other member of the military, regardless of rank.

Early the next day, Charlie sought me out and told me that the investigation had concluded. The investigating officer had recommended to the convening authority, who was the wing commander in this case, that the charges be dropped. This was not an unexpected reaction, as far as I was concerned – I knew we had them by the proverbial short hairs. So we were told that we were to appear at an appointed time and place later that morning to receive non-judicial punishment, which was to be administered by the wing commander. Anyone in the service has the right to demand trial by a court-martial and does not have to accept non-judicial punishment. The reason for the rule is that it can ruin a military career once it appears on the record of any officer. After consultation with my clients, I advised Charlie that such a course was not acceptable. Within a matter of minutes, the word came back that the wing commander wanted to have a group chat to speak with us, and that he had abandoned all thought of any formal action of any kind since we all demanded to be tried by court-martial rather than undergo non-judicial punishment. Plus, I passed the word up that I intended to depose every senior officer aboard, including the Navy officers.

We appeared en masse to meet with our erstwhile leader. The entire time I served in the 75th, he always looked drunk to me, and this morning was no exception. The session took place in a stateroom. We all stood at attention as the colonel told us that he thought we were too dammed smart for our own good and other similar vignettes, all the while glaring through his glassy eyes at me. At this time, on the table there were several cartons of the sort in which the White Horse Scotch was packaged. As the final act of this counseling session, the colonel went to an adjacent porthole, opened it, and with great ceremony picked up each carton and flung it out. As he did this, the wind blew each of the containers high into the sky. There was a gagging as we all tried not to laugh, but I couldn't contain it, and the place went hysterical. That night, the father-in-law verified to us that the boxes were empty and the cocktail parties were back in business. That, plus my winning a wallet in the Christmas Eve bingo game, were the highlights of my voyage to Korea.

I have included a letter dated January 9, 1953, from Warren Mengis to his parents in which he describes our journey from Texas to Korea, but does not stress his constant sickness at sea.

Warren Mengis, Charlie Weir & Bob Shaines

Lt. W. L. Mengis, AO 224 900 6
Hg. Sq. 75th Air Base gp.
A.P.O 970 % P.M
San Francisco, Calif.

Korea,
21 Jan '53.

Dear Mom & Dad,

This is the first time that I have been able to latch on to a typewriter...sure feels good not to have to scratch out a letter. Guess I'm just allergic to writing "by hand". Dad, I got your letter yesterday, and it was the first letter I had received in 10 days from anyone...I was beginning to think that all my relatives had writer's cramp. Still haven't heard a word from Luther since my arrival in Korea. He is extremely busy, I know, but I'm going to 'scortch' him nevertheless unless he writes pretty soon.

I, too, came down with a touch of flu and was confined to the hospital for several days. What a pain in the neck. The hospital facilities are alright, but being confined with nothing to do is downright irksome. Fortunately, my case was mild...temperature around 100° for one day only with nausea and headache for several days. I'm feeling O.K. now and am back at work...although confidentially there's not much work to do. Spent all day yesterday reading Shakespeare. As a matter of fact I'm getting disgustingly cultured!

We also had a USO show here Monday, which helped to break up the monotony. No big names, but it wasn't bad at all...lot of laughs; little singing, little dancing, little acrobatic work, and lots of jokes. It was doubly appreciated in view of the fact that we have no moving pictures over here, or other entertainment of any kind.

Since I don't know when I'll be able to get hold of this typewriter again, here are the highlights of my trip over — some of which I have already mentioned. We boarded ship about 6 a.m. on the 5th of December at Corpus Christie, after a four hour ride down from San Antone by bus. The ship was the USNS W. H. Gordon, a 17,000 ton troop carrier. My quarters, with 9 other first lieutenants, was just about amidship on A deck (one deck below the Prom Deck), and they were very comfortable.... we had very nice bunks, with mattresses, blankets, sheets, pillows, etc. We raised anchor about 4 p.m. that afternoon and it took about an hour and a half to get out of the channel at Corpus and out into the Gulf. That night everything was very calm, but the next day we ran into some swells that put quite a few of the boys over the side or in the latrine. I felt a little "queasy", but that's all. On the third day out the weather got quite rough as we ran into a little storm...it was warm by this time... and the compartments where the men slept were quite hot and smelly, which caused quite a bit of seasickness. This was the only serious threat I had... but found that when I hit the sack everything was O.K., so I spend the third day in the sack except for meals.

-1-

01-21-1953 letter Warren Mengis to mom & dad-pg1

On the fourth day the weather was nice again and we got into Panama that morning. Since we had priority as a troop ship, we went right on by Coco Sola into the bay and on to the locks. Before reaching the locks there is a stretch of what appears to be a Bayou with overhanging jungle, birds, etc. Actually, I guess it is a very deep canal, although it is not built up on the sides. The hills seem to jump out of the ground in that part of the country...saw a very pretty waterfall before reaching the first locks. Everyone was amazed by the density of the jungle. The locks were the least interesting part of the passage, I thought, even though mechanically they are something to marvel about. We couldn't see much of the troop accomodations down there, but what we saw looked pretty good. There sure was a nice golf course on the right of the first locks. Next we went on into the lake which connects the two locks, and it was really beautiful. Water was very blue. The locks on the Pacific side (called Mira Flores I believe) were about the same. As soon as we got through, we docked at Rodman Naval Base and about 8 p.m. I managed to get off the ship with the other officers. All enlisted personnel went off first, but there wasn't much for them to do. As soon as I got to the Officer's Club I tried to call Chris...what a mess! I called every operator I could think of; ended up with about six different numbers; and tried them all one at a time until I finally got Chris about an hour and a half later...and then I couldn't hear him because by this time allthe officers were drunk and raising hell. He and Marie drove over from the Atlantic side with Robbie, however, and we spent about an hour together before it was time for me to report back to the ship.

At 8 a.m. we left Panama and started up the coast line of Central America. This went on for about four or five days, with fair weather, until we reached a point somewhere around the U.S.--Mexico boarder, and then we angled out into the Pacific in a northern circle around the Hawaiin Islands. From this point on we had one storm after another, some of which got so bad no one could go out on deck for fear of being thrown overboard...I never felt wind so strong before in all my life...it would literally throw you around. During all this time life had been singularly uneventful...we played bridge, chess, went to movies at night, and ate three squares a day. In addition I had managed to get a disgusting little chore called "Junior Officer of the Deck" which consisted of four hour tours all over the ship...that is, one tour over the ship every thirty minutes for four hours. We were on four, off eight, on four, and then off 24, and back on again. All in all I caught about 22 four hour tours. It wasn't bad during the day, but sometimes at night, specially the 12 to 4 graveyard shift, I had to rugged time. I got seasick on two of these graveyard shifts when I went down into the ship's brig which is the foremost compartment on C deck in the bow. After I got off duty, I got a bacon sandwich from the galley, lay down, and then ate my sandwich. Felt fine the next morning.

We picked up the albatross when we were north of Hawaii, and they followed us on into Yokohama. Guess there must have been 25 or 30 of them. The bad weather didn't seem to bother them at all.

01-21-1953 letter Warren Mengis to mom & dad-pg2

On the 23rd we cross the International Date line, and consequently, there was no 24th. The 23rd became Christmas eve for us...we had midnight mass aboard the ship in the officers' mess. The next day all of us got presents that had been collected by the Red Cross and put aboard in Frisco before the ship came down to Corpus Christie. Most of the packages contained cigarettes, pocket novels, candy, camphor ice, mints, lead pencils, toilet articles, etc. It was pretty nice to open all the little packages... as they were individually wrapped in Christmas paper.

We were a day late getting into Yokohama because of the storms, and I sure was glad to see dry land again. The harbor there is tremendous and there is a great deal of activity. One thing that immediately impresses you about the Japanese people is their industry...they work like beavers. I have already told you about my visit into Yokohama, which is not much of a town as our towns go, although there are plenty of people. The ship was dry as a bone, Pop, no beer, no whiskey, no nothing; consequently I had quite a thirst when I arrived. Three of us went into town and had a nice steak, four or five beers apiece, played the slot machines, had five mixed drinks all on ten bucks and had a nickel left. You ought to see those taxi drivers in Yokohama...they drive on the left side of the road of course, but they're even worse than taxi drivers in the States...if someone gets in the way, he's a dead pigeon. I am enclosing 500 yen as a souvenir for my scrapbook. The exchange is 360 yen to $1.00.

The next day, which was the 30th, we left Yokohama; went down the Coast of Japan until we got to the channel between the main Island and the Southern Island, and cut through to Korea. The Gordon dropped us off in Korea, and the last leg of our journey was made by LST. The newspaper I sent illustrates this part of the trip. Boy, was it cold! It seems funny now, but when it's just freezing outside, you hardly bother to get your coat. It snowed again three days ago...about an inch...but it has been warm ever since (that is, about 28 to 30 degrees).

We've got our room all fixed up now. Bamboo mats all around the walls and on the floor; shelves built across the ends of all the bunks; closets built, and so forth. The house girl clean up every morning and does all the washing and ironing...she even starches our shirts and khakis. Completed our bar the other day too. All we need now is a brass rail. Haven't got it completly stocked yet, but we're working on it. With a bar in the room we don't have to go out in the cold for a night cap.

It's about chow time, so I'm going to quit for now. I want to get a shower in today while it remains warm...I take them during the middle of the day when the sun is warmest. Why don't you send this letter around to all the family?

Love,
Warren

P.S. I'm glad to hear about Panama trip... When do you plan to go? Thanks for info about car payment from Luther.

01-21-1953 letter Warren Mengis to mom & dad-pg3

Louisiana State University Law Center
Baton Rouge, La. 70803-1000

Jan. 9, 1992

Tel: (504) 388-8846
Fax: (504) 388-5773

Dear Bob,

I have enclosed the letter I wrote to Mom and Dad in January of 1953. It's a copy so you can keep it or throw it away. It may help to bring back some memories of "our crossing". I also have in my scrap book the newspaper spread of the 75th setting up in Korea...there are quite a few pictures including one of Col. McShane. If you don't have it, I'll make you some zerox copies.

When the OSI report on Schreiber, Kinder and Toth came to Charlie Weir, he asked me to read it and give my opinion as to whether we could have Toth picked up in the U.S. and flown back to Korea for trial. He had been discharged and was a civilian. I told Charlie that it could not be legally accomplished under the then provisions of the UCMJ. As you probably know, Charlie and I were overruled by some Colonel at 5th Air Force. When things were heating up for you and Charlie, I was transferred to Iwakuni. I saw Lt. Schreiber after that, but I cannot remember where. It seems to me that it was at Tachykawa. I never consulted with him.

One of my friends here at the Law Center, Paul Baier, teaches constitutional law and about three years ago he mentioned the litigation involving Toth, the habeas corpus proceedings. He was totally amazed when I told him of my involvement. I looked up U.S. v. Schrieber, 16 CMR 639 and U.S. v. Kinder, 14 CMR 742 to refresh my memory.

I use to hear from Charlie once and awhile, but have heard nothing from him for six or seven years. I guess he is still in Oklahoma. Good luck with your book.

Warren

01-09-1992 letter Warren Mengis to Bob

CHAPTER 2

Air Force Goes Marine Green

THE AIR FORCE bases in both North and South Korea were each given a designation of "K" and a number. In all, there were 57 of them during different phases of the war. Some ended up in the People's Republic of North Korea, such as K-21, K-23, K-24, and K-25 – the first three located around Pyongyang and the latter at Wonsan. Three of the 57 bases, although designated, were never completed. The bases varied in size from outposts of a few dozen men at a radar station in the mountains to full-sized air bases, such as K-13 at Suwon, which housed both the 8th Fighter Bomber Wing and the 51st Fighter Interceptor Wing in 1953.

Life on the K bases was for the most part quite crude, ranging from the use of tents to Quonset huts to some buildings and even some hangars. USAF personnel generally lived in tents with floors of wood, concrete, or, in many cases, dried mud covered with straw mats. At some bases, there were Quonset huts for offices and assembly points such as briefing rooms or mess halls. The latter were often turned into courtrooms when necessary. Except for folding canvas cots, there was no furniture supplied, so the skills and enterprise of the airmen and officers were used to create all of the furniture, both in the sleeping-living quarters and in the offices and courtrooms. Much of it was created from scrap wood and packing crates as these supplies became available. Most of the large crates turned out to be made from Philippine mahogany, as they were transported from the Philippine Islands to Korea via a large air base at Baggio. The skills of these American men were astounding. They fashioned chairs, tables, desks, benches, and cabinets from scraps of wood with hand tools, having no such thing as power tools in those days.

The tents and huts were cold in the winter and stifling hot and humid in the summer. There were no such things as screens to keep out insects. The dusty, unpaved streets between the tents and huts turned to mud in the spring and fall seasons. While aircrews did their best to fight boredom and carried out tension-filled missions, maintenance personnel worked long hours to keep the worn and damaged aircraft in service.

When I was stationed at the 8th Fighter Bomber wing at Suwon, I shared quarters with a group of other lieutenants, most of whom were pilots of an all-weather fighter bomber largely used as a night fighter, a bomber, and to fly missions during inclement weather. My bunkmates would often return from their missions and head to the latrine to vomit for a few hours, whether from relief, terror, or plain airsickness. Make no mistake – these young airmen wanted to live and survive and, despite the verve and swagger they often exhibited, they confessed to me the sheer terror they often felt when flying at supersonic speeds through darkened or stormy skies while evading MiG-15 fighters flown by experienced Russian pilots seeking to destroy them. At other times, they were flying at incredibly low altitudes over mountainous terrain in order to complete a bombing run while facing anti-aircraft fire.

In a letter written to his sister dated January 8, 1952, Lieutenant Charles Hinton, a combat pilot with the Fifth Air Force at a K Base in Korea wrote:

"Dear sis . . . The Commies have .50 caliber machine guns, 20mm, 40mm, 85mm and 105mm anti-aircraft guns and some son of a bitch with a rifle shot us down. . . . I reckon you don't need to tell mom about my hairy story." (From fact sheet National Museum of the U.S. Air Force).

Thousands of young men like Hinton fought and died in the Korean "police action," as it was then called, and later called the "Forgotten War." The hardships endured included not only crude living and working spaces, but also intense weather in every season, the ever-present guerrilla forces, and anti-government forces. The last of these were also anti-American; they proliferated in every part of Korea, and included deserters from the ROK military as well as North Korean and Chinese regulars who infiltrated the South.

To all of us who had not experienced war on a battlefield, in the sky, or at sea, this was an intense war against a determined adversaries that included communist North Korea, Red China, and their Russian backers. It seemed like we were inserted into a vortex of misery, death, injury, deprivation, and confusion. While the Air Force did not train its personnel to be members of a ground-fighting force, in many instances these airmen were called upon to fight or die as infantrymen, such as when bases were overrun by advancing forces or put under attack by guerrilla fighters or infiltrators from the regular forces opposing us. The arms available to us were often .45-caliber pistols, carbines left over from World War II, or used machine pistols as supplied to the paratroops in that war. In spite of everything, these young men measured up and exceeded expectations in their fighting ability.

One unforgivable thing that stands out and disturbs me to this day was the lack of equipment, vehicles, weapons, clothing, tools, and supplies that accompanied the 75th Air Depot Wing to Korea. When we disembarked after midnight on December 31, 1952, at K-10 just outside of Chinhae, it was agonizingly cold, and we were tired, hungry, and dispirited. Our first friendly visitors the morning of our arrival included the commanding officer of the First Marine Combat Service Group. We learned from some of the ex-Marines now serving in our wing that, in a combat zone such as Korea, all accountability for supplies ceased. This Marine Corps policy meant that whatever equipment was brought into a combat zone did not have to be accounted for by any sort of documentation – it was all expendable. Supply officers were not required to fill out reams of paperwork explaining what happened to various supplies under such conditions. They considered all military stores within the bounds of good sense to be combat-expendable items, just like bullets. This policy turned out to be our good fortune.

After taking a tour of our base and observing all of us shivering and struggling to keep warm in our flimsy summer uniforms, the Marine officer concluded that we were obviously poorly clothed, ill-equipped, and damned uncomfortable. This gentleman made what to some of us seemed like a statesman-like decision, one for which several thousand of us will be forever grateful. He had compassion and he had his men deliver to us winter uniforms, including overcoats, fur hats, lined gloves, winter boots, and many other items such as snow shovels and anti-freeze for our vehicles to make our lives more comfortable. Of course, the Air Force was a brand new branch of the military, and there was no longstanding rivalry with any other branch of the service.

To really appreciate what happened, you need to know that one of the missions of the First Marine Combat Service Group was to supply and equip the Republic of Korea Marine Corps. The Korean Marines had a training base in close proximity to K-10. All of the forces in Korea were said to be part of the United Nations Command, which included the Marines, both U.S. and ROK, as well as the U.S. Air Force. The United States had set out to provide for and equip the Korean marines as a part of our cooperation with the United Nations. It had been made clear to all of us who served in that war that we were there as United Nations troops and not as United States forces. Because of their supply mission, the Marines had abundant stores of warm and serviceable winter clothing on hand, much of it too large for the average Korean male at that time. This cold-weather gear was transported to K-10 that same day and distributed to the freezing forces of the 75th Air

Depot Wing. By evening, it looked like a Marine division had landed at Chinhae. All of this gear was emblazoned with the globe-and-anchor insignia of the United States Marines and was worn proudly and gratefully for the duration of our stay in Korea.

In addition to the lack of equipment, we were woefully untrained for the hardships and combat that many of us had to face. I am thankful for the Boy Scout training of my youth and the ROTC training that I received in college and law school, as otherwise it would have been difficult to make do with what supplies we had available. Many in my outfit seemed to be unable to cope with the surroundings and lack of creature comforts. It is difficult to describe the number of men who simply broke down and cried in their despair over how to survive in that milieu. We picture the American fighting man as the well-trained Marine or Navy Seal or Army Ranger, but in reality, when a reserve wing such as the 75th Air Depot Wing was activated, it was for the most part untrained for the conditions in which it had to function and in some instances it was poorly led. Good leadership in a military organization can help the lower ranks make do under most adverse circumstances. Some of the senior officers were alcoholics and out of touch with reality much of the time. That is not to say that there were not many capable officers, but they were for the most part subordinate to some erratic and alcoholic commanders. The 75th Air Depot Wing had been activated and scheduled to go to Bordeaux, France, as a part of the U.S. NATO forces. At the last minute, our mission was changed to go to Korea.

It is not readily ascertainable how many military officers are actually incompetent or severely impaired from alcohol or drug use, but like athletes on steroids, it has become a well-kept secret. We inherited several officers who stayed on in the Active Reserves to earn their pensions. This included several former lieutenant colonels and colonels who reverted to enlisted grade in order to gain their last few years of active service and entitle them to a pension. Military pensions were based on the highest rank or grade at which the individual served for a continuous two-year period. These folks never anticipated seeing active service again, let alone, in a war zone and were not prepared mentally or physically for the rigors of such active service. Hence, they did not prepare their troops or themselves for what lie ahead. It seems that after World War II and the establishment of the United Nations that not many in our Defense Department contemplated that the United States would be involved in a shooting war so soon.

CHAPTER 3
Myoshi's

AFTER OUR EXTENDED voyage across the Pacific Ocean, the USMS *General Gordon* docked at Yokohama, Japan. Everyone was to have three days onshore before we resumed our trek to Korea and the war. It was sort of a present to the men of the Air Force for being good sailors and making it that far.

The evening before we were to go ashore, we were treated to a training film. After the evening meal, all of the officers and, I presume, the enlisted men assembled for a movie. Since attendance was mandatory, we all speculated that it would be the armed forces' latest version of a Japanese travel documentary. Knowing that the Department of Defense annually spends millions of dollars producing training films on a vast variety of subjects, we assumed that this film was to be about Japanese customs and how to avoid offending the indigenous population. In military parlance, that means the native or domestic population of a particular place.

Since very few of us had been to Japan before, we figured we would be shown how to get around, how to watch where and what we ate, and something about the local currency and customs. All this, we assumed, would be presented with the idea that we wouldn't embarrass the United States government or the United States Air Force. If you were never in the service, you can't imagine how fastidious the various branches of the armed forces were, and I presume still are, in trying to ensure that their people don't commit common social faux pas in foreign countries. They tried to do this in the early 1950s with training films.

With the foregoing in mind, we settled back with our coffee cups in hand and prepared to watch and learn as much as we could about Japan, its people, its mores, and its culture.

A Navy officer gave us a short talk, which to my memory told us how to get public transportation from Yokohama to Tokyo. The thing that stands out most is that he explained that we should get off at Shinbashi Station. I thought to myself that, armed with such a vital piece of information, we should be able to easily master the intricacies of one of the world's largest cities. Then came the famous film. It turned out to be a movie that the Army used during World War II on venereal diseases. The acting wasn't bad, and it was sexy enough that if we weren't horny before, the film moved most of us in that direction. The upshot was that, even if you didn't have getting laid on your mind, you were made to feel that you should have. This bit of important information was then followed by a talk from one of the wing physicians, who explained that everyone leaving the ship would have to leave with a "pro kit."

I don't want to sound naive, but I thought to myself, "What the hell is a 'pro kit?'" Being too embarrassed to ask, I figured that I would wait until the time of disembarkation and examine the much-vaunted piece of military gear.

Bright and early the next morning, my pal, a first lieutenant from Oklahoma named Howard Smith, and I prepared to disembark. As we stood in line, a medical corpsman handed us each a "pro kit." Smitty and I had discussed this and decided to ask for two apiece. They were given happily. After we left the ship and walked a couple of blocks to the train station, we stopped and looked at this most important and heretofore secret piece of military equipment. It turned out to consist of a pack of six rubbers, a tube of salve, and a handkerchief. Of course, we then got into a discussion about Oriental women in general and, in particular, the rare venereal diseases that they could transmit. On board, there were stories of guys languishing in VA hospitals because their venereal diseases. These men were said to be infected with Asian germs so virulent that they couldn't be let loose so as to infect others. In the service, the fastest thing in the world is a rumor. The more absurd it is, the faster it travels.

We then figured that if the carrying of prophylactics was so important to the higher-ups, there would be some degree of shame attached if we didn't use them. Honestly, we had been talking of seeing the Imperial Palace and other similar tourist destinations before the famous film episode aboard ship.

We eventually located the train station and headed for Tokyo. We even remembered to get off at Shinbashi Station. It wasn't long before we met an American soldier who gave us directions to the Imperial Palace. At that point of our trip, we still maintained some decree of decorum and discretion about our sightseeing. One of us then mentioned that we ought to visit the Imperial Hotel. I think it was me, as I had just read a book that mentioned the hotel having been designed by the famous architect Frank Lloyd Wright. I was also impressed by the fact that it had been built to withstand the shock of a major earthquake. I told Smitty that the hero in the book had met a gorgeous lady in the bar of the Imperial Hotel. So off we headed with high expectations of meeting some sultry and exotic women at the fabled Imperial Bar.

We eventually located the hotel with the help of a couple of bicycle rickshaw drivers. It was a beautiful building, as we had expected it to be. We went inside and headed straight for the bar. We sat down, and a waiter approached us. Wanting to seem sophisticated, we both ordered sake. It was served warm in a small container. As we sat there, we noticed very few people in the bar. We started chatting and were engaged in an intense but informative conversation with a Pan American Airways pilot about the pleasures of Japan and Tokyo in particular. He told us that he regularly traveled to Tokyo in his job and wanted to know if he could help us with information. After the sake, which neither of us were used to drinking, we began drinking bourbon. As the time rolled on, the pilot asked us if we had ever seen a Japanese-style hotel room. We said no, and he took us to see his room, which was a traditional tatami room with mats on the floor and a bedroll that is rolled out for sleeping. He even shared with us a viewing of a Japanese-style toilet, which was essentially a hole in the floor. After that, he instructed us in the use of such a facility, warning, "Keep your feet out of the way, or you will poop on them." There was a particular way to use the Asian toilets that had to be learned if you were from a place with sit-down commodes.

We returned to the bar and, after a few more drinks, we got up the nerve to ask him what he meant by the "pleasures of Japan." Smitty had been a Bible salesman in Muskogee, Oklahoma, and I was young and not worldly wise, being from New Hampshire. In reality we were just a couple of horny young men, looking for adventure in a strange land. We finally asked our new found friend where we might find some women. With that, he asked the bartender for a telephone. One was produced right at the bar, and he proceeded to make a phone call. He then accompanied us to the front entrance of the hotel and talked to the doorman, who in turn had a discussion with a taxi driver. The pilot bade us goodbye, told us to have a good time, and disappeared back into the hotel.

The taxi driver gave us a smile and a knowing look before taking off through the narrow streets of Tokyo. After about a half hour, we arrived at what seemed to be the outskirts of the city. In front of a massive wooden gate, the driver blew the horn in a distinct rhythm, signaling an elderly Japanese man to open the gate. The taxi proceeded inside. Immediately, we could see beautifully landscaped grounds. It looked like an elegant park. We drove a short distance, and the driver got out and removed our overnight bags that had been placed in the front passenger's seat. An old lady approached and bowed deeply. The taxi driver told us that he had been paid for the trip by the airline pilot and refused our money. He bowed, smiled, and left. The lady told us in English that she was the "mamasan" and said that we should follow her. We went inside a Japanese-style house. There were several houses with paper windowpanes on the grounds, along with many pools and gardens. We were told to remove our shoes and not to worry, as no one would take them. We sat on the floor and were offered tea or sake. We chose sake and tried our best not to appear nervous. Neither of us was wise or experienced in the ways of the world, particularly not in this part of the world or in this type of facility. Neither of us wanted to admit our inexperience with women to the other.

Once we were put at ease, another mamasan appeared and spoke to us in excellent English. She asked us if we wanted dinner, and we immediately felt relieved. We actually sighed with relief and uttered a loud "yes" at the same time. We were famished, nervous, and, now knowing what to expect, we began to feel more at ease. The lady then clapped her hands, and two young women dressed in kimonos entered the room. They sat down on the cushions and began chatting with us in broken English. There were no chairs or tables, only cushions on the ground and a square hole cut out in the floor. This hole was where one put the feet, and a small table, sort of like a low-lying, short-legged coffee table, covered the floor opening.

The young ladies departed, and two more entered the room. That scenario was repeated five times in all. The mamasan then asked each of us which girls we liked the best. Being nervous and not really knowing what in the hell was going on, neither of us could remember the names of any of the girls. So the mamasan left, returned with all ten of the girls, and told us to discreetly tell her which one we each liked the best after they left the room. This entire production took over an hour, and by now we really were hungry, thirsty, curious, and a lot less nervous.

We were told that if we wanted dinner and breakfast in the morning, it would cost us each fifteen dollars for the night. We were told that there was to be no tipping and that, once we paid that sum, everything we needed or wanted was included in that price. We paid.

The girls we had chosen appeared. We had an introductory drink – sake, of course – whereupon the girls guided us to a house. When we went inside, we again removed our shoes at the front door, entered, and were led by the young women, who took each of us by the hand. We were asked to stand, and each young woman proceeded to undress us down to our undershorts. They produced terrycloth kimonos and towels, then bade us to follow. We proceeded to another building and entered a room that seemed to be steaming. Nearby, we saw a pool of water that looked like an enlarged hot tub built into the floor. We were totally undressed and bade to remove our underpants, which we did somewhat shyly so as to cover ourselves.

The two girls disrobed and were naked. They produced two small stools and sat us on them, then began to apply soap and water and scrubbed each of us with a brush. The girls rinsed us off by splashing us with very hot water from small, wooden buckets. Both of us being virile, young, and by now quite horny, we had a hell of a time concealing just how aroused we were. The girls began to joke about this in Japanese, but the pointing and joking between them left no doubt as to the object of their conversation. I thought that this was, up to that time, the most embarrassing moment of my life. The erections would be very short-lived. After the scrubbing and rinsing, the girls washed and scrubbed themselves in similar fashion.

We then all went to the steaming pool. The girls dropped in very gently and adroitly, then motioned for us to follow. We did. It was the hottest water that either of us had ever experienced, and, even now, it hurts to think about it. I have seen lobsters cooked in water that wasn't as hot as that seemed. The shock of the water was so great that my body became instantly numb. All sexual thoughts instantly disappeared. All

I could think of was how a lobster must feel when dropped into the boiling pot of water. I said to Smitty that they must be trying to punish us for some evil deeds that our fellow servicemen had inflicted on their country during the last war. In a matter of minutes, we recovered as our bodies became accustomed to being scalded and we became used to the heat. After that, I experienced a sensation of complete relaxation. I had very little sexual experience and was totally unaccustomed to being with a naked woman. Even so, I had no desires in that respect after being in that pool for fifteen minutes. I lost all sense of time. After a while, maybe forty-five minutes, we left the pool, were dried off by the girls with towels, and were robed in silk kimonos and given sandals. We then were led back to our house.

In the house, we sat on the floor with our feet in a pit, at the bottom of which was a charcoal fire beneath a wooden grate. We had a cool drink, not sake, and some other girls served dinner. All of this took place to the lilting rhythm of soft Oriental music in the background. Following dinner, the girls played a game of charades with us which involved various sexual innuendos, such as one or the other of the girls exhibiting some part of their rather attractive anatomies to us. These girls were pretty enough to have been finalists in the Miss Japan contest, if they had one.

After midnight, Smitty's companion got up, said goodnight, and took him up to the second floor of the house. The girl who was to be my companion for the night slid open a paper screen, and we entered what was the bedroom. Having been introduced to a Japanese-style bedroom by our Pan Am benefactor some hours earlier, I was at least familiar with the setup. The tatami bedroll came out, the kimonos came off, and I regained in my masculinity. I really didn't know what to expect, but I made it through the night; but I was so tired from the ocean trip, the excitement of being in Tokyo, the nervousness of my encounter with the Japanese girls, and having survived a scalding in the Japanese bath that I laid my head down and instantly fell into a very deep sleep. I think I dreamed about the fabled Arabian Nights.

About midmorning, I awoke to the sound of music and shortly after coming awake I was served breakfast in bed, which was even accompanied by the offer of a parting sexual tryst. The latter I declined as I was too embarrassed. I believe that women are much more sophisticated in interpersonal relations than men. Sixty years ago the mores of American society did not condone extramarital sex. Our clothes were produced, having been cleaned and pressed during the night, and our shoes were at the door, newly polished. A taxi was called for us and, with much bowing, embracing, and happy chatter, we left this Oriental paradise. We later learned that the name of the place was Miyoshi's, that it was a resort, and that it catered to Allied officers, diplomats, and airline pilots only. It actually had a small golf course. This had been one hell of a fast introduction to Japan and the Japanese culture.

Oh yes, with all of that I almost forgot, when we returned to the ship, we were given new "pro kits," and we proceeded to douse ourselves with the tube of salve before wrapping our sexual organs with the handkerchief. Over the next several months, we had a lot of very long and hearty laughs at our own expense about that episode and our needless show of concern for our health.

Howard Smith & Bob Shaines

CHAPTER 4
Uniform Code of Military Justice (UCMJ)

IN HIS BOOK *The Coldest Winter,* the late David Halberstam wrote that, for many Americans, except perhaps for a high percentage of those who actually fought there, Korea became something of a black hole in terms of history. Likewise, Clay Blair, in his book *The Forgotten War,* shares a similar sentiment. Both of these authors and their fine chronicles of that conflict concentrated their writing on what was happening to the armies and marines engaged in the battles and paid little or no attention to the air war or, for that matter, the Navy's role in the war. The facts are that the U.S. Air Force in the beginning of the war was poorly equipped with World War II leftovers, such as the P-40 and a few jets such as the F-80 "Shooting Star." The U.S. pilots, many of them newly minted lieutenants, were up against experienced pilots of both the Soviet Union and of communist China who were flying the latest version of MiGs.

To add to the vacuity of information about the Air Force, little was known about the legal history that came about from the war. The Uniform Code of Military Justice came about as a result of Congress enacting Public Law No. 81-506, also known as the Military Justice Act Of 1950. The new Code (UCMJ) became effective on May 31, 1951.

In June of 1950, the Korean War began. The Air Force recalled large numbers of reservists to serve on active duty. The newly created Air Force JAG Department had almost no one trained in the new Code or its procedures. In addition, the department was sorely undermanned.

The Judge Advocate General of the Air Force, (called "TJAG") General Reginald C. Harmon, initiated the JAG school at Maxwell AFB in Montgomery, Alabama, to train its members, both old and new, in the military justice program. He thereby founded the Judge Advocate General Staff Officer Course. At the time the first course was taught, beginning in January 1951, the Manual for Courts-Martial, 1951 had not been printed. The first class used only mimeographed draft copies for study purposes. The initial staff had to prepare the lectures and the courses as best they could. Also, guest lecturers from the Air Command and Staff Officer course, which was also taught at Maxwell (the site of the Air University), taught military courses to the JAG students so that they were trained in military tactics and problems as well as legal subjects. Note: TJAG refers to the General officer designated as the Judge Advocate General of the Air Force by the president.

I attended the JAG school in the summer of 1952 before embarking for Korea. All of us early graduates received credit not only for graduating the JAG school, but also for having completed the Air Command and Staff Officer course. When I was twenty-two years old, I had completed credits for my law degree from Boston University School of Law and had received my diploma from the Air Force JAG course and from the Air Command and Staff Officer course (ACSC). The ACSC was largely attended by majors and lieutenant colonels. As a result as a very young lawyer and officer I had credentials far ahead of many of the senior officers under whom I would serve. I was also as a graduate certified as competent to serve as trial or defense counsel in general courts-martial. I was one of the early few in Air Force JAG so certified, yet my practical and trial experience was nil. My credentials far exceeded my practical abilities as a lawyer or as an air force commander or staff officer.

The JAG and the Air Command and Staff Officer Courses were also physically demanding, and many of the older officers suffered badly in the heat of the Alabama summer in 1952. In Montgomery the temperature exceeded one hundred degrees Fahrenheit most days. The weather was also very humid, as Maxwell Air Force Base was bordered by a river. In addition to that, the only air conditioning was in the classroom where most of our subjects were taught. We went to sleep sweating and woke up sweating. For a young, well-conditioned man it was fine, but many suffered badly and more than a few of the senior officers came down with orthopedic injuries, including torn muscles, strains, and even fractures from the rigorous obstacle courses and the evasion and escape training of the day. These were courses taught by NCOs who were inclined to be merciless. They said it was for our own good, as many would end up serving in Korea, although I don't recall meeting any of my senior classmates while serving in Korea. Let us say that service in Korea, with few exceptions, was reserved for the younger JAG officers. Strange as it seems my roommate at the Air University was a Royal Thai Air Force Colonel by the name of Obri Si Vissesimet. He was a nice guy but a poor handball player.

Warren Mengis and I were originally assigned to the Air Materiel Command in Dayton, Ohio, and then were told that we would join the newly activated Texas AF Reserve Wing, the 75th Air Depot Wing. We were then told that the 75th Air Depot Wing was to be activated and was to move to Bordeaux, France, as a part of the U.S. response to the Cold War in Europe. We were also told that we would receive intensive instruction in the French language. In reality, the 75th had been designated to transfer to Korea to support the 5th Air Force. Warren and I had received a visit from the TJAG , General Reginald Harmon, who told us that since we were both single, he wanted us to join the 75th for its war mission in place of other officers with families who had been initially scheduled for such duties. Both of us gladly agreed to do so, with the promise that we could choose our station of choice upon our return from Korea.

In peacetime, the JAG officers' duties involved claims against the Air Force, personnel law, legal assistance, contracts, and other legal issues arising in the military community in which they were serving. Military justice was a small part of their duties. In wartime, all that changes. The focus becomes military justice due to the very large mobilization of forces and essentially the drafting of reservists, many of whom are reluctant to be called upon once again to serve on active duty and who report with a "chip on their shoulder." There was also the early Air Force policy of letting sentenced prisoners out of their confinement in prisons if they volunteered to serve in Korea. Those matters greatly increased the need for Air Force JAG officers who were trained in the new procedures and rules of law pertaining to military justice and the armed services of the United States in 1951, and who would serve as trial counsel and defense counsel using the new Uniform Code of Military Justice. The students at the Air University included balding or gray-haired reserve lawyers recalled from civilian practice, young lieutenants appointed directly from civilian life, and a number of majors, senior captains, and lieutenant colonels. Many of the latter were on flying status as well. The Air Force was hard-pressed to meet the staffing needs of trained JAG officers to serve in Korea. Life in Korea was hard, and the average Staff Judge Advocate was involved in on-the-job training.

For the first time, lawyers with degrees from accredited law schools or members of the bar were required to serve as counsel in general courts-martial and, as stated before, to serve in any general court one had to be certified as competent by the TJAG. Non-lawyers could still be assigned as counsel in special courts. However, if the trial counsel was a lawyer, then the defense counsel had to be a law-school graduate or a bar member (TJAG} refers to the top lawyer in the Air Force called The Judge Advocate General).

The position of law officer, a precursor to the military judge, was created to preside over general courts-martial. While not yet called a judge, the law officer in fact made rulings during the trial on motions and evidentiary matters, instructed the court members as to the law, and acted as the trial judge. The non-lawyer court president still controlled much of the trial.

The Uniform Code also gave staff judge advocates increased responsibility to instruct the convening authorities as to their duties. The idea was to do away with the potential for unlawful command influence. Defendants now had enhanced rights against self-incrimination. The idea was to grant to criminal defendants in the military certain rights not granted to civilian-criminal defendants until a decade later, when the U.S. Supreme Court decided *Gideon v. Wainwright* and *Miranda v. Arizona*. It was the intent of Congress in enacting the Uniform Code of Military Justice to provide servicemen and the dependents who were subject to the code with the most protections available to one accused of a crime in this country. The actual workings of the system were still mired in the old traditions where the commander's word was supreme and and so many commanders were against the liberal ideas of the new Code and the idea of taking advice from lawyers was repugnant to them.

When the Air Force Judge Advocate General's Department came into existence, each branch of the service had its own system of justice. The Army had the Articles of War; the Navy and Marine Corps had the Articles for the Government of the Navy. On June 25, 1949, Congress passed an act that made the newly formed Air Force subject to the Articles of War. The Air Force later adopted the Manual for Courts-Martial, U.S. Army, 1949. There was no law officer or military judge. Usually, the senior member of the court, who was the president, ran the trial with the help of a voting member, who was a lawyer, if available. Counsel did not have to be a lawyer and, in many cases, was not. Appeals were not made to an appellate court, but to a board of review of the Office of the Judge Advocate General.

COMMAND INFLUENCE

In an effort to meet the pressure of groups protesting the abuses of the military justice system during World War II, including private citizens and veterans' organizations as well as the American Bar Association, Congress agreed to create a system to promote public confidence and to protect the rights of the accused military members. This led to the UCMJ, enacted on May 5, 1950, and the publication of the MCM, effective May 31, 1951.

While commanders were still permitted to convene courts, Article 37, UCMJ, prohibited the convening authority from influencing the court. Article 98, UCMJ, made the unlawful influence of the court-martial a crime. However, due to the newness of the justice system in the Air Force, the pressures placed upon both commanders and lawyers to keep in place good order and discipline, and the fact that the same commanders also were rating the officers assigned to them in the JAG Departments, command influence was alive and well. It was my belief that if a commander wanted a conviction, he got it. Don't forget, the same commander also appointed the court members. Hence, if theft was an issue, woe unto the accused charged with theft. If AWOL (absence without leave) was a problem, woe unto him who was so accused. A conviction and harsh sentence were imminent to keep order and discipline intact.

We were in the recycling business in Korea. We would convict men, and they would be given six months in confinement, a bad-conduct discharge, and a reduction in rank to basic airman. Then they would be recycled back to active duty in Korea in a matter of months, many times to the same squadron from which they were convicted. The exigencies of war play strange games even upon the justice system. Expediency ruled the day. So, it was in wartime Korea in the early 1950s. Most of the commanders, who were also the convening authorities for military courts, were holdovers from the days of command influence in convicting the accused who fell into the web of military law.

For the judge advocate who went to Korea, the conditions were harsh for working, traveling, and living. There were very few paved roads, and those that did exist were often dirt tracks that were pitted and had unfilled bomb craters in many places. Bridges were often temporary, as one side or the other had destroyed the original bridges in battle. The cities of Pusan and Tague were crowded with refugees and insurgents living in the streets. Sanitation was nonexistent, and the constant stench of human excrement permeated most places. Seoul was a bombed-out shell of a city with no buildings standing, except for the rare exception in the main district of the city. There were no roofs, even on the buildings with four walls remaining intact, during the few times when I was in Seoul.

Amidst all of this ruin, the JAG officers, being in scarce supply, had to do extensive travel in the areas to fulfill their duties in the unoccupied parts of South Korea. This often meant traveling by Jeep, truck, or train to an air base where there was likely to be military air transport services or cargo planes with sufficient room to accommodate a few passengers. This meant bearing the risk of being shot at or apprehended by the roving guerrilla and insurgent bands that permeated the south. Those of us who served in Korea were awarded battle stars for each six months of service in the war zone. Flying often meant lying on top of cargo or sitting on the floor of a cockpit. Sometimes it took days of waiting to get a flight to a destination. The weather was also a factor, as winters in Korea are often inclement and flying was out of the question, as the cargo flights were not outfitted with the latter-day instrument landing systems and sophisticated radar devices. Often, the destination was a small, steel-matted field. We became accustomed to sleeping in hangars, waiting to be called by the operations officer with a flight, or hanging out in operations to ask a pilot of a transport or bomber for a ride to the next destination.

Meanwhile, there always seemed to be an ongoing poker game in the hangars where we and others waited. There were always several cases of C-rations stacked in a corner, and there always seemed to be a diesel-powered stove to heat the cans of stew, franks and beans, or whatever was in the boxes. These delays often took days. The travel orders were to travel by the most expeditious means to our destination. Very often, this meant flying in a combat zone with no parachute, although they were required for all who boarded an aircraft in Korea. However, many times we would bypass the operations officer and wait for our ride in a secluded area of the runway designated by the pilot as he taxied for takeoff. With the help of a crew member, we would be hoisted by our armpits into the airplane and given a ride to a chosen destination.

There always seemed to be a camaraderie among us junior officers, whether JAG, aircrew, or pilots.

One of my more memorable flights involved a trip from Fukuoka, in the south of Japan, to Tachikawa Air Base outside of Tokyo. A young pilot was introduced to me by a fellow Portsmouth, New Hampshire, officer, Louis Fusigni, who happened to sit next to me at the lunch counter in the operations facility hangar at Fukuoka. Louis was in the class ahead of mine at Portsmouth High School. Lou was kind enough to arrange for me to board the plane at the end of the taxiway thereby getting me a ride to Tokyo. The plane took off in a driving rain. When we were an hour or so into the flight, we were hit by a severe thunderstorm and buffeted about fiercely. I was standing in the cockpit, as there was no room to sit in the cargo area.

As we were approaching Tokyo we could see the top of Mount Fuji through the rain and clouds. On the final approach to landing the plane was struck by lightning. The starboard engine caught fire and was burning intensely. Efforts to douse the fire from the cockpit were futile. The two young lieutenants flying the plane told me that they were going to sound the bailout alarm so that the two crew members who were not in the cockpit could bail out by parachute. The senior pilot told me not to worry as both pilots were going to stay with the plane and bring it in for a safe landing if possible. But they wanted to give the crew a chance to bail out over Japan, just in case. I recall the plane commander telling me that I was his responsibility and, if he chose to take me on board his flight without a parachute, he would be damned if he was going to abandon me and his plane now. If we didn't make it, it was his responsibility. Such was the courage of these young pilots. If I was to die, he would go with me. So don't panic, he said. Amazingly, I never doubted his ability or his resolve. We landed at Tachikawa with a full array of crash fire engines and ambulances running alongside of us, spraying foam on the fiery wing that gratefully remained in place for the descent and landing. We never even exchanged names, but parted with hugs and tears of joy as brethren in the fight.

I always loved to have to travel to Japan, as it was a way to get out of the war for a few days and experience life among the living instead of life among the dead or those liable to die. All of South Korea was a battleground in the days of the war, and there were no safe zones. Among the hundreds of thousands of refugees from the north were the dead and dying, to say nothing of our own combat troops and those of our allies. At every base large enough to handle transport aircraft capable of flying to the United States, there were steady streams of ambulances loading the dead, the dying, and the seriously wounded.

Rufugees in Riverbed, Tague 1953

Korean Orphans, Chinhae 1953

CHAPTER 5
Korea After World War II

AFTER THE SURRENDER of the Japanese Empire in 1945, Korea was divided between the Soviet Union and the United States under the U.S.-Soviet Joint Commission as agreed to by the Moscow Conference of Foreign Ministers. The Koreans had no say in the matter. It was understood in the agreement that, following five years of international rule, Korea would then be governed by Koreans. However, during this period, each side developed its own political ideology. In the North, a communist regime came to power with the Soviet puppet Kim Il Sung as the leader. In the South, the United States put in place its own puppet leader, Syngman Rhee.

In December 1945 and throughout 1946, thousands of people engaged in violent rioting against the so-called democratic government in South Korea. Under United States military rule, the Army refused to recognize the existing political organizations that had been established by the Korean people. The United States Army Military Advisory Group in Korea (USAMAGIK) – also called KMAG, which stood for Korean Military Advisory Group or "Kiss my ass goodbye," by the GIs assigned to that organization – They had recognized foreboding signs in the fact that the Rhee government was unpopular and was faced off by an aggressive communist regime in the North.

As a result of these policies and two additional factors – that the

Japanese had recruited thousands of Koreans into their armed forces during World War II and that the Japanese had looted Korea, stripping it of any manufacturing base and looting its agricultural resources, resulting in mass starvation of the people – guerrilla groups formed to fight the South Korean government of Syngman Rhee. The Japanese recruited the Korean police during the war, and this same group that were members of the Japanese Police during the Japanese colonial period in Korea remained in power during World War II and continued on as the Nationalist Police under the Rhee government. Syngman Rhee and the United States naively installed numerous pro-Japanese officials as the senior members of the South Korean government. In South Korea, a right-wing group known as the Representative Democratic Council emerged and was vehemently anti-American. It was said that democracy reigned in South Korea so long as no one opposed Rhee, who was an autocratic dictator. This was in contrast to the communist regime in North Korea, which for all purposes was controlled by Joseph Stalin of the Soviet Empire and his client Mao Zedong, the leader of The People's Republic of China.

The American GIs who rushed into battle to save South Korea in the summer of 1950 had little if any knowledge of Korea – except that thousands of Koreans had fought against us in the Pacific as Japanese forces and that the Korean guards in most of the Japanese prison camps where the Americans were held were among the cruelest to the Allied and Chinese prisoners. These folks were not our friends, but our strategic interests demanded that we oppose communism wherever and however its expansionist interests threatened us, or so our national leaders believed.

In June of 1950, when the forces of the communist north invaded the south, the U.S. Army leaders believed that North Korean regulars were hidden among the thousands of refugees streaming to the south. The U.S. Army was allowed to fire on these columns, killing and maiming thousands of civilians, including women and children.

Against this background, the U.S. Air Force commander in Korea asked for a ruling as to whether his airmen could be excused from the strafing and bombing of the refugee columns; although requested to do so by the Army. Many of the pilots ordered to attack the refugee columns objected on humanitarian grounds and, despite the requests that they be permitted to halt the air attacks, they were ordered to continue to do so.

Many officers and men conscripted into the Republic of Korea (ROK) army felt no loyalty to their government and supported the various oppositional forces. None of this internecine conflict among the Koreans of the South was known or otherwise communicated to the GIs who so gallantly fought against terrible odds to save the South. Most of these Americans entered the battle for the South with little training, no combat experience, and they were poorly equipped with arms and munitions. Further, most were going into battle for a country they had never heard of before arriving there and where no one, save the indigenous population, understood the local dynamic – this included the American generals in Tokyo, Korea, and Washington. Because the primary focus of American foreign policy and military preparedness was directed at preventing the expansion of communism into Western Europe, little thought went into measures to prevent the spread of communism in Asia. Foreign policy in Korea was pretty much ceded to the Army and General Douglas MacArthur.

The events in this book unfolded as a result of insurgent and guerrilla action directed against the American forces in the South. While our forces were, for the most part, made up of untested youngsters who were told that they were fighting for democracy and against the hated communists, most of those who were there questioned the wisdom of those who put them into harms way without proper training or equipment.

Those of us who served in Korea during the Korean War were told to think of our mission as a patriotic duty. But I often heard from my buddies that we really didn't understand why we were there and that the whole country wasn't worth a damn to us. This was our view, even though the Korean soil was soaked with the blood of over fifty-eight thousand American and Allied dead. We were told we were there as United Nations Forces fighting to keep South Korea from following into communist hands. In reality Korea was not strategically significant to the United States. Its importance was to be that it was the only hot war fought between the United States and the Soviet Union during the cold war era. The Soviets fought via their Chinese and Korean proxies for the most part although the Soviet Air Force was directly involved.

In 1952, there were three munitions- and bomb-supply depots near Pusan, which was Korea's largest wartime seaport city at that time. These three depots included an Army depot, a Marine depot, and an Air Force depot manned by the 543rd Ammo Supply Group of the 75th Air Depot Wing, Far East Air Materiel Command, known as FEAMCOM. The commander of the 543rd Air Police Detachment assigned to guard the Air Force depot was Lieutenant George C. Schreiber. In the weeks before September 26, 1952, guerrillas had infiltrated both the Army and Marine depots and caused massive explosions and loss of life of some of the Army and Marine guards. In the aftermath of those events, the Air Police guards at the 543rd were in a high state of alert and anxiety, and performed their duties with great trepidation and some degree of pure fear. Everyone believed that the perpetrators were either North Korean irregulars or Chinese infiltrators. In retrospect, they could well have been black market operators or forces of South Korean dissidents who hated both the Americans and the Syngman Rhee government.

Before the outbreak of the Korean War, the North Korean army was equipped with more than two hundred and fifty tanks, one hundred and fifty Russian-built YAK fighter aircraft, one hundred and ten attack bombers, two hundred artillery pieces, plus YAK trainers and about thirty-five reconnaissance planes. Additionally, the North Korean navy had several small warships. The invading army consisted of two hundred thirty one thousand troops, with a reserve of another thirty thousand kept in North Korea. North Korea had a logistics system that was able to move supplies in keeping with the military's advance southward. Thousands of refugees fleeing to the south in tandem with the communist troops' advance were compelled to carry supplies for the advancing army.

According to Roy E. Appleman in his book *South to the Naktong, North to the Yalu*, the South Korean army had ninety-eight thousand soldiers, of whom sixty-five thousand were combat troops. South Korea had no tanks, twelve liaison-type aircraft, and ten AT-6 trainers. The United States withdrew its entire army garrisons from South Korea in 1949, except for a small cadre of advisors. The intent was to leave the defense of the South to the Koreans.

The North planned its attack very well, and it was done with surprise across a broad front that included attacks from the sea, the air, and the land. Within a matter of a few days, the South Korean forces were routed. Thousands deserted and went into the countryside or defected to the north to later fight with the Kim Il Sung forces. Seoul was occupied on June 28, 1950. Two days later, the largest battle fought exclusively between the North Korean and South Korean forces occurred. The south suffered seven thousand dead, and sixteen thousand were taken prisoner. Most of those captured later fought for the North, and many other South Korean troops deserted into the countryside to fight as bandits or simply go into hiding.

The only thing that saved the South was the fact that a large American force was stationed nearby in Japan. On June 27, 1950, President Harry S. Truman ordered the United States air and sea forces to support the Rhee regime in South Korea. On the same day, the United Nations (UN) issued Resolution 83, which recommended that member states militarily assist the Republic of Korea. Some at the UN argued that, since the initial clashes were between North Korean and South Korean forces, the upheaval was a civil war and therefore was not subject to UN intervention. At this very time, the Soviet Ministry of Foreign Affairs made the decision to boycott the United Nations on the premise that the boycott would prevent action by the UN Security Council. The Security Council acted without the presence of it permanent member, the Union of Soviet Socialist Republics (USSR, and the forces, including the Americans, entered the fray as United Nations forces. It was President Truman's belief that if South Korea was allowed to fall to the communist North without opposition from the "free world," that no small nation would have the courage to resist aggression by its stronger communist neighbors. He then ordered General Douglas MacArthur to transfer ammunition, weapons, and equipment to the Republic of Korea (ROK) Army and to use air cover to evacuate U.S. civilians. He also ordered the Seventh Fleet to protect the Republic of China (Taiwan). The Taiwanese government had asked that it be permitted to participate in the war, but its request was refused on the grounds that their entry would embolden the People's Republic of China (communist China) to enter the war.

The first U.S. force to come to the aid of South Korea was the Army's 24th Infantry Division, which was based in Japan as an occupying force. These soldiers were largely ill trained and ill equipped for battle. The vaunted General MacArthur, who felt that he was responsible for defeating the forces of Japan, was no match for the North. In the first battle at Osan on July 5, 1950, the division, which was under strength, suffered 1,416 dead and 785 taken prisoner. The 24th retreated to Taejon and, when that city fell, it suffered 3,602 battle casualties and another 2,962 taken prisoner, including Major General William F. Dean, the division commander. Eighteen American fighter aircraft were shot down, along with twenty-nine US bombers, as compared with five North Korean aircraft. By August, all of the South Korean, U.S., and British forces had been driven back into the so-called Pusan perimeter, which constituted about ten percent of the Korean Peninsula. The outer limit of the perimeter was the Nakdong River.

52

The North advanced no farther. By August, there were five hundred American medium tanks landed at Pusan, and by September, the ROK and UN forces outnumbered those of the north. ROK and US B-29 bombers were knocking out supply depots, oil refineries, bridges, and rail facilities in North Korea, cutting off the Northern forces' supply lines. In addition, the Navy blockaded the North Korean ports and bombarded them from Navy ships at sea. The UN forces then rapidly drove the North Korean army back to the Yalu River, on the border between China and the North. China then entered the war and, once again, the communist forces moved south and captured Seoul. The battles were vicious and took numerous thousands of lives on both sides until July 1951, when the UN forces made the decision to halt any further pushes north at the 38th parallel. Thereafter, there was little territory exchanged, and the war consisted of bombing the north and air battles over North Korea between American and Russian pilots together with some People's Republic of China pilots flying Soviet aircraft with North Korean markings.

Peace negotiations started on July 10, 1951, and lasted until July of 1953 when an armistice was agreed upon. Numerous battles were fought over small patches of territory during that period as each side tested the resolve of the other to continue the conflict. It was similar to the trench warfare of World War I.

When parts of South Korea were under North Korean control, it was reported that thousands of people were systematically rounded up and killed, including South Korean government officials and anyone deemed to be hostile to the communists. At the same time, the South Korean military, the Nationalist police, and some paramilitary forces executed tens of thousands of leftist inmates and alleged communist sympathizers, including the massacre of political prisoners at the Daejeon prison. According to R.J. Rummel, a University of Hawaii professor, about four-hundred thousand South Koreans were conscripted into the North Korean army. In addition, when the North retreated from the conquest of Seoul in September of 1950, their army took with them as captives and slave laborers, some eighty-three thousand civilians who were never heard from again.

During this period, some U.S. Army officers photographed assembly-line like executions of thousands of people at Daejeon, where between three thousand and seven thousand bodies were buried in mass graves. One U.S. officer gave his approval that if the North Koreans approached Pusan that he would allow the slaughter of thirty-five hundred political prisoners by a South Korean army unit that he was advising. . There was no indication that the United States Military advisors had ever tried to halt any of these mass executions. It has been stated that South Korea massacred between two-hundred thousand and 1.2 million civilians suspected of membership in the Bodo League, an organization of reputed left-leaning people or communist sympathizers.

The Korean Central News Agency of the Republic of North Korea claims that the United States and its allies killed at least thirty-three thousand prisoners of war and that tens of thousands were crippled or wounded while in UN captivity. On May 27, 1952, it was claimed that some eight hundred prisoners were killed by flamethrowers at the 77th camp on Koje Island. Other atrocities were also alleged by the north, including the machine-gunning of prisoners for practice shooting at moving targets. I visited several POW camps during my tour in Korea, and saw signs of brutal treatment of prisoners, but no killings. From my observations, I have to believe that brutality was normal in these camps. On one occasion, I witnessed a prisoner who had stopped to adjust his shoes being kicked violently in the scrotum by a guard. The guard had a smile on his face, while the prisoner was in obvious pain.

The North was also accused of mistreating its military prisoners through beatings, starvation, forced labor, summary executions, and death marches. A U.S. Congressional Report alleges that two-thirds of all American prisoners of war in Korea died in captivity.

I bring out this bit of history because much of it had been unknown until recently, when the South Korean Truth and Reconciliation Commission and the U.S. Senate Subcommittee on Korean War Atrocities (of the Permanent Subcommittee of the Committee on Government Operations) released new information.

My purpose in bringing out the sheer number of mass murders by both the north and the south, with U.S. and Soviet concurrence, is to contrast and to highlight the political nature of the charges against Lt. George Schreiber, Airman Thomas J. Kinder, and Airman Robert Toth for premeditated murder of an Oriental male, Bang Soon Kil, under extreme circumstances. With much of the Korean populace and the U.S. news agencies following these trials, it was obvious to the American reporters covering Schreiber that the case against him seemed to be somehow contrived. Many of those reporters and members of the military believed that he was, in fact, innocent of the charges. It appeared as if the United States needed a scapegoat to pacify the South Korean government. The press so reported during the trial that in fact the trial was a sham designed to appease the South Korean government. The South Koreans complained that the American forces were murdering and abusing its civilian populace at will, such as bombing and shooting them and turning loose guard dogs on them to maim and injure both women and children. These accusations were far reaching and it almost became the policy of the South Korean government to criticize the United States for having no regard for Korean lives.

CHAPTER 6

Assignment to the Case

IN MAY OF 1953, I was becoming accustomed to the routine in the 75th Legal Office. For me it involved a lot of travel in South Korea and Japan and participating in a lot of court-martial preparation and trial work. I was very happy with my duties and I liked my boss, Major Charlie Weir. He was kind, a good teacher, and a man with incredible patience and excellent ethics. Charlie would give me an assignment, and then tell me why it was important and what he expected of me. The result was that, no matter what it was he asked of me, I felt good about it and wanted to do my best to prove to him that his faith in me was not misplaced.

Charlie called me into his office one day in May 1953 and said that he had an assignment for me that came from the staff judge advocate of 5th Air Force, Colonel Charles L. Loewenberg. The 75th was under the direct command of Far East Air Materiel Command (FEAMCOM). This meant that, under the normal chain of command, the higher headquarters for the 75th was at Tachikawa Air Base in Japan and that our general court-martial convening authority was the commanding general of FEAMCOM. However, in February of that year, the commandant of FEAMCOM transferred his authority over military courts and military justice for the 75th Air Depot Wing to the commanding general of the 5th Air Force in Korea. What this meant is that, for the purposes of conducting courts-martial, we were under the jurisdiction of the 5th Air Force and its staff judge advocate, Colonel Loewenberg. It also meant that I got to take several trips to Taegu, which is where the headquarters was located.

Charlie said, "Bob, I've been asked to assign you to the defense of a premeditated murder case involving a lieutenant in the 543rd Ammo Supply Squadron. I don't know much about the case. I've been assigned as defense counsel for an airman who is to be charged in the same case. Since the interests of our clients may be different, I don't want you to discuss any details of the case with me." I was a bit taken aback for a few reasons. I was just out of law school, had never tried a murder case before, and was being told that I was representing another officer who was going to be on trial for his life.

I said, "Charlie, are you sure they asked for me?" He replied, "Yes, Bob, for you. You and Warren have amassed quite a record at 5th Air Force JAG in the number of cases you have tried, and you're certified to try general courts-martial. There aren't very many certified trial counsel in South Korea, and you are one of them."

Our trial load was horrendous. One reason for this was that the 75th ADW was the organization that ran all of the Air Force bomb dumps in Korea. This meant that a lot of manpower was needed to handle the vast amounts of munitions that were being used by the United Nations forces, for we supplied not only the U.S. Air Force but most of the other UN air forces with bombs and munitions, including rockets, machine-gun ammunition, and the like. These supply depots were strategically placed within a few miles of an operational air base, a rail line, or a seaport. The result was that our wing was heavily staffed with lower-grade airmen who moved and handled this stuff. It was a backbreaking and dangerous job. In addition, these depots were the favorite targets of the many guerrilla units of the Chinese and North Koreans that proliferated South Korea in 1952 and 1953. In fact, we were so hard up for manpower in 1952 and 1953 that the Air Force had a policy of letting its prisoners in the stockades in the Zone of Interior (the United States) volunteer to return to active duty by going to Korea to work in a bomb depot or as stevedores. In exchange, if the man served with honor, his prior sentence would be remitted and he would be allowed to serve out the remainder of his enlistment. In many cases, substantial prison sentences were cut short, and the man had the opportunity to avoid a bad conduct discharge or worse. So a great many of these people were such volunteers, and the offenses among this group in South Korea were numerous. Hence, Warren and I were among the most active trial counsel in the theater. However, the common cases were assaults, thefts, drunkenness, marijuana, heroin, and opium use, and offshoots of the above, including an abundance of insubordination cases.

Many of these cases were disposed of by summary or special courts-martial. In those days, the Uniform Code of Military Justice required that all counsel in a general court-martial be certified, but there was no such requirement in a special court-martial. Consequently, we would very often serve on courts as legal advisors or would oppose non-lawyer prosecutors. The idea was that the defense counsel should be the more-qualified counsel, giving the accused the best chances. In practice, the staff judge advocate who assigned these duties was the guy who recommended to the convening authority that the prosecution take place. In most cases, the convening authority was the SJA's boss, the wing commander. The SJA had a vested interest in seeing that the accused was convicted, since he'd look like a chump if there were too many acquittals. It always seemed to me that the cards were stacked against the accused, even though the system enacted by Congress was designed to be fair and to correct just such abuses of military justice.

With the foregoing knowledge in mind, I said to Charlie, "If it's a case of premeditated murder, why don't they give this guy counsel with some experience?" He replied, "It's out of my hands. Call the colonel."

I called Colonel Charles Loewenberg, and he told me that Major Weir was to defend Airman Kinder and that I would be assigned as the assistant defense counsel for a Lieutenant George C. Schreiber of the 543rd Ammunition Supply Squadron, stationed at K-9 Air Base in Pusan, Korea. He also said that no charges had been brought against either man at that time, but that he was reasonably sure there would be such charges soon. He also said that the cases would engender a great deal of notoriety, and he wanted to be sure that the counsel were knowledgeable about the cases in a timely fashion. He added that I should regard the case as my primary duty for now. He had arranged with the wing commander for unlimited travel orders for me, and the military defense counsel was to be Major Jesse O. Bryan IV, the staff judge advocate of the 3rd Bomb Wing (Light) stationed at K-8, Kunsan, Korea. Armed with this information, I sought counsel from Charlie Weir. Charlie said that I had better get over to Pusan and talk to the former commanding officer of my client, which I did the next day. Schreiber had been detached from his former duty post in February, and was sent to 5th Air Force headquarters in Taegu on temporary duty later that month. He was then reassigned to the 75th Ammunition Supply Squadron at K-10 in March, arriving at K-10 on April 1, 1953. I had not met him until notice of my assignment as assistant defense counsel.

The drive over to Pusan was an event every time. The roads were not paved and were rutted. The route went over at least three mountains, and it always seemed to me that it was a series of roller-coaster rides over a washboard. It was a lot better if we could get a 6x6 truck, but the motor-pool officer lost too many of them to the black-market thieves that proliferated in Pusan to let a lowly lieutenant take one, so it was usually the inevitable Jeep ride. My traveling companion was generally an Airman Peterson from Minnesota. Pete usually traveled with me in Korea. He was my assigned clerk typist and a rugged and good kid the same age as me. We got along well and looked after one another on our numerous trips together. The one thing he couldn't do well was drive the Jeep. So, even though in normal military parlance he would be known as my driver, I always ended up doing the driving.

We arrived at K-9 and eventually located the Air Police headquarters. I asked for the provost marshal, and the sergeant said to wait a minute. Out came a major, who introduced himself as commander of the AP Squadron and Provost Marshal Lee H. Vanderhoven. He proceeded to question me as to who the hell I was and why I wanted to talk to him about Schreiber. After I told him I was to be Schreiber's lawyer, he immediately called the Air Police commander at the 75th to verify that I was who I said I was. After he satisfied himself that I meant no harm, he readily talked about Schreiber. The major told me that Schreiber was his best officer and that Schreiber was being harassed by the Office of Special Investigations, known as the OSI. He also said that this case had been investigated for several months, then closed after the investigating officer had recommended that no action was necessary or warranted. He continued that some "asshole, ass-kissing lieutenants" at 5th Air Force JAG had asked the SJA to let them reopen the investigation. The result was my being there, and that was a sure sign that these "assholes" had succeeded. The major was a big Dutchman, and he left no doubt as to his feelings in the matter. He felt it was a railroad job and that the Korean government wanted to get him as well as his men, including his favorite officer, George C. Schreiber.

Major Vanderhoven recounted for me the duties of his men and of Lieutenant Schreiber. He said that his organization was responsible for guarding and securing the ammunition depot, which was one of the largest in Korea. He also told of the great job that Schreiber had done among the Air Police guards in raising their morale, training them, and looking after the welfare of his men. Major Vanderhoven then recounted how, in the last month before the incident at the root of the proposed charges, two ammunition depots near the 543rd had been blown up by guerrillas with a loss of life of some of the men on guard duty. As a result, there was considerable unrest and fear among the Air Police detachment in the 543rd. Schreiber had calmed their fears and, through appropriate training of the men, had turned his unit into the best Air Police unit in Korea. He was very proud of Schreiber and felt that he was being prosecuted because a "pissant" by the name of Kinder had told a story to his mother upon his return home after his tour of duty. The result of all this was that Lieutenant Colonel Al Nice had come down from 5th Air Force headquarters and conducted an investigation. The investigation was closed on Colonel Nice's recommendation that no action was warranted. The matter had come to life again, Vanderhoven said, only as a result of Kinder's mother complaining to the Chief of Staff of the Air Force in Washington. He also noted that the Korean Foreign Office was involved at this point, as he had experienced trouble in the past with the Koreans complaining about the Air Police guards abusing civilians by turning guard dogs loose on them. He then unwound a tale of bad relations between him and the Korean National Police. He said that every time his men apprehended a Korean national and turned him over to the National Police, one of two things happened – the Korean police would turn the person loose, or they would torture the "poor son of a bitch to death." There was no middle ground. The result was that the biggest thieves in South Korea were the National Police and that the chief of police ran the black market in Pusan.

I knew from my own experience that at K-10 the civilian guards outside of our gate were largely poor refugees or farmers impressed into service by the police as guards, and that any time the National Police wanted to stage a raid, they would enlist the cooperation of the local police guards. One night, they stole several vehicles from the 75th motor pool, and we had accused some of the guards of involvement. I accompanied the Air Police to Chinhae with the two Korean police guards and spoke to the chief of police. He advised me without the flick of an eyelid that, as a sign of his indignation, he would personally see to it that they were to be tortured to ascertain the identity of the thieves. All the while, we had OSI reports attesting to the chief's involvement. The chief was called "Tiger Kim" at his own request.

So, I was no stranger to such information. I felt after my discussions with Schreiber's commander and with the Chief of police in Chinhae that such information would be helpful in representing and discussing the proposed charges with George Schreiber. I told this to Schreiber, who was somewhat cautious with me, although I felt like I knew him a little bit. We were to get to know one another thoroughly before our ordeal ended. George was a tall man, six feet six inches in height, with a firm grip and ready smile. He was very guarded in his statements to me.

Major Vanderhoven suggested that I stay overnight at the 543rd, offering to show me around the base and the bomb dump in the morning. Since it was late in the day and we were told not to be on the road after dark, I agreed to stay. The accommodations at these places were primitive even by standards of the K bases. The men all slept in tents and the officers in huts with tin roofs. The officers' mess was always the showplace, though. It seemed that every mess sergeant wanted to please his officers, so they made a real effort to decorate the mess and to do their best with the food available. They always had a bar set up as well, since there was no officers' club at these places and it was the only place the officers could use as a club. The plumbing was always nonexistent, but sinks were built using inverted helmets. There were counters and a large steel barrel of water that sometimes was heated over a primitive stove. A spigot was welded into the lower part of the barrel. The 543rd was no different. It was always fun for me to visit these posts because the officers always went out of their way to make me feel comfortable and welcome. I could never pay for a drink anywhere I went in Korea as a guest visitor. Major Vanderhoven made sure that this visit would be hospitable, and it was.

Since he was an airman second class and pulled very little rank,

I always had to make sure that Pete was taken care of. So I made it a habit to ask the commander of the unit we were visiting to speak to the first sergeant about accommodations for Pete. The result was that the top soldier usually took him under his wing and looked after him. Pete was a very good poker player and had no trouble occupying his free time while waiting for me.

After returning to K-10, I had my client to myself and was eager to talk with him. I wanted to find out about what had caused the Chief of Staff of the whole Air Force to be involved in his case, and why everyone who knew George Schreiber had such strong beliefs in his innocence.

At that point in my legal career, I didn't have any standard manner of dealing with clients who were about to be charged with premeditated murder and who were fellow Air Force officers. At that time, Schreiber was a first lieutenant and of almost equal rank to me. I predated him in rank by about seven months. He was the first officer that I had been assigned to represent. Usually, a major or lieutenant colonel was assigned to represent an officer as defense counsel, and a very experienced first lieutenant or a captain was assigned as assistant defense counsel, particularly in a capital case where the death penalty was authorized. George began the conversation by questioning me about my education and experience. He asked if I knew Major Bryan, the defense counsel. I told him that I not only didn't know him, but that I had never heard of him. George then spoke of how the "bastards" were out to get him and how he felt that the military wasn't about to provide him with a proper defense. He continued by saying that, since his life was at stake, he was going to hire a civilian defense counsel to assist Major Bryan and myself in defending him. He didn't say anything to make me feel bad, and I encouraged him to hire the civilian defense counsel. From what I had seen of military courts, even with a staff judge advocate as fair and ethical as Charlie Weir, the accused had the cards stacked against him. This was simply because the commander who convened the court was usually convinced of guilt. Otherwise, he wouldn't convene a court-martial to try someone in the first place. This was particularly so in a combat zone, where there was usually a shortage of qualified officers to carry out the mission, let alone sit as a member of a court-martial. If an officer sat on a number of courts and more than two of those tried by the courts were acquitted, it would be reflected in the officer's fitness evaluation. Though nothing was ever said about it, every career officer knew how things worked. So, in effect, once the charges were preferred, it was a foregone conclusion that there would be a conviction at trial then the convening authority could exercise his compassion if the court went too far by exercising clemency after the staff judge advocate reviewed the record of trial. So it went like this – the court would convict, the commander would feel he was right, and any errors or miscarriages would be handled upon review by the SJA. I even noticed that when I would get a few acquittals I was switched to being the trial counsel, as the prosecutor is called in military law. Schreiber and I discussed these facts openly and frankly, and I agreed with him that if his family could afford it, he should hire the best civilian lawyer that he could. I assured him that I would work no less diligently on his behalf and that, while I didn't know Major Jesse O. Bryan IV, I felt he would be of similar mind. With these preliminaries out of the way, we began to discuss the events that led us both there.

George told me the same story that he would eventually tell at his trial. On the night of September 26, 1952, he was awakened from his sleep by a phone call from the sergeant of the guard, Airman Toth. Schreiber had been on medication for some time, and that medication made him exceedingly drowsy and sleepy, so it was difficult for him to really wake up. He said that Toth told him that a Korean had been picked up in the bomb dump, some kind of struggle had ensued, and the Korean had to be subdued before being brought in by force to the Air Police operations office, where he was presently being held. Schreiber told the sergeant that he would be there shortly, then returned to his room to get dressed. At that time his roommate, First Lieutenant Edward G. Penabaker, returned to the room. Penabaker, who was the squadron duty officer that night, asked him where he was going, and Schreiber told him that they had a Korean at the Air Police operations who was picked up by the Air Police. Schreiber finished dressing, and Penabaker either preceded him or accompanied him to Air Police operations. He really didn't know what time it was, but thought that it was midnight.

When Schreiber arrived at operations, the guard was being changed, so that's why he surmises that it was about midnight or 2400 hours. The first thing that he noticed when he entered the office was that the Korean was on the floor, and that four or five airmen were inside the doorway. He wasn't sure who was there, but knows that Toth was there because he spoke to him. He looked at the Oriental and asked Toth what had happened. Toth informed him that this man had been picked up in the bomb dump and tried to get away, but that Toth caught him and brought him in. In the process of bringing him in, Toth had said, the man reached and grabbed hold of his .45-caliber pistol. He said something about stopping the vehicle, looking at him, and hitting him with something. Schreiber understood why Toth would have resisted the efforts of the man to grab his weapon. Schreiber said he then leaned over the man to determine his condition. The lighting was poor, as there had been a power loss and the place was lighted with a gas lantern. He observed a bruise on the man's face and some blood in his hair, which led him to determine that the man had sustained a cut or bruise about his head and face. He turned to look at Sergeant Toth and asked if the man possessed identification of any kind, as he wanted to check to see if the man had been picked up before. Toth informed him that the man bore no identification. He did not recall how the man was dressed, other than that he had on dark clothing. He told me that it was very unusual for a Korean not to have an identification card, as one was needed to get into the area because it was under military control. However, since there was no evidence of sabotage in the bomb dump and the man had no ID, he would normally turn him over to the national police, which he had previously done with other Koreans. He believed the National Police were working with many of the people that his men had apprehended. In short, Schreiber shared my opinion that the National Police were at best thieves, if not worse. He then said, "I told Toth to take this man out – get him out of here, which Toth proceeded to do."

The questioning continued. Schreiber remembered Ed Penabaker, his roommate, being present, as well as Sergeant Addleman. He said that there were one or two other airmen in that office, but didn't recall just who they were or what they were doing there. He did not see Airman Kinder there at this time, but as Toth was taking the Korean out, Kinder came in and walked into the gun room. He told Kinder to take his carbine and his ammo clip and to accompany and assist Toth. He then said that, as Kinder was walking out, he turned around and said in what Schreiber thought to be a joking way, "Is that an order, Sir?" Schreiber then said, "Yes, that's an order." After that, Kinder left.

Schreiber then called for some coffee, sat down at a table or a desk, and talked to Sergeant Addleman. I asked about Penabaker, and he said that Penabaker was there for only a few minutes and left. Schreiber did not leave the office, but may have gone to the entryway. He said that there were airmen coming in and going out during this period.

He remembers himself and Sergeant Addleman sitting at the desk with no one else near them at that time. He couldn't identify who passed in or went out. He believes that he was discussing a shift change with Addleman when he heard shots fired. At that time, he noticed Sergeant Rumpf sitting at a desk and ordered him to go to the bomb dump and investigate the shots. He told me that there were no means of communication between operations and the bomb dump, and if shots were fired it was necessary for someone to be sent to investigate the circumstances. In a period of between five and ten minutes, Sergeant

Rumpf returned and told him that a Korean had been shot in the bomb dump. He called the K-9 dispensary and asked for an ambulance to be dispatched to meet him at the AP squadron area since it was dark and the ambulance driver would not know where the bomb dump was, as it was in the mountains.

He said he then got into a Jeep and that there were others with him, whom he didn't recall. He proceeded to the main gate of the squadron area to await the arrival of the ambulance. In a few minutes, the ambulance arrived and he headed out in front of it, leading the way to the bomb dump. As he rounded a curve at the bomb dump, a guard in the road signaled and pointed a direction to him. He pulled up to an area about five hundred yards from the ammunition dump itself and saw several people there. There was a figure on the ground. The ambulance pulled up to where he stood, and two medics jumped out. He saw an airman named Renteria and his guard dog approaching the figure on the ground. The dog appeared to be highly agitated, and he opined that the dog was a very vicious dog. He remembers going up to Renteria and telling him to keep the dog back and to stay with him. He said that he didn't want anyone to get chewed by the dog while taking care of the individual on the ground. He saw the corpsmen place the man on a stretcher, place him in the ambulance, and drive away. It was very dark out there, as there was no moon, no lights, and the location was in a valley. He then asked what had happened and someone said, "Kinder shot a gook." He got into his Jeep and returned to Air Police operations. He doesn't remember getting out of the Jeep at operations, but decided to go to the K-9 dispensary. It struck him as peculiar that the dispensary was in complete darkness with no lights on. He saw several people running about in a hurried fashion. He waited between five and ten minutes before he was able to get someone's attention to obtain information as to the man's condition. He didn't know who it was, as it was dark in the room. He was told that the man was being treated, was either drugged or a little drunk, and had a gunshot wound, but that he would be all right.

After leaving the dispensary, Schreiber returned to the 543rd Operations Office and inquired as to Kinder's whereabouts. Either Rumpf or Addleman told him that Kinder had gone to chow with some of the other men and had then gone to bed. He then told Rumpf and Addleman to check on the man at the dispensary in two or three hours to determine his condition so that he would know when he arrived on duty in the morning. He then returned to his quarters and went to bed. He awoke between 7:30 and 8:30 in the morning and, after breakfast, went to the Air Police operations building. After he arrived, he asked how the injured Korean was doing and learned, by either a written or a verbal report, that the Korean had died during the night. The clerk typist on duty then took the information from the logbook and typed up an incident report for him to sign for the commanding officer. A report was prepared for the commanding officer in similar fashion each day.

That morning, he received a telephone call from the 17th Air Police investigator. He was told that they wanted to see Airman Kinder regarding the previous night's incident. He told the caller that he would be over with Kinder as soon as he could locate him. He found Kinder as soon as he could, and the two got into a Jeep and started over to the 17th Air Police office. Kinder asked him where they were going, and he told him that they were going to the 17th Air Police office. He explained that the office had called, said they were investigating an incident in this area, and wanted to talk to him about the incident of last night. Kinder asked, "What shall I tell them?" Schreiber said he replied, "Tell them what happened."

I asked him, "What did Kinder tell you?" He said, "He told me – or previously, I don't know whether it was the night before when he had been over here or in the Jeep the next morning – I was told by Kinder, I believe by Kinder, that this Korean came at him and he shot him. We went over to the 17th Air Police, and I met the provost marshal of the K-9, and the Squadron Commander of the Air Police squadron there, and an Air Police officer, and two other officers there. The investigators took Kinder into an office of some type asking about the incident, I surmised. People outside were asking me about it. The provost marshal was discussing the incident in general – discussing a number of incidents which we were having at the bomb dump in the gasoline-storage area, the general problems encountered in that area."

Kinder came out, and Schreiber saw him making what appeared to be a written statement. Then they left. He said that they returned to the operations office, and he believes that Kinder went back to bed. At the office, he believes he spoke to Sergeant Addleman. He recounted that someone was constantly shooting at the men in the bomb dump, that they had men who had been knocked down by intruders, and that this incident appeared to be the "coal on the fire." He said that his men were talking about a battle shaping up with people in the hills. He said, "To be perfectly frank, I was becoming more afraid of their action in the hills."

That day, he prepared lesson plans, made out reports, and made duty-roster changes. He had a normal training class planned for the day. The men were all talking about the incident of the previous night and appeared to be visibly upset. They seemed to be showing more bravado to hide their fears. He cautioned the men not to let their imaginations run away with them, not to make more of the incident than it was, and not to excite their fears by discussing the incident. Later, he went to the bomb dump where the incident occurred and talked to some airmen who had been fired upon by a burp gun from a distance of about forty yards. The men were shaken and afraid to the point where they were throwing up. His men were becoming so fearful that, when they saw a Korean in the street with a knife, they were worried about getting knifed. With all of this going on, he said he instructed his men not to talk about the incident anymore. He told of how he continued to have problems with infiltration into his area by men in the hills around the bomb-dump area, but continually trained his men to cope with the problems.

He told me that he received a spot promotion to First Lieutenant from General Rustow, the commanding general of his command, when the general came to inspect his unit. I asked Schreiber when he first became aware that there was any investigation going on as to the events involving the death of the Korean man. He told me that sometime during the last week in January 1953 he was told about an Office of Special Investigations inquiry into the matter. He had been on temporary duty in Japan for about nine days at a provost marshals' conference and, on his return, some of his men told him that they had been interrogated by an OSI agent. He reacted by telephoning Lieutenant Penabaker and advising him of this information. He also reminded Penabaker of his rights under the Uniform Code of Military Justice against self-incrimination. He said he felt that, since Penabaker was a friend of his, he wanted him to know what was going on. At that time, Penabaker had been transferred to another base. He also questioned his men as to who had been interrogated and who had actually given statements. At a training session for his men, he excused those who had not been on duty the night of September 27, 1952, and then proceeded to remind the men who had of their rights against self-incrimination.

He told me that it may have been the morning after the shooting when he first discovered that Kinder had shot the Korean. The OSI first approached him for information on the incident around the February 15, 1953. When I asked if he felt that he had done anything wrong with regard to the incident, he said that he did. What he told me was that he should have obtained medical treatment for the Korean before he asked his men to escort him to the gate and release him.

He said that he wrote a letter to Sergeant Robert Toth, who had already rotated to the United States for discharge from the Air Force, on or about February 7, 1953. In the letter, he advised Toth of the investigation and also reminded him of his rights against self-incrimination. He said he sent the same letter to Airman Kinder in the United States. In those letters, he wrote, "Remember, I am the responsible officer. You are reminded of your rights under Article 31. It would be better for all concerned if no one would make a statement."

He went on to say that he told all of his men that he wanted them to tell the truth if they made a statement and not to perjure themselves. He then told me that he told his men, "If anyone was in trouble, I will back you up to the limit. Remember, I am the responsible officer. I will help you." He explained these words and actions to me by saying that he felt that the welfare of these boys was his concern since they had been, and some were still, under his command. He told his desk sergeant to type up the letter and to send it to anyone who was present on September 26 or 27, when the event occurred.

He told me that he became concerned once he learned that the OSI was involved, saying, "I know the methods the OSI uses – I have seen the methods the OSI uses on airmen. I knew that these kids would be shaken up if they had anything to be shaken up about." He denied that he had falsified any entries in the logbook for the night in question.

The facts as I was able to gather them from various sources were that the 543rd Air Police Unit was comprised of very few trained men when Schreiber arrived. There were about sixty policemen in the unit. Their duty was to provide guards for the bomb and ammunition supplies that were stored in the area, which consisted of revetments, or storage areas, spread over an area of almost two miles in length in the hills near K-9 Air Base. The bomb dump was very vulnerable to guerrilla attack. The guards were mostly untrained and were eighteen to nineteen years old. When Schreiber arrived, there was no commissioned officer in charge, and there were about six noncoms trained in Air Police work. Schreiber had recently graduated from an Air Police school at Tyndall Air Force Base in which the instructors were experienced FBI agents. He had been briefed as to the intelligence situation surrounding his new place of duty at the 543rd and, to put it succinctly, things were a mess. There was a lack of discipline. No formal training existed for the men, and they were all terrified for their lives.

After his arrival, he had a personal and private interview with every man in the unit. He initiated formal training programs in Air Police work, established a physical training program, and initiated courses so that those men who lacked high school degrees could take courses through the Armed Forces Institute to obtain degrees and receive their diplomas. He greatly increased the morale of the unit and had the respect and admiration of both his men and his commanding officers.

As I would come to learn, Schreiber was given this job at the 543rd after an evaluation by the provost marshal of FEALOGFOR (Far East Air Logistics Force formerly known as FEAMCOM). FEALOGFOR was responsible for furnishing approximately ninety-seven percent of all the logistical personnel for Air Force units in the Far East during that time. It had bomb dumps in Japan, Guam, Bataan in the Philippines, Okinawa, and two in Korea. Of all such installations, the bomb dump at K-9 was the most troublesome. The Koreans were giving us the most difficulty with theft, sabotage, and pilfery. Losses were averaging about $50,000 per month. People were trespassing at the bomb dump every night. There was no fence around the storage area because it was too large, and there weren't sufficient engineering personnel to erect one, although some barbed wire was in use. There was a danger of explosion from the bombs, and it was known that there were several hundred guerrillas operating within a few miles of the 543rd area.

In January of 1952, a radar site in the area had been attacked, and five U.S. Marines who had been guarding it were killed. A number of the guards in the 543rd had been attacked and fired upon by unknown shooters. There was virtually no internal security at the 543rd. On June 16, 1952, an Army ammunition dump a few miles away had been infiltrated and blown up. The dump had been operated by the 8th Army, and more than fifty people had been killed in the explosion and attack. On June 30, 1952, an explosion had been reported at the Air Force dump. Schreiber had been briefed on these events before his arrival at the 543rd. He arrived there around September 1, 1952, after being told by the FEALOGFOR provost marshal that his assignment was the most important of all such jobs in the Far East. Additionally, Far East Air Materiel Command (FEAMCOM) had a new name – Far East Air Logistics Force (FEALOGFOR.)

When Schreiber arrived, he couldn't tell if his men were in the United States military or not. They wore no uniform hats. There was a lack of insignia of rank or identification. Their hair was long, they were not clean-shaven, and they wore any clothing they wished. There were fifteen Air Policemen and ten sentry dogs. The rest were Korean national police. Schreiber requested and was assigned additional men and sentry dogs. He let all of the Koreans go. He then set about to measure the most efficient use of the men and dogs. There was no basic policy on the use of the dogs in any particular time or for any definite number of hours. He started to experiment to see if the sentry dogs could work for twelve hours at a time instead of only the six-hour guard shifts of the handlers. He compiled statistics on the alertness of the dogs and on the rations that they needed if they worked the additional hours. At the end of thirty days, he submitted a written report to the provost marshal giving a detailed and complete report of the progress of his experiments. At the end of sixty days, he gave a full and conclusive report on his experiment up to that time. Subsequently, all of the results of his experiments were published and disseminated to the Far East units that used sentry dogs, including those of the Air Force, the Marine Corps, the Navy, and the U.S. Army. He began writing articles on the use of sentry dogs, military discipline, and training on the job. He went on to write twelve different articles in all, which were published in the *Far East Air Force Bulletin*. It was estimated by the provost marshal that George Schreiber averaged between eighteen and twenty duty hours a day. The provost marshal for the Far East Logistical Forces would eventually rate him as his most valuable officer, ahead of even a lieutenant colonel in his command, and he would testify that he had about six positions that he would like to put Schreiber into. Schreiber was rated by this very senior officer as "far ahead of any police officer or provost marshal assigned to me, including one lieutenant colonel I had for two years. I consider Lieutenant Schreiber a superior officer."

This was an overview of my client and the story from the viewpoint of my client. He never wavered from it and I believed it then and I believe it now. Most criminal defense lawyers have told me that they rely on the presumption of innocence of their clients and never ask for the story from their clients.

Air Force photo of George

CHAPTER 7
Foreign Claims Commission

IN ADDITION TO my duties as a JAG trial counsel or defense counsel, I was designated by the commander of FEAMCOM (Far East Air Materiel Command, later FEALOGFOR) as Foreign Claims Commission Number Three. We were in Korea as part of a United Nations force and technically not as an American Expeditionary Force. This distinction was important, as will become evident later. As a Foreign Claims Commission officer, it was my duty to investigate damages and injuries or deaths caused to civilian persons or property in South Korea in which the Air Force was in any way involved. I had an interpreter, a vehicle, and airman Peterson from the 75th JAG office assigned to me. We had to travel throughout South Korea as part of our investigative duties. I then had to travel to FEAMCOM headquarters at Tachikawa Air Base near Tokyo once each month to have my reports reviewed. These duties entitled me to carry special orders allowing me to travel anywhere in the Far East by the best possible means in pursuit of my duties. This was a benefit that very few officers in the Air Force possessed, as it allowed me to travel as I deemed necessary. So long as I didn't abuse the right, my boss, Major Charlie Y. Weir, was tolerant, as I put my duties in the 75th JAG office as having priority on my time.

My claims commission job required that I travel to Taegu, where 5th AF HQ was located in February of 1953. What I saw and experienced there left an indelible mark on my memory and on the way that I view my life. It has shaped my thoughts on life and death and my dealings with people. It taught me to cherish every day as a separate experience, to live my life in "day tight cells," and to never complain about what we in our society might deem as depressing or upsetting issues or circumstances. With this in mind, I try to cherish each day of health and life and thank my Creator for the opportunity to be of service to my family, friends, and clients without complaint.

What triggered my memories of war-torn Taegu was a newspaper article that quoted a letter I had written to my Rabbi, Baruch Korff, at Temple Israel in Portsmouth, New Hampshire. On February 14, 1953, *The Portsmouth Herald* published an article on page one that quoted my letter to Rabbi Korff. The article also included a photograph of me.

The article read: "'Korea is a land to be pitied with all the pity the human mind can give.' That's the way a Portsmouth officer of the Air Force sums up his impressions after two months in Korea. Lt. Robert A. Shaines, 23, son of Mr. and Mrs. Edward I. Shaines of Hillside Drive, gives a vivid and dramatic account of the suffering he's seen among the thousands of victims of a war-land. 'I have seen families living in holes in the earth, . . . babies playing almost naked in icy puddles, . . . old ladies fighting little boys over scraps of garbage from our mess halls. . . . Inhumanity runs rampant here.'

In a letter to his friend and Pastor, Rabbi Baruch Korff, Shaines told of the shocking conditions war has brought on the Korean people. Shaines, a legal officer with the Air Materiel Command, said in his letter that, 'There are thousands of refugees working at UN bases. Many of these held responsible jobs before the war,' he wrote, 'but now must perform menial tasks to stay alive.'

'The tragedy,' he commented, 'is illustrated at my own air base, where an old man who once taught economics at Seoul University now cleans latrines, and a Ph.D. in physics sweeps the floors in wing headquarters.'

Shaines compares the crowded conditions in Korea to 'a garden too heavily seeded . . . flower begins strangling flower, until only the hardiest survive. God can provide the means to live for only so many organisms in a given area.'

He praised the fortitude of the Korean people. 'It really reaffirms one's faith in the Lord to realize that people do exist for something besides materialism and greed,' he wrote.

In spite of the war, Shaines said the Koreans are looking to the future. 'They revere education and are constantly studying. The little boys who work in the mess halls from 5:30 AM to 8:30 PM attend school for four hours in the evening. These are the more fortunate boys. Their bellies are full . . . they have a place to sleep . . . they can learn. That helps one reaffirm his sense of values and faith in mankind.'"

It is a rare day that passes when I don't place myself in Taegu, Korea, in 1953, standing on a bridge in below-freezing weather and looking down upon the thousands of people groveling to stay alive in a dry riverbed. The sight and smell of death is a constant memory to me and a reminder to thank my God for my present condition each day of my life. I believe that the scene of stacks of the dead and dying waiting to be carted away and the stench from those souls never leaves anyone who has had such an experience. All in all, it is how we use that experience that guides us throughout life. There are those who are afflicted with post-traumatic stress disorder who can never quite recover from such an experience. And there are those of us with faith in a higher power who use the experience to guide our thoughts and deeds as a message to be thankful for life's blessings.

As I promised at the start of this chapter, I said that I would explain the distinction between being in Korea as a UN force and not an American force. Of the many tragedies of severe destruction of property, death, and injury that I investigated and for which I estimated the amount of compensation to be paid to the victims, none was ever paid. The reason for this is that the United States took the attitude that, since we were present at the behest of the United Nations, that body should be the one to make reparations. The UN never voted to do so, nor did the U.S. Congress. I am certain that those people who endured injury, the loss of a loved one, or the destruction of their property at the hands of the neglect of Air Force personnel forever thought of the Americans as perfidious.

Lt. Robert A. Shaines, Tokyo 1953

CHAPTER 8
Article 32 Investigation

AFTER THE UNITED States Congress enacted the Uniform Code of Military Justice, thereby for the first time in our history establishing uniform laws for the trial of military personnel for crimes and military offenses committed anywhere in the world. That same law also mandated the publication of the Manual for Courts-Martial, United States, 1951. The Manual was ever after referred to as the MCM, and the law itself is known as the UCMJ. Since that time, Congress has amended the UCMJ and several revised editions of the MCM have been published pursuant to an Executive Order of the President of the United States (e.g., Executive Order 11476, June 19, 1969, Richard M. Nixon).

Section 29 of the Manual provides:

"INITIATING AND PREFERRING CHARGES. a. Who may initiate. Charges are initiated by someone bringing to the attention of the military authorities information concerning the offense suspected to have been committed by a person subject to the code. This information may, of course, be received by anyone, whether subject to the code or not.

b. Who may prefer. Any person subject to the code may prefer charges even if he is under charges, interest, or in confinement. When a commander is empowered to convene courts-martial and has an official interest in the disposition of the case, it is customary for him to direct a commissioned officer of his command to make a preliminary inquiry into the suspected offense and to prepare appropriate charges if the facts shown by the inquiry warrant the preferring of charges."

In this case, the events giving rise to the court-martial of George Schreiber occurred on September 26 and 27, 1952. The charges were preferred on June 6, 1953, by Colonel Herman E. Hurst of headquarters, 75th Air Depot Wing in the case referred to trial by general court-martial by order of the commanding officer of the 5th Air Force on July 1, 1953.

The official record begins with an order dated July 14, 1953, addressed to Major John A. Webb, 17th Bombardment Wing (L). That order directed Major Webb to investigate the charges that were attached to the order, those charges being made against second Lieutenant George C. Schreiber, HQ. 75th Supply Group, APO 970. The orders went on to say:

"2. Your investigation will be conducted in conformity with paragraph 34, MCM, 1951 and Article 32, Uniform Code of Military Justice."

The UCMJ provided that such investigations would be conducted within 48 hours, and any delay in the investigation has to be explained in the report. As a practical matter, the time parameters were not a problem in the usual military case, since the events being investigated usually took place on a military or naval installation and all of the witnesses were readily available to the investigating officer. In this case, many of the witnesses had returned to the United States or were at other duty stations in the Far East. Major Webb was an experienced judge advocate officer and was the investigating officer in the Kinder case. Hence, he was familiar with the stories of many of the witnesses whom he would be required to interrogate in the Schreiber case. He was not impartial, nor was he unaware of the seriousness of the conflict between statements of various witnesses.

In this case, after Kinder arrived back in the States, he told his mother a story of how he murdered a Korean civilian. Burdened by conscience and in the naive hope that, if he could lay the blame for his actions on his superiors, Airman Toth and Lieutenant Schreiber, he would either not be punished or would get off with a lighter sentence. He told a story that was to result in charges being preferred against Toth and Schreiber. Since Kinder's mother complained to the Office of the Chief of Staff of the Air Force, the charges in effect began at the top and worked their way down through the echelons of command, rather than the other way around, which was the usual manner of events and the one contemplated by the drafters of the UCMJ.

In the military, the suggestion of a commander is generally regarded as a mandate to those subordinate to the commander. In fact, when the information was first presented to the attention of the commander, 5th Air Force, an investigation into the events was conducted by Lieutenant Colonel Al Nice, an experienced judge advocate officer. Nice performed his investigation and recommended that the matter be closed and that no action was warranted. That's where things stood for many months until Kinder's mother made known to the authorities her son's new version of the facts. As time went on, Kinder gave several versions of the "facts," changing them as needed depending upon whom he was talking with. One fact is certain – he shot the Oriental male who would be described as Bang Soon Kil. He understood the gravity of what he did and, for a significant period of time, persisted in his many fictions both to himself and to others officially and unofficially.

His court-martial trial took place at Taegu in July of 1953. Many of the witnesses at his trial were ordered to remain at Taegu to testify in the preliminary investigation required by Article 32 of the code and to remain there for the purpose of testifying at the Schreiber trial, which was preordained to happen due to the obvious efforts of the hierarchy at 5th Air Force headquarters to comply with the requirements of the

Uniform Code of Military Justice. That headquarters operated under the same set of rules under which most military justice systems had operated for centuries, which is to give the accused a "fair trial" before pronouncing him "guilty."

For two centuries, the military and naval services of the United States operated under a system known as "drumhead justice." The Uniform Code was designated by its drafters to eliminate the injustices and criticisms under which the military and naval services convicted and condemned its victims without due process until that time. Hence, it was very important to the Air Force, which had only been an independent branch of the services since 1948, to do things correctly – particularly in a case like this where the press of the world would ultimately take notice. Article 32 itself reads in part as follows: "No charge or specification may be referred to a general court-martial for trial until a thorough and impartial investigation of all matters set forth therein has been made. This investigation shall include inquiry as to the truth of the matters set forth in the charges, consideration of the form of the charges, and a recommendation as to the disposition which should be made of the case in the interest of justice and discipline."

In this case, Colonel Charles Loewenberg designated the trial counsel in May, at least a full month before any charges were preferred against Schreiber. I had been advised of my assignment as assistant defense counsel in June, after charges were preferred, and no impartial investigation was to take place until after Kinder had been tried and convicted of the murder by his plea of guilty as part of a deal made with the commander, 5th Air Force.

What we were all to learn was that the Air Force had cut a deal with Kinder that would reduce his sentence to confinement for a period of not more than two years in exchange for testimony against Schreiber and Toth. This was pretty fair motivation for a 20-year-old murderer "to tell the truth." It got even better as the events unfolded.

Even though the 75th had an impossible workload for its

legal officers, Charlie Weir was assigned to the Kinder case as chief defense counsel, and I had been given my orders by Colonel Charles Loewenberg to commence representation of Lieutenant Schreiber as informal defense counsel.

In May of 1953, the war in Korea began to heat up. The negotiations at Panmunjom were stalled and going badly. The Chinese started an offensive that would take them to the area just outside of Seoul across the Han River. One of the air bases closest to the new military action by the Chinese was K-13 at Suwon, just south of Seoul. I was suddenly ordered transferred to Suwon and K-13. At the same time, President Syngman Rhee, the president of South Korea, had ordered his generals to set free several thousand Chinese and North Korean prisoners of war in the area as a defiant gesture against the Americans and to show his disdain for the armistice talks at Panmunjom.

Martial law had been declared throughout South Korea, and the diplomats were trying desperately to appease the South Koreans and, at the same time, avoid open military confrontation with our Korean allies. On May 30, Rhee advised President Eisenhower that the acceptance of any armistice terms that allowed the Chinese to remain in Korea meant "a death sentence for Korea without protest." Rhee was demanding that all United Nations and communist forces leave Korea at once. On June 7, he declared martial law in South Korea, recalled his chief of staff from Washington, and canceled all military leaves. Rhee, for the most part, did not trust his own generals, and certainly didn't trust the Americans. Against this backdrop of events, I was ordered to leave K-10, which is where Schreiber was posted, and traveled almost 300 miles to K-13 to a new duty station with the 8th Fighter Bomber Wing.

It was difficult to travel in South Korea at best, but at that time in early June of 1953, the Air Force had launched an all-out series of air strikes on North Korea, and all the bases were on full alert because the Chinese and North Koreans were employing guerrilla and military efforts to show their strength and military control of the battlefields in order to influence the armistice talks. I had a difficult time leaving behind my friends at the 75th and also my client, George Schreiber.

After I arrived at the headquarters of the 8th Fighter Bomber Wing, I learned that the staff judge advocate, a lieutenant colonel, was being sent to Japan and then home because he was unable to perform his duties as a result of a serious alcohol problem. I talked to the staff judge advocate on one or two occasions to try and learn what the status of the legal office was, but these talks availed me little information and much less solace. Here I was, the youngest and most inexperienced legal officer in all of the 5th Air Force. I was charged with assisting a fellow officer in the defense of his life and also sent to be the only legal officer in one of the foremost combat units in the Korean theater of operations, taking over a job which called for the rank of lieutenant colonel or even full colonel on the Table of Organization. (The TOO was a document by which units of the Air Force were staffed.)

Shortly after my arrival at K-13, I was summoned to a meeting with the commander of the 8th Fighter Bomber Wing and his executive officer, who in this case was also the deputy wing commander. Both of these men were combat pilots, and they let me know that immediately. The wing commander said to me, "I don't know a damned thing about military law or the duties which you will perform in my name, but as of right now you are the acting staff judge advocate of this wing. I will say this only once – you can sign my name to any document or order you need to. I am too busy fighting a war to be concerned with the administrative shit. But if you get me in trouble, it'll be your ass, not mine."

The deputy echoed this message, and I was for all intents and purposes on my own. I tried to explain my dilemma to them. They both smiled and told me that my first obligation was to the 8th FBW, my second was to them, and then, if I could, I should feel free to deal with my obligations to Lieutenant Schreiber. Suffice it to say, I achieved considerable judicial experience at K-13 because I handled almost all of the wing's military justice problems via non-judicial punishment, convincing the squadron and group commanders of the folly of trying to convene a military court at K-13 at that time in history. Fortunately for me, the 51st Fighter Interceptor Wing was stationed across the airfield and shared the base with the 8th. The staff judge advocate of the 51st was none other than Al Nice, the same lieutenant colonel who had originally investigated the Schreiber case and advised that no charges be brought. His advice and counsel to me were invaluable, as he was a fine man and an excellent military lawyer. The person responsible for my new assignment was the staff judge advocate of the 5th Air Force, Colonel Charles Loewenberg.

Adding insult to injury was the fact that K-13 was a favorite trysting place for "bed-check Charlie." The Chinese and North Korean air forces did not venture too far south of the 38th parallel at that time due to the very heavy concentration of UN airpower. However, they had a nasty habit of flying down some old and slow propeller-driven aircraft to harass us. These planes were known as "bed-check Charlies" because they would come down at about 2:00 or 3:00 in the morning, flying low and dropping small but sometimes lethal bombs. As a result, we would have to spend parts of many nights in slit trenches hoping that the bombs would not strike anything or anyone. I recall one such raid when "Charlie" exceeded his wildest expectations and planted a bomb right in the center of the major fuel depot, lighting up the night sky like the 4th of July, which it may have been, in fact.

With Al Nice's help, I was able to reestablish communication with George Schreiber and also with Major Jesse O. Bryan IV, my senior military counsel in the Schreiber case. Jesse was an experienced military lawyer and was serving as the staff judge advocate of the 3rd Bomb Wing (L), based at Kunsan on the west coast of South Korea, about 150 miles from K-10 and 150 miles from K-13. To say the least, communication and coordination of the defense team and the interaction with our client was to be challenging and difficult. Jesse was a native of Alabama. He was forceful, handsome, and fiery and took no foolishness from anyone, including the 5th Air Force staff judge advocate, Colonel Loewenberg. I learned from both George and Jesse that George had hired a civilian defense counsel, a Michael A. Braun of Tokyo, Japan. Mike was married to a very beautiful Japanese woman and had experience in military law by serving in the U.S. Army. He was forceful, energetic, and liked both Jesse and me. We would come to work well together. Mike would go on to become a senior executive with Mitsubishi in his later life and career.

The Article 32 investigation was to take place at 5th Air Force headquarters in Taegu, and I was not present. Major John A. Webb was described to me by an officer who knew him, but whom I choose not to identify, as an "intellectual idiot." When I first heard that term, I was puzzled. Bear in mind that I was young, inexperienced, and not very worldly-wise. I had a hard time reconciling the fact that an intellectual could also be described as an idiot. So, in my naivety, I asked for an explanation. I was told that, in the law, one very often comes across individuals who are well schooled from a textbook point of view, but don't have the slightest clue as to how such information should relate to the secular world. In other words, there are lawyers who possess a sense of justice, fairness, and what the law should be trying to accomplish in any given set of facts, and those who choose to interpret it literally to the exclusion of common sense, fairness, and justice. I have revisited that term many times in my life, as it applies to lawyers and judges with whom I have dealt over the course of my legal career, and am sad to say I have met and dealt with too many "intellectual idiots" over that span of time.

Having recently experienced an Article 32 investigation on the boat ride over to Korea, I was well versed in the way in which the investigating officer can influence the outcome of charges against an accused in the military. The investigating officer in a case with charges such as those Schreiber faced was supposed to be like the inquiring magistrate used in many European countries and also like a one-person grand jury – tasked with preventing the accused from standing trial in cases where the facts don't justify it. Major Webb was not such an investigating officer, and his performance of his task was a farce. He went through the motions because the book and the law said he must.

It was my experience in the military that most line and operational commanders at that time were totally uneducated in the requirements of military law and justice, and didn't have the time or the interest to become so educated. In fact, they placed all their reliance on the staff judge advocate of the unit to carry out their mandated duties for them and in their name. In fact, the convening authority, instead of being advised by an independent professional, defaulted his duties under the Uniform Code to his staff judge advocate. What happened was that, in matters of military law and justice, the lawyer was also the client. In this case, Colonel Charles Loewenberg was the commanding general of the 5th Air Force, in actuality for all intents and purposes of prosecuting the charges against Schreiber. This was not the scenario that the Congress intended, but then many times the real-world application and enforcement of laws are not those intended by the lawmakers. The intended application of the code was to make sure that the accused was afforded all of the steps mandated by Congress, but ceremony took precedence over substance. In other words, like in the Old West, they wanted to give the accused "a fair trial before they hung him." Form was everything, facts and fairness notwithstanding.

CHAPTER 9
Office of Special Investigation (OSI)

THE AIR FORCE Office of Special Investigation (AFOSI) was and is a field operating agency of the Air Force that provides professional investigating services to commanders at all levels throughout the Air Force. At present, the AFOSI identifies, investigates, and neutralizes criminal, terrorist, and espionage threats to personnel and resources of the Air Force and the Department of Defense using special agents.

Today, the AFOSI is a highly trained force of over three thousand active-duty, reserve, and civilian personnel serving in several hundred locations worldwide. In addition to rigorous physical and firearms training, AFOSI personnel are trained on subjects including polygraph use, behavioral sciences, computer use, forensic investigation, cyber-terrorism, terrorism, economic crime investigation, criminal investigation, and intelligence gathering. It was an OSI officer who first alerted General Douglas MacArthur's headquarters in Tokyo of the North Korean attack in June of 1950 at the beginning of the Korean War. Service in the AFOSI is the second most popular career choice of enlistees. In addition to the AFOSI, today there is an organization called the U.S. Air Force Intelligence Surveillance and Reconnaissance Agency.

AFOSI was founded on August 1, 1948, by Air Force Secretary

W. Stuart Symington, who patterned it after the Federal Bureau of Investigation (FBI). The first AFOSI commander was Special Agent Joseph Carroll, an assistant to FBI Director J. Edgar Hoover. Joseph Carroll was charged with providing unbiased and centrally directed investigations of criminal activity in the Air Force. Originally, the members of the AFOSI were officers and enlisted personnel who volunteered for the service. They wore no indicia of rank, but in Korea they wore a plain uniform with no identifying markings. The special agents of the OSI performed the investigation into the killing of Bang Soon Kil on September 27, 1952, at Pusan, Korea.

Witnesses were scattered throughout the United States and Korea. Statements from these witnesses formed the basis for the Article 32 investigation and the recommendations of the investigating officer to charge Schreiber, Toth, and Kinder with conspiracy to commit premeditated murder and the commission of premeditated murder.

Article 32 in the Manual for Courts-Martial, 1951, provided:

(a) No charge or specification shall be referred to a general court-martial for trial until a full and thorough investigation of all these matters set forth therein has been made, etc.

(b) The accused had a right to be present and represented by counsel and could cross-examine witnesses if available. "The investigating officer shall examine witnesses requested by the accused." etc.

The problem was that the witnesses that Schreiber wanted to have testify were in the United States, and the witnesses to be called by the prosecution were far-flung, most outside Korea. The Article 32 investigation was in reality a perfunctory farce despite Schreiber's requests to be allowed to depose witnesses in the United States. So why weren't any challenges posed at trial to this miscarriage of justice? The provisions of Article 32 (d) provided as follows:

"The requirements of this article shall be binding upon all

persons administering this goal, but failure to follow them in any case shall not constitute jurisdictional error."

The manual itself provides that the investigating officer should carry at least of the rank of a major in the Air Force. It says: "He is required to conduct a thorough and impartial investigation and is not limited to the examination of witnesses and documentary evidence listed on the charge sheet or mentioned in the papers accompanying the charges. He should extend his investigation as far as may be necessary to make it thorough. . . . Any failure to comply substantially with the requirements of Article 32 which results in prejudice to the substantial rights of the accused after the trial – such as a denial of a reasonable opportunity to secure witnesses for use at trial or an opportunity to prepare his defense – may require a delay in the disposition of the case or disapproval of the proceedings."

With this high-minded rhetoric, the Article 32 investigation was performed by Major Webb, who was under orders to complete his investigation and submit his recommendation in four days. When all of the important witnesses were back in the United States, Schreiber's requests through counsel to move the matter to the United States for investigation and trial were denied, as were the opportunities to depose witnesses. The command was under the gun from the Air Force chief of staff to get his case tried and to have Schreiber convicted without ceremony. So came General Anderson's orders, and hence Colonel Loewenberg's orders, all to the prejudice of good order and justice. We later made these arguments in defense of Schreiber, but to no avail.

Ernest W. Gibson, a former governor of the state of Maine who served as judge advocate officer in the U.S. Army during World War II, described his experiences as follows:

"I was dismissed as law officer because the man was acquitted. . . . When the commanding general wanted him convicted, yet the evidence didn't warrant it, I was called down and told that if I didn't convict in a greater number of cases, I would be marked down in my efficiency rating; and I squared off and said that wasn't my conception of justice and that they had better remove me, which was done forthwith."

The Uniform Code of Military Justice was enacted by Congress to prevent such abuses as command influence. Many lawyers returned from World War II disillusioned with the concept that there was actually justice available in the military and that the system intended to administer justice was deemed arbitrary and subject to substantial command influence. Unfortunately, in the early days of the U.S. Air Force, most of the senior commanders were holdovers from the big war and never shook off their ideas as to how justice was to be dealt with in the newly formed Air Force. In addition to this situation was the fact that very few Army JAG officers transferred to the Air Force, so there was a shortage in the Air Force of trained lawyers equipped to manage the justice system under the Uniform Code of Military Justice, as provided in the Manual for Courts-Martial, 1951.

The investigation into the Bang Soon Kil killing was going on at Williams Air Force Base, Arizona, where a Sergeant Leroy Gillette was interviewed. He said he'd heard rumors of what happened and was asked about the whereabouts of a Staff Sergeant Fulghrum. Gillette had called the OSI the night of the shooting and wanted to call the attention of the OSI investigators to the fact that the hole in the deceased's jacket did not match the hole in his body. Fulghrum had brought this to Gillette's attention. Fulghrum was, at that time in March of 1953, at Ent AFB in Colorado Springs, Colorado, and did not know the whereabouts of Airman Third Class Kenneth Stoops or Captain Orton Stokkey.

And so it went. In my experience, most of the OSI's special agents that I met in Korea were noncommissioned officers, poorly trained but highly motivated to obtain convictions. Almost all of the witnesses questioned by the OSI investigators in the Schreiber case complained that their words were twisted or somehow manipulated by the investigators to indicate guilt of the parties being investigated. After three or four inquiries by OSI investigators, they didn't know fact from fiction.

CHAPTER 10
If I Tried to Run

AFTER BEING ASSIGNED to the Schreiber case, I was called in by the wing commander. At that meeting, I was told that Lieutenant Schreiber was under quarters arrest – that he was confined to his quarters except for meals, medical treatment, church services, or legal consultations. Since his military defense counsel, Major Jesse O. Bryan IV, was at Kunsan and his civilian lawyer was based in Tokyo, it was necessary that Schreiber do some traveling to properly prepare for trial.

Since most of Korea was involved with active hostilities, it was very difficult for a civilian to obtain permission to travel within the country in 1953 – that is even if one could get civilian travel arrangements. None of the major airlines were flying there that year. Air China, which I believe was a CIA airline, was the only airline that I ever saw coming in or out of Korea while I was there. The only airfields in the country were under military control.

In addition to Mike Braun not being able to travel to see Schreiber, Jesse Bryan sent word to me that he had duty commitments that made it almost mandatory that George and I travel to see him at Kunsan or Taegu. The upshot was that George was, in effect, placed in my custody for the purpose of trial preparation. The commander told me that I was to remember that the charges against him were premeditated murder and that it was not unusual for people in that position to harbor thoughts of escape. Since we were in Asia, there were lots of places where someone in George's predicament could try to flee to and hide. Hence, he said that for pretrial-preparation purposes he had authorized unlimited travel orders for George and me. He also said that I would be expected to have my sidearm with me at all times, as I would be responsible for George and was to treat him with respect, but also remember that he was a military prisoner in my charge.

Nothing at JAG school, law school, or in ROTC training ever taught me how to handle this situation. Here I was, assigned to defend the man as a lawyer and, at the same time, given orders to act as his police guard even to the point of wearing a .45-caliber pistol at all times I was with him outside of his quarters. Obviously, the only reason for that was that I was supposed to use the weapon if my client made a move that looked to me like he was going to try and escape military custody. I was even provided with a pair of handcuffs and a key. While today I can see all sorts of ethical problems with such an arrangement, at that time being young, dedicated to duty, and obedient, I had no difficulty with my orders and set out to obey them as best I could under the circumstances.

At that time, I didn't know George and set my guard accordingly. That is, when he was at K-10 and we weren't actively conferring on his case, I would turn him over to the custody of the base police. Of course, since he was an Air Police officer himself, I don't believe that they were overly strict with him.

Since one of my additional duties as a trial lawyer at courts-martial was as Foreign Claims Commission officer in a significant area of South Korea, I had unlimited personal travel orders. This meant that I could travel anywhere I needed to in the Far East. I really think the reason for that is that Warren Mengis didn't like to travel and Charlie, my boss, couldn't and didn't want to travel any or more than he had to. The Air Force had three Foreign Claims Commission officers in Korea at that time, and I was known as number three. The idea was that we were there as United Nations troops, but if, in the course of conducting the war, the United States forces inflicted any unnecessary injury to civilians or their property, the injured party could present a claim for payment of compensation against the United States. The United States took the position ultimately that the proper party to pay was the United Nations, and it turned out that the UN didn't pay anybody. However, I put together some very nice files documenting a lot of damage. I was instructed not to tell the victims or their families that no payment was ever likely. The whole gist of this was that I became very knowledgeable about how to get around Korea and Japan. I came to know which operations officers could be relied upon to get me to where I wanted to go, and which just didn't give a damn.

I traveled in Korea by train, Jeep, and airplane and to Japan by air. The system worked like this – I would go the motor pool officer and check out a Jeep if the trip was within one hundred miles of K-10. In such cases, I was required to have an airman ride shotgun and would also bring along the interpreter assigned to me. If by air, I had to arrange a ride through base operations at whatever air base I was near. This often meant waiting for weather to clear, combat operations in the area to quiet down, or, in many cases, for the right type of aircraft to come in or go out. Over time, I became familiar with the sergeants in the various base-operations offices and was given priority treatment over higher-ranking officers. The military had an unwritten rule that "rank has its privilege," better known as "RHIP." This meant that, no matter how important to the mission it was for me to travel, I could count on being "bumped" by rank. The exception was that if the ops sergeants knew you and liked you, they would give you priority over everyone. On the other hand, if there was to be a good poker game that night, I could always arrange to be "bumped." The import of all of this was that I could get George and myself around the theater of operations with minimal hassle.

Thus armed with the know-how, my pistol, and my client-prisoner, George and I took quite a few trips. We eventually became quite close as well.

When first confronted with each other, I had an understanding with George. If he gave me his word as an officer and a person that he wouldn't try any escape moves, I would put the pistol away unless we were in an area where sidearms were mandatory. And I certainly would not entertain the idea of cuffing him. He gave me his word, and I accepted it.

One morning while we were having breakfast at the downtown officers' club in Tokyo, where we stayed on our visits to see Mike Braun, George said, "Bob, if I tried to run, what would you do about it? Would you really try to stop me?"

This question took me by surprise, and I became uneasy and a bit suspicious. I tried to act nonchalant and calm. I took my time, because my first thought was, of course, that I would try to stop him. At the same time, I thought, I sure as hell wouldn't blame him if he did try. My sympathies and feelings were with him and not the Air Force, which had put both of us in this predicament. I finally said, "I'd try to shoot you in a spot that wouldn't hurt or do too much damage." But then I said, "I am a poor shot with the .45, and you'd better not try to find out just how bad." Over the years, I have pondered the riddle posed that morning and still don't really have the answer to the question. Fortunately for us both, he never tried to go. I trusted him implicitly, and he knew it. Although, in retrospect, if the tables were turned, I really believe that George would have acted like the perfect cop and would have told me not to try him that way. In spite of his predicament, he never once to me bad-mouthed the Air Force or the system that put him there.

CHAPTER 11

Formal Charges Under the UCMJ

UNDER THE UNIFORM Code of Military Justice, once it is determined that charges should be brought against a member of the armed forces, a charge sheet is prepared. The charge sheet is served on the accused, which is the term for the defendant under the UCMJ. The charge sheet is dated and identifies the accused and the prosecution witnesses. It includes some documentary evidence and the accusation in military terms, and is signed by an accuser under oath.

In Schreiber's case, the charges were signed by Colonel Herman E. Hurst, the executive officer of the 75th Air Depot Wing, and were dated June 6, 1953. Colonel Hurst further attested that he served the charges on George Schreiber on June 6, 1953. In the same document, it stated that the case was referred to a general court-martial appointed by a special order issued by the commanding general of the 5th Air Force, Major Billy S. Holland. Holland also attested that he served a copy of the charges on "the above-named accused" on July 31, 1953.

Of course, Schreiber had already known of the charges for several months, as I had been assigned to take him into my custody in May of 1953 in order to assist in the preparation of his defense. George was placed in my custody while on quarters arrest by Colonel Hurst upon being informed that he was being charged with premeditated murder and conspiracy to commit murder along with Robert W. Toth, who was at that time a civilian, and Airman First Class Thomas L. Kinder.

The victim was never identified as a Korean or a Chinese man. He spoke no Korean so far as we were able to learn throughout our trial preparation and at the trial, so some bright light at 5th Air Force JAG decided to name him "Bang Soon Kil" and described him as "an Oriental male." This is how the nameless victim was named and identified for the trial and for eternity.

Once the charges are brought, the UCMJ provides that an investigating officer make an investigation, pursuant to Article 32 of the code. Major John A. Webb of the 17th Bombardment Group (L) was appointed by the general, who was also the "convening authority," the person who ordered that the charges be tried before a general court. A copy of the Investigating Officer's Report is included in the appendix to this book. In this case, it listed fourteen witnesses as present and seven as absent. It also listed several documents that were examined by the investigating officer and shown to the accused and his counsel. Since the trial of Schreiber was a foregone conclusion, I did not attend the Article 32 Investigation, but it was attended by Jesse O. Bryan IV, the senior military counsel for the accused. Major Webb's report is dated July 24, 1953, just about ten months after Kinder committed the shooting.

Following these formalities, Major Webb recommended that George Schreiber be tried for the offense with which he was charged by general court-martial. Both Toth and Kinder were charged with the same offense. Toth, who was out of the Air Force and working at a steel mill in Pittsburgh, was taken into custody while leaving work by several agents of the Office of Special Investigations, the Air Force version of the FBI.

We used to work with OSI agents in Korea, as they were the detectives who brought to light many of the cases we JAG officers tried as either the prosecution or the defense. Hence, we kidded with these guys by saying, "I am a member of the OSI, sister service of the FBI."

These agents wore no symbols of rank, and in the zone of the interior (the U.S. mainland) always wore civilian clothing. In Korea, a combat zone, they wore uniforms and fatigues with no badge of rank. Hence, we never knew if we were talking to a sergeant or a colonel, and that was the idea. However, most agents were of the rank of staff sergeant or tech sergeant.

Kinder was the first to be tried. He was tried at 5th Air Force headquarters in Taegu before a general court-martial. He entered a plea of guilty and was convicted. He was sentenced to life in prison, given a dishonorable discharge, and was to forfeit all pay and allowances. What we didn't know was that his defense counsel and my boss at the 75th JAG office, Major Charlie Y. Weir, had made a deal. If Kinder testified against Schreiber as the prosecution wanted, he would be released from confinement and restored to full duty as an airman second class with no loss of pay and allowances. As part of the deal, he would be demoted to two stripes instead of three. He incurred a loss of one pay grade for his part in the murder, thanks in large part to his willingness to testify against Schreiber.

This was kept from Schreiber and his counsel for obvious reasons, since it was Kinder's testimony that proved to be most damaging to Schreiber both in the investigation and the trial.

CHAPTER 12

Pretrial

ON JULY 14, 1953, the investigating officer, Major John A. Webb, delivered the formal notice of investigation under Article 32 of the Uniform Code of Military Justice to George Schreiber.

Article 32 of the Uniform Code of Military Justice provided that no charge of specification could be referred for trial before a general court-martial until a thorough and impartial investigation of all matters set forth therein had been made. It also said, "This investigation shall include inquiry as to the truth of the matter set forth in the charges, consideration of the form of the charges, and a recommendation as to the disposition which should be made of the case in the interest of justice and discipline." The accused also has the right to be represented at the investigation by counsel, including civilian counsel if provided by the accused. The article goes on to state, "At that investigation full opportunity shall be given to the accused to cross-examine witnesses against him if they are available and to present anything he may desire in his own behalf, either in defense or in mitigation, and the investigating officer shall examine available witnesses requested by the accused. If the charges are forwarded after the investigation, they shall be accompanied by a statement of the substance of the testimony taken on both sides and a copy thereof shall be given to the accused."

The object of the Article 32 investigation was to permit a fair and impartial investigating officer to independently examine the charges against a person accused of a military crime and to act in part as the grand jury would act in a civilian setting. Article 32 also required the investigating officer to make a recommendation to the convening authority as to whether or not the charges were correctly asserted, bringing attention to any mitigating circumstances that would result in a less-serious charge being brought or that would lead to the trial being heard before a lesser military court such as a special or summary court-martial. For example, the maximum punishment that a special court-martial could impose was a bad conduct discharge, confinement and hard labor for six months, and forfeiture of all pay and allowances for six months. A general court-martial could impose any sentence, including the death penalty.

The Manual for Courts-Martial stressed the importance of a "fair and impartial" investigation and also stated:

"The officer appointed to make such an investigation should be a mature officer, preferably an officer of the grade of major or lieutenant commander or higher, or one with legal training and experience. Neither the accuser nor any officer who is expected to become the military judge or a member of the prosecution or the defense upon possible trial of the case will be designated as investigating officer."

The Manual also specifies that the investigating officer should "extend his investigation as far as may be necessary to make it thorough." It makes reference to permitting the accused a reasonable opportunity to secure material witnesses and to properly prepare for his defense and says, ". . . a failure to comply with the provisions of Article 32 may result in a miscarriage of justice."

One serious problem that was evident to the defense at once was that Major Webb was also the investigating officer in the Kinder case. He had at this point investigated that case and knew that Kinder and Schreiber had very different versions of what went on the night the Oriental male called Bang Soon Kil was killed. He was also a JAG officer in 5th Air Force, and the network let it be known what Colonel Charles Loewenberg was thinking almost as soon as he expressed it. Hence, the investigating officer was neither fair nor impartial, and several important witnesses had returned to the United States or had been transferred out of the Korean theater. Oh yes – the investigation under normal conditions was supposed to be completed within 48 hours and, if not, reasons had to be advanced in writing.

The fact is that I had worked for Charlie Weir ever since I was assigned to the 75th Air Depot Wing, and we felt we could trust one another. Even though I was now the acting staff judge advocate of the 8th Fighter Bomber Wing stationed at Suwon, about 300 miles away from K-10, I had occasion to travel to K-10 to help prepare for trial. On one occasion, I tried to pump Charlie for information that I felt could be helpful to George. Charlie was upset with me and brushed away from the subject by telling me, "For Christ sakes Bob, I have the responsibility for the kid's life and I'm not going to tell you a damned thing."

This was the testiest that Charlie had ever been with me, and I felt that he was holding back on me. I then used my "source" at 5th Air Force headquarters and quickly learned that a deal had been prearranged between Colonel Charles Loewenberg and Charlie so that Kinder would serve a maximum sentence of two years no matter what sentence the court handed down, including the death penalty. As mentioned earlier, the deal provided that if Kinder testified against Schreiber as a prosecution witness and helped gain a conviction, he would be returned to active duty and have his sentence remitted.

One of the advantages of having been young and willing to travel was that I got to know a lot of the non-commissioned officers and even played cards with them in my travels around Korea. The result was that I had a good relationship with many of the seasoned master and tech sergeants that really ran the various legal offices in Korea and always knew what was going on at any given time. The Sergeants always knew

I had imparted this information to my senior defense counsel, Major Jesse Bryan and Mike Braun, as soon as I could. When the actual Article 32 investigation took place on July 21, we all knew it was a farce. The interesting thing about the military is that so many of the ranking officers felt that they could do anything they wanted as long as they adhered to the letter of the law and to the regulations. The idea behind the law was of little consequence to such people as long as they were in no personal jeopardy. It was called "going through the motions."

The Schreiber case had been initiated at the highest level of the chain of command of the Air Force, the Office of the Chief of Staff. Once that system was put in motion, it was inevitable that the case would get very special attention. In the armed forces, the document known as the efficiency report or fitness report is of primary importance, since most promotions and good assignments are the result of good reports. The people who make out the reports are aware of this fact and wield unusual power over subordinates upon whom they opine in this way twice a year. These reports were referred to as "ERs" in the Air Force. Hence, if an officer took care of his superior, he could reasonably expect the superior to take care of him. In the JAG corps, the senior command JAG officer rated those under him. In this case, Colonel Charles Loewenberg was responsible for the ERs of Majors Webb, Bryan, Weir, and myself. Before my sudden transfer to Suwon, Charlie Weir produced my ER. {efficiency report=ER}

In June of 1953, Charlie called me into his office and advised me that I was being transferred to the 8th Fighter Bomber Wing at Suwon. Suwon was about 18 miles south of Seoul and a few miles west of the Han River. I point that out because, at Suwon, I was at an active Air Force combat base and a few short miles from the front lines. Whereas at K-10, I was at least 320 miles away from the front and the base was a supply depot that was not actively engaged in doing battle on a daily basis. The reason given for this move was that the staff judge advocate at the 8th was ill and in need of hospitalization, and the wing would be without a legal officer once he went for his treatment. So off I went, a green lieutenant to replace an experienced lieutenant colonel in a job that the manning tables provided be filled by three legal officers.

There was indeed a shortage of qualified legal officers in the Air Force in Korea in the year 1953. When I reported in, the wing commander of the 8th Fighter Bomber Wing immediately summoned me. Both he and his deputy were there, dressed in flight suits with colorful scarves around their necks. Both were full colonels. The commander shook my hand, noted how young I was, and proceeded to tell me that he knew nothing of the Uniform Code of Military Justice and cared little about the administrative duties of his office. He went on to say that he was a combat pilot first and a commander second, and that he and his executive officer, the deputy commander, hated desk jobs. They both gave me the following admonition. "You can take whatever action you see fit to take in your area of responsibility and can sign anything you need to in my name. Just keep our asses out of trouble, or you'll wish you had." I then inquired as to the whereabouts of the SJA whom I was about to replace. I was told that he was probably where he usually was, "in the sack, sleeping it off." Later that day, I learned that the illness from which the man was suffering was severe alcoholism and fatigue. He was gone shortly.

I now faced a problem. I was inexperienced, as lawyers go. I had no mentor to guide me at the 8th FBW, and I had responsibilities to George Schreiber, who was facing a possible death penalty in a case that I thought was rigged against him. In addition, I had a hell of a time arranging transportation out of the base at Suwon, as it housed not just the 8th, but also the 51st Fighter Interceptor Wing – together, the two most decorated Air Force units in Korea and the home of the "aces." An ace was a pilot credited with at least five kills or the shooting down of at least five enemy aircraft.

The result of all this was that I was unable to travel to 5th Air Force headquarters in Taegu to attend the pretrial investigation. And although as assistant defense counsel I was responsible for the preparation of any trial briefs and motions and the law and defense requests, at Suwon I had no access to a military legal library. I somehow felt that the SJA of the 5th Air Force had calculated all of those impediments to my carrying out of my defense role in the Schreiber case. To make matters worse, his assigned military counsel, Major Bryan, had his tour of duty in Korea extended by necessity in order to handle his duties in the Schreiber case. Major Jesse O. Bryan IV never complained about this very major change in his plans to be reassigned to the United States, but in fact I believe he welcomed the challenge, for he was not complimentary in the expression of his feelings toward Colonel Loewenberg.

When Congress enacted the Uniform Code of Military Justice, some former abuses and criticisms of military law were addressed. One of the major abuses in the past had been complaints of undue command influence. With this in mind, Article 37 of the code was enacted into law. This section forbade any authority convening a military court from admonishing, censuring, reprimanding, coercing, or by any unauthorized means influencing the conduct of counsel, court members, and investigating officers in the conduct of their duties related to any military court or tribunal.

The article also addressed the widespread abuse of indirectly taking care of the miscreants who wouldn't do the commander's bidding in such cases by providing the following:

"In the preparation of an effectiveness, fitness, or efficiency report or any other report or document used in whole or in part for the purpose of determining whether a member of the armed forces is qualified to be advanced in grade, or in determining the assignment or transfer of a member of the armed forces, or in determining whether a member of the armed forces should be retained on active duty, no person subject to this chapter may, in preparing any such report (1) consider or evaluate the performance of such duty of any such member as a member of a court-martial, or (2) give a less favorable rating or evaluation of any member of the armed forces because of the zeal with which such member, as counsel, represented any accused before a court-martial."

In fact, the code also made it an offense punishable by court-martial to violate the provisions of Article 37. The trouble was that most military commanders were not familiar with the code, and even the old-time military lawyers had not familiarized themselves with its various provisions and proscriptions, as it was a relatively new and completely revised way of dealing with military law and justice. For centuries, military justice had been known as "drum head justice," named after the old Army tradition of drumming the accused from the post after conviction by a military court or tribunal.

A couple of points should be noted here – namely, the accuser in the case was Colonel Herman E. Hurst. He was the deputy commander of the 75th Air Depot Wing, and in reality knew almost nothing about the case. The Uniform Code provided that any person subject to the code could be the accuser. The 75th Air Depot Wing was attached to the Far East Air Logistical Force, which had its headquarters at Tachikawa Air Force Base in Japan and was not a part of the 5th Air Force. Under ordinary circumstances, the convening authority for a general court-martial would have been the commander of the 75th Air Depot Wing, Colonel W.C. Sams, or the commanding general of FEALOGFOR (Far East Air Logistical Force). But because of the extreme interest of the press, the Korean government, the United States State Department, and the Air Force in this case, the jurisdiction had been retroactively ceded by the commander of FEALOGFOR to the commander of 5th Air Force.

In fact, while the commanders nominally are the actors in the paperwork which accompanies the bringing of charges as in the Schreiber, Kinder, and Toth cases, the person actually doing the work of making the decisions was the staff judge advocate of the command – in these cases, Colonel Loewenberg. In reality, the advisor became the actor, taking action in the name of the commander. Most commanders react no differently than did my commanding officer at the 8th FBW, and make it clear to the staff that they are concerned about two things – the primary mission of the unit and keeping their asses out of trouble with higher authority. The appearance of fairness counted a hell of a lot, more than actually being fair, even if a man's life was at issue.

If there is one major criticism that I can level at the Air Force, it is that the more senior in rank one became, the more arrogant and publicity conscious one became. This was true at every level of command, so far as I was able to observe. Added to these concerns was the need for every general officer to be able to point a finger at a convenient subordinate scapegoat if things went wrong and the ability to lie to protect one's ass. This is no different from our politicians from the president on down, and is a sad reflection on our society and its various pecking orders. But to the career military person, this lesson is vital in order to succeed and to have a successful career. There is little room for do-gooders in a military organization, even if it is your job to assure such a thing as a fair trial. In enacting the code, Congress tried to deal with the problem. But in practice it was business as usual – the SJA was required to be loyal to the commander who promoted him and on whose staff he served, since even among the military lawyers and judges they were Air Force officers first and lawyers second, with a few notable exceptions. Fortunately for Schreiber, both Jesse Bryan and I still had those notions, as did Al Nice, the lieutenant colonel who first investigated the charges against Schreiber in this case and recommended that no action be taken against him.

In a noteworthy civilian criminal trial, forces are at work to ensure that the accused defendant receives a fair trial and, if he is acquitted, kudos go to the defense lawyers for doing a good job. It's usually regarded as a sign that the system is working. In the military, when an accused is acquitted, it is a sign to the convening authority that there was a foul-up and someone must answer for the mistake of letting the guilty go free. The U.S. Congress recognized this problem and made it a military offense for a commander or anyone else to take retaliatory action in the form of poor evaluations in efficiency reports for zeal in the performance of one's duties as a counsel for an accused. But, in practice, one had to live with and interact daily with one's superiors and not one's congressman.

The last witness named in the Notice of Article 32 Investigation was Special Agent Frank J. Lanza, 24th District OSI (IO) USAF. The Office of Special Investigations in Korea was both a criminal investigation section and a counterintelligence unit of the Air Force. Its members wore no military insignia and no uniform, except the same uniform or military-type clothing that accredited war correspondents or American Red Cross workers wore. The 24th District was the Korean theater of operations. It had assigned to it both criminal investigators and intelligence personnel, and it answered to its own hierarchy and not the usual chain of command. It was agents of the OSI who literally kidnapped Toth from his job in Pittsburgh, Pennsylvania, and transported him back to Korea against his will to stand trial for the murder of Bang Soon Kil. It was the same OSI that undertook to reinvestigate the case at the instigation of the Air Force chief of staff.

In the normal criminal case, the defendant or his counsel are entitled to obtain a copy of the police investigator's reports, which contain the statements of witnesses against him in order that the defendant might properly prepare his defense. In this case, no OSI agent appeared at Schreiber's Article 32 investigation and Special Agent Lanza's name was crossed out as a witness in the notice of the list of witnesses. As we were to find out, the OSI reports never were made available to the defense in the Schreiber case and to this day have not been available.

As events unfolded, it became increasingly clear to the defense team that the witnesses had been intimidated by their OSI interrogators to the point that they did not know the truth of the facts about which they were to testify. Many even accused the OSI of brainwashing them with lengthy and repeated questioning and threats of prosecution to the point that, when they were in court, they could not distinguish between what they actually saw and recalled and what the OSI agents told them they were to have seen and recalled.

Despite such repeated stories and complaints, to my knowledge no action was ever suggested to remedy these grave accusations of prosecutorial misconduct, and I feel sure these practices continued unabated by the OSI agents. It always seemed to me that it was an OSI technique to intimidate and to frighten people with whom they were dealing with the idea that, if someone were scared enough, the truth would come out. In retrospect, it was the same technique that we have ascribed to the KGB all of these years.

An illustration of just such a case was the statement made by Technical Sergeant Kenneth A. Borchardt during his interrogation by Major Webb in the Article 32 investigation. After being sworn in as a witness and asked if he was familiar with his rights under Article 31 of the code (the military equivalent of the 5th Amendment that protects members of the armed forces from being forced to make statements that may tend to incriminate or degrade them), he was asked by Webb for a second time if he was sure that he understood his rights, a sure indication that Major Webb didn't believe his prior statement. (Webb had already interrogated him in the Kinder Article 32 investigation.)

Borchardt testified that the night of the September 27, 1952, was his first time on duty as a member of the 543rd Air Police, that he didn't know Kinder, and that he didn't remember seeing him that night. He said that when he reported for duty, the first assignment that Schreiber gave him was to accompany Toth and two other persons in a truck, and that he didn't know the identities of the other persons at that time. He said that the truck proceeded to what was identified as Post 12, and the other persons, who were Kinder and the Korean, got out. Webb at that point asked him if he would submit to a lie-detector test, another cue that Webb didn't believe him. The questioning then continued as follows:

Investigating Officer: "When you started driving away before Kinder got out, was there any words said between Kinder and Toth?"

Witness: "That I don't remember. We left Post 18, sir, and we proceeded back to Post 12. On the way back, there was a guard on either Post 13 or 15 who stopped us and stated he heard either a shot or shots fired by Post 12. We then proceeded towards Post 12. When we got to Post 12, we drove up into the road going back to the depot. We drove part of the way and then we stopped. At this time, I seen Airman Kinder standing on the left-hand side of the road, and on the right-hand side of the road a little bit above us was a body lying there. I then got out of the truck and walked over to where the body was lying on the right-hand side of the road. To the best of my knowledge, he had on either a T-shirt or a white shirt. I seen bloodstains on the back of his shirt, directly below the right shoulder blade. I lifted up the shirt, and I seen a bullet hole there. At this time, Sergeant Rumpf came up to the area. It was either Sergeant Toth or Airman Kinder who said that the Korean was shot. I don't remember what else was said there."

Borchardt continued to tell how Lieutenant Schreiber and others came with an ambulance and that the body was removed. He said that he didn't believe that Kinder said a word, but that he might have been talking to Sergeant Toth when the ambulance arrived. He said that his last job had been as an Air Police investigator before his assignment to the 543rd.

Webb then asked, "Did you make any statements to the OSI?"

Borchardt, the experienced Air Police investigator, replied, "I made two statements to them – the first time when I was called in by Mr. Grindstaff and Mr. Specks, and one other. In the first one, I was in there for two and one half hours, and they kept pushing words in my mouth. I went back over later when I remembered correctly. The second statement is the one to the best of my knowledge and belief."

What a powerful indictment of the validity of the statements obtained by the OSI. Here was an experienced Air Policeman, a trained investigator, and a senior noncommissioned officer testifying under oath in a murder investigation about the fact that he had been abused by the OSI into making a written statement that was not reflective of the truth as he recalled it.

CHAPTER 13
Trial Preparations – Witness Interviews

THE FIRST MEETING between Jesse O. Bryan IV, Michael A. Braun, and myself following the Article 32 investigation was at 5th Air Force headquarters in Taegu to coordinate our efforts in preparation for Schreiber's impending trial. Inasmuch as the orders to reinvestigate the cases of Kinder, Toth, and Schreiber came directly from the Air Force chief of staff in Washington, who directed the commander of Far East forces, Lieutenant General Samuel Anderson, to convene a general court-martial to try Schreiber, Toth, and Kinder, their conviction was almost certain. A three-star general (Anderson) doesn't buck a four-star general, the chief of staff. We knew we would be working under a handicap, just how much of one we didn't realize. We were somewhat guarded but hopeful that we could appeal to a court of officers, in Schreiber's case, to use common sense in adjudicating his case at the trial. After a detailed discussion as to what needed to be accomplished, each of us was given our assignments on what we had to do, where we had to go, and whom we had to interview.

I was assigned to interview Sergeant Robert Toth, who was in confinement at K-2 Air Base near Taegu. Toth had been honorably discharged from the Air Force and awarded a Bronze Star medal for meritorious service in Korea as an Air Policeman. I got a Jeep and drove to K-2. I advised the NCO in charge of the confinement facility that I was there to interview Robert Toth. We located the base confinement facility, which was a low, cinder-block building with barred windows and no screens or window panes, just bars. An Air Police sergeant led me down a corridor, and I came to a small cell that was more like a cage. In it was Sergeant Toth.

The cell itself was filthy. There was a bucket for a toilet. There were all kinds of crawling and flying insects in and about the cell. Toth was physically disheveled. He was wearing dirty Air Force fatigues and looked like he hadn't shaved for a week. His hair was wild. His eyes were wilder. When he saw me, he started yelling at me, cursing me out with all kinds of vile language. After he exhausted himself screaming at me, I told him who I was and he began saying, "Fuck you. Fuck the Air Force. Fuck them all. Fuck Schreiber. I hope he dies." He absolutely refused to talk to me in any way, shape, or manner and just kept railing at me. Actually, if he could have gotten loose, I believe that he was so out of control and so angry that he would have tried to kill me. He was a total package of human violence, vitriol, and hatred for anyone in the Air Force. Bear in mind that he had been kidnapped by the Office of Special Investigations of the Air Force from his civilian job in Pittsburgh, spirited aboard an Air Force plane, and taken to Korea to stand trial as a prisoner accused of premeditated murder. I understood his anger.

Eventually, he calmed down and told me that Schreiber was the only officer in the entire damned Air Force whom he respected and that he would help in Schreiber's defense. Ironically, at this time, Toth's sister had hired a lawyer in Pittsburgh and had petitioned the U.S. District Court there for a writ of habeas corpus, which the court granted. The court ruled that the OSI agents had no right to apprehend Toth, who was then a civilian, and forcibly remove him to Korea to stand trial for murder. The judge ordered that Toth be released from confinement, but ruled that he could be kept in Korea pending the appeal of his ruling by the Air Force. The Air Force, through its lawyers, assured Toth's sister and the court that Toth would be given his liberty at 5th Air Force headquarters and treated respectfully. This was all show, as he remained in a flea-infested cell like a caged animal in extreme heat, as he was when I first talked to him. Toth would later make legal history when his case reached the United States Supreme Court, but that part of the story comes later.

I was also assigned to talk to Master Sergeant Raymond F. Addleman, who would turn out to be a very pivotal and key witness at the trial. I was also tasked to interview Airman Thomas Kinder, who was also charged with murder. He was represented by my old boss at K-10, Major Charlie Weir. Charlie very sharply told me that he would not let Kinder discuss anything with me. I later learned that it was Kinder who had returned to the United States, and in a fit of remorse, had told his mother of the shooting of the victim, Bang Soon Kil. In concocting his story he had blamed it all on Lieutenant George C. Schreiber, claiming that he was only following orders when he shot and killed the victim. He told this tale after his tour of duty in Korea had ended and he was stationed in the United States. Kinder thought Charlie Weir had made a deal with Colonel Charles Loewenberg and General Anderson that would allow him to plead guilty, testify against Schreiber and Toth, and, in exchange, have his sentence remitted and be returned to active duty in the States. This is precisely how that all played out. I still remember Charlie Weir saying to me, "Sorry Bob, but I had to do it." Schreiber was obviously the target of the prosecution, and Kinder's "deal" was necessary to prosecute and convict him.

The next fellow I had to interview was Technical Sergeant Kenneth A. Borchardt, who was then stationed with the Air Police squadron at the 543rd Ammo Supply Squadron. He had arrived at the 543rd on September 24, 1952, and had met Schreiber that day for the first time. He then worked with Schreiber for several months until the charges were made and Schreiber was placed in quarters confinement with me as his keeper. Borchardt was a burly man. He was an Air Force veteran, a career non-com. He professed that he wanted to help Schreiber in any way he could, but was adamant that he was going to tell the truth under all circumstances. He is the fellow who testified that Schreiber said, in essence, "get rid of him" in such a way that it connoted to him that Schreiber meant to take the man out and kill him. During my interview with him, Sergeant Borchardt seemed rather kindly and benign, and he gave the appearance of being very forthright. He told me that he thought that Schreiber wanted this guy killed, and that this message was pretty clearly conveyed to all the non-coms who were standing there. I had asked him about Schreiber's mental condition, and he professed that he didn't know very much about it. He said he was a great fan of Lieutenant Schreiber, and that George was a fine officer.

Airman Second Class Thomas Kinder, who was represented by Charlie Weir, was promised a release from prison after he helped to convict Schreiber. He only talked to me in Major Weir's presence. Kinder honed to the line that he was not going to make any pretrial statements. He indicated to me that he didn't trust the Air Force or Major Weir. He also had little trust for a general who would go along with the deal he had made, so he refused to make any statements detailing the events leading to the killing. I think that was probably on Charlie Weir's advice.

In June of 1953, I took Schreiber over to the Tokyo Army Hospital in Japan to have him examined for mental capacity. As you know, in any capital murder case there is always an issue as to whether or not the accused was capable of forming criminal intent or "mens rea." If the accused was incapable of forming criminal intent, then it couldn't be murder in the first degree, or in the Air Force, premeditated murder. The AF psychiatrist, Colonel Gatto, took a complete medical history from Schreiber and was very much aware that Schreiber had been suffering from hives. Because of this ailment, Schreiber had been on very heavy doses of ephedrine and Benadryl, an antihistamine, which George said made him very, very groggy so that all that he wanted to do was sleep. Schreiber said that he had no memory of the events of September 27th, and that he had no ability to really think.

As it turns out, Colonel Gatto wrote up a report that was very favorable to Schreiber, coming to the conclusion that Schreiber would not have had the mental capacity to premeditate. Based upon the reported dosage of Benadryl that Schreiber took that night, Gatto concluded that Schreiber's capacity to pay attention to detail or the happenings around him could have been greatly affected. He mentioned in his report that Schreiber was suffering from severe anxiety due to the stress of guerrilla activity at his command post. He likened it to a state of combat stress. He felt that Schreiber's mental capacity was definitely impaired by the use of prescription medications and his severe anxiety state due to the stress of his duties. As it turned out, he was ready and willing to testify as such, and did so. He didn't tell me what his testimony was going to be. I know he wanted to think about it. He didn't give me a written report at that time.

I spent some time in the waiting room while Schreiber was being examined, but I was present as counsel when the Board of Psychiatrists talked to Schreiber. The board didn't ask Schreiber anything about the offense. I cautioned Schreiber to discuss only his mental status on the night in question. The board was very respectful and did not want any admission from Schreiber. They were there to assess his ability to participate in his defense and to have premeditated a killing on September 27, 1952.

Colonel Gatto subsequently called me and advised me that he was going to be helpful to Lieutenant Schreiber. He said he liked George and felt that he was not guilty of the offenses. How he so concluded, I didn't know, but I was glad that he felt that way.

CHAPTER 14

The Defense Team Comes Together

I HAD MET and worked with Mike Braun at his home in Tokyo on my various trips to Japan in preparing for the trial. Mike and Jesse Bryan had not met in person, but had conversed by phone. Each was apprehensive about the other and, like trial lawyers most places, each wanted to have a prominent role in representing George during the trial. This period of preparation is called planning the trial, which includes designating and agreeing upon who will cross-examine which prosecution witness, the nature of the cross-examinations, and the matters to be covered by the cross-examinations.

There is the matter of dealing with exhibits to be offered by the government prosecutors. It is axiomatic and taught in every law school trial course that a good lawyer never asks a witness on cross-examination a question that he or she doesn't know the answer to be elicited. This means that the trial lawyer must have read every statement of the witness, in most cases must have had an opportunity to interview the witness, and must be sure of how the questioning will assist in the defense of the accused (client). There was also the issue of what defense witnesses would be called to testify, what they would say, and, again, who would handle the witness. There was the matter of defense exhibits to be viewed and discussed between counsel. A trial strategy had to be developed, and counsel had to confer with one another rather intensively and become knowledgeable of one another's trial style. Some lawyers are abrasive with opposing witnesses, and others are charming and smooth. Nevertheless, a scenario for Schreiber's defense had to be developed.

Since the three defense counsel on Schreiber's team had never sat down to accomplish any of this as a trial team, we were ill-prepared to defend a capital murder case. Our client's life was in jeopardy, since the court could impose the penalty of death if the members so voted. In real life, the defense preparation in such a case would normally take a matter of months. In Schreiber's case, we had scheduled a Monday and Tuesday work session, which meant that we would have the 10th and the 11th of August to prepare for trial together. Mike Braun had told me that he believed that he could be in Taegu on August 9, 1953, a Sunday. He in fact arrived on August 11, a Tuesday, at 6:00 p.m. He had to get authority to leave Japan and a visa to return after the trial. Since there was no air service, he had to arrange for military orders to permit him to fly on an Air Force flight to Taegu. He received those orders on Sunday, August 9. There was no scheduled air service on military flights. All of this caused him delay in arriving in Korea. When we walked into court on the August 12, Jesse, Mike, and I had only conferred for about two or three hours before it became evident that my two senior defense lawyers were exhausted. Jesse had just finished a long and important trial by general court elsewhere, that same week.

Mike had tried to obtain from me as much information as was feasible during my sporadic visits and by phone. Mike had met George once in June when we were in Tokyo for George's psychiatric exam, which was my idea, not my senior counsel's. I had met and discussed the case with Colonel Gatto; neither of them had done so. I was familiar with all of the witnesses, having devoted several weeks to preparation of the defense case; they were not. While it was evident that neither of them wanted me to have a starring role in the trial, I was the only member of the defense team who knew the witnesses, had interviewed most of them, and had a handle on how the case for the defense should be tried. I knew the case in full; they did not. They were going to have to wing it and use whatever skill they possessed to put on a defense.

Since I was outranked and out-classed by age and experience, I kept quiet about having a part in presenting the case at trial. I did my best to assist and inform them about what I knew and what I thought as to the strengths and weaknesses of the witnesses, both for and against us. At that time, I had a great many special court trials behind me, and I had become a pretty good trial lawyer, if I may say so. I knew how to cross-examine witnesses, how to pick up on the strength of my case and weakness of the other side, and I could present a very good closing argument to the court members. I had a very strong penchant for defending my clients and winning cases, even though I had been at it for only about 11 months. I believed that I could have been the lead defense counsel and could have done a compelling job in presenting the defense case. I kept my thoughts to myself, as I didn't want to appear to be a "know it all." Besides, if I stayed in the Air Force, I didn't want someone like Jesse to think poorly of me. One thing I did learn in the Air Force is that if a major or any senior officer has an ego, it is unwise to try and challenge it. Jesse could have been a movie star. He was handsome, and his mellifluous, Southern, good-old-boy drawl was captivating. Mike was a no-nonsense type of professional who spoke with a New York accent. He was sharp and also ego-driven. Both of these men were motivated to put on a good show.

There were members of the press who came in from Chicago and other major cities to witness the trial. There were at least three news services also represented. In all, there were probably a dozen major press representatives covering the trial. Jesse and Mike saw the trial as a stage upon which to advance their professional skills and reputations. I saw it as an opportunity to learn but, above all, I knew Schreiber was innocent, and I wanted an acquittal.

By Sunday night, it became evident that we still didn't have all of the documents from the prosecution and some reports from the psychiatric team in Tokyo. This gave us some good arguments, as these files had been withheld from us along with some depositions taken from defense witnesses in the United States. It became my task to outline the defense case for these lawyers and to let them figure out our defense strategy. It was obvious to me that we were far from ready to proceed to trial. Jesse and Mike had agreed upon a trial date of August 12.

On the night that Mike arrived, Jesse and I went to the visiting officers' quarters and woke up Major Farnell, the law officer. We appealed to him for a continuance so we could try to organize our defense for George. He was reluctant to do so, but when we told him about the shenanigans of the prosecution withholding documents and how Mike couldn't get to Korea until 6:00 that evening, he started to soften. Major Farnell asked how long we wanted for a continuance, and Jesse replied that we wanted until 1:30 p.m. on the August 13. That would hardly give us time to prepare, but it was better than no time.

George Schrieber, Mike Braun & Bob Shaines

5th AF Headquarters-Place of Trial

Scribes on sidewalk, Tague 1953

Tague City Center, 1953

CHAPTER 15

The Prosecution's Tactics Begin

THE REAL PURPOSE behind our filing the motion to continue was that, on the afternoon before the trial was to start, two very significant events had happened. The first was that the local Associated Press correspondent had approached me and informed me of a press release issued by Lieutenant General Anderson that day. The American and the Korean press were set to cover the trial in depth. The Chicago papers had picked up on the events preceding the trial and, since Schreiber was from the Chicago area and a basketball player of note for Valparaiso University, his case was noteworthy even at this point in time for the Chicago press. The Korean press believed that the United States was abusing its citizens in a brutal way, and this trial and its events would be a grand opportunity to exacerbate those claims. There was no love lost between the Korean politicians and the representatives of the United States. In fact, there was downright hostility between the Korean president and the United States' diplomatic and military representatives. The opportunity to show up the Americans was particularly satisfying to the Syngman Rhee government. The Kinder and Schreiber cases were to the liking of the diplomats trying to appease the dictator. Toth had become a celebrity of sort due to the manner in which he was apprehended and brought to Korea.

Once Jesse and Mike heard that a press release had been issued asserting Schreiber's guilt and conveying the prosecution's version of the evidence – and especially upon learning that the release had been issued in the name of General Anderson – they became livid. In essence, the convening authority, General Anderson, had publicly declared our client, George Schreiber, guilty of the charges.

I was assigned to try and get a copy of the release, if feasible. Faxes had not yet been invented. Mimeographs were the order of the day for multiple copies of documents. We needed to know what the commanding general, the convening authority of the Schreiber court-martial, had said. It was damned unusual to hold a press conference about a murder case when the trial was going on in his command with his officers sitting in judgment. We met in the officers' club at 5th Air Force headquarters and, over a drink, we tried to brainstorm what was up. We postulated that General Anderson, like most of his peers, was acting in a manner to placate his chief of staff at the Pentagon. If he sought worldwide publicity, this was his chance to get it. The Toth case was in the federal courts in the United States, challenging the jurisdiction of the Air Force. The Schreiber and Kinder cases had already received the attention of the secretary of the Air Force, and the charges were prompted from the Office of the Chief of Staff of the Air Force. As it would turn out, Anderson had said all of this in his press release.

At the same time, the diplomats of both Korea and the United States had taken notice of the cases. In a normal situation, the general would have been advised by his staff judge advocate to remain low key the case and keep his mouth shut so as not to prejudice the court or its members. Such was not to be the case. Both the general and his staff judge advocate had egos that relished the spotlight, and neither was about to give up the chance at such publicity. Just because Schreiber's life or freedom was at issue was no reason not to advance what they believed Air Force headquarters in Washington wanted done with these accused airmen. In short, they cared nothing about a fair trial, but concocted what in olden days would have been seen as a lynch mob. They were of the command influence generation of commanders. We knew it and were determined to try and show that Schreiber could not and would not get a fair trial at 5th Air Force headquarters in Taegu, or for that matter anywhere in the Far East Air Force region and probably at no place under the military justice system.

A place like 5th Air Force headquarters in Taegu is like a small town. All the players get to know one another very quickly. The court members and the defense were all billeted in the same visiting officers' quarters. We all ate in the same place and drank at the same bar. Space was limited, and facilities were even more limited. Taegu was a city swollen with almost a million impoverished refugees, and it just wasn't safe to venture from the military compound areas, even if there was someplace to go. The war correspondents shared the bar at the club with the members of the military, so in short order everybody involved with the case knew who everybody else was. It was in this fashion that the AP correspondent asked me if I knew what the press conference was all about.

That same discussion between Mike, Jesse, and me also resulted in Jesse reminding me that we had never received a written report from the Air Force psychiatrist in Tokyo whom I had taken George to see on June 18. As we discussed this, I said that I had never seen the report, but that Colonel Lucio D. Gatto, the psychiatrist, had said that he would try and help George in any way that he could. Remember, time, distance, and lousy communications had hampered the defense team from communicating and consulting as a team. In addition, I had been transferred away from the base to which George was assigned just weeks before the trial. Jesse had just finished a major trial and was preparing to return to the United States to handle some details involving an appeal of the other case. Mike was a civilian lawyer in Tokyo, and communications between Korea and Japan were difficult even for the military, let alone for a civilian. I was left with the task of traveling to where Jesse, Mike, or George was, then trying to relay the information in a reasonable fashion between all of us. I was also incredibly inexperienced in many ways and had the propensity to trust everybody. So, when Billy Holland the prosecutor assured me that I would have a copy of the psychiatric report as soon as it was available, I took it for granted that I would. After all, he was a major and a lawyer, and thus should be trustworthy in that regard. As we lawyers say, I was satisfied with his bona fides.

With this information now in front of us, we decided to go to see Colonel Loewenberg, the SJA. It was late in the afternoon on August 12. We went to the legal office and asked Jake Hurley, the executive officer, if we could see the colonel. He pointed us to the colonel's door. It was a Dutch door, and the top half was open with the bottom half closed. Colonel Charles Loewenberg was seated at his desk. He looked up and gave us a stern and unfriendly nod, as if to ask by what colossal nerve we wanted to talk to him. Jesse first asked about the press conference and was told that the colonel didn't know anything about it – and even if he did, it was none of our business. Jesse then asked if a psychiatric or other medical report involving Schreiber and addressed to either him or to me had been received at the 5th Air Force JAG office. Colonel Charles Loewenberg said that he knew of none. While the reported conversations seem innocuous enough when I write of them now, the atmosphere in that office at that time was highly charged. Everybody there, staff and officers, knew that there was open hostility between the colonel and the defense team. Jake Hurley made no secret of telling us that Colonel Charles Loewenberg had a lot of ass-kissers in his organization, but was universally loathed by most of his subordinates. He was arrogant to a fault, and was a close pal of Brigadier General Underwood, the vice commander of the 5th Air Force and the man in charge at Taegu. Loewenberg was in the power position. He was technically our boss and had to approve our transfers and promotions. He could and would make life miserable if he didn't like someone. We were told he severely reprimanded Major Farnell for granting us the additional time in which to prepare.

We were about to beat a hasty withdrawal from the JAG office when both the chief clerk and Jake Hurley gave us a nod that they would meet us outside the office in a few minutes. They told us that the colonel was lying on all accounts. Jake Hurley met us a few minutes later at the officers' club bar. He said that the sergeant had told him that a press release had been prepared for General Anderson at the legal office, and that about a week ago he had delivered to Loewenberg a report addressed to me from Colonel Gatto. He continued that the report was in the lower, left-hand drawer of the colonel's desk.

Emboldened by that information and by the drinks, we formulated a plan. Jesse told me to get a screwdriver and a flashlight and to meet him outside of the headquarters building after dark at about 8:00. I did. Jesse then said, "Let's go get the report." It was surprisingly easy. The guards saluted us, and we walked into the building. Down the hall we walked to the legal office, where we tried the door and, to our surprise, it was unlocked. We turned on the lights as if we belonged there and approached the colonel's office. Again, the door was not locked. Jesse then told me to look in the desk. I did, and there on top was an envelope addressed to me. It had been opened. I put it in my pocket, and we closed the door, shut off the lights, and left. My heart was pounding. I trusted Jesse's judgment implicitly. He was a major and a lawyer. I pondered what we were going to do about the situation. How would we handle it?

It was obvious to us that someone had left the doors unlocked and cleared the way for us. We didn't use the screwdriver or the flashlight. We had achieved our initial objectives. The report was favorable to Schreiber, and we finally got it officially through Major Holland, the trial counsel. We now had to contact Colonel Gatto, talk with him, and get him to Korea at once. This we accomplished.

I telephoned Gatto from the Associated Press office, then told him what we had discovered and how much we needed him now. He told me not to tell anyone, but that he would somehow be in Taegu in the morning. He was.

30 June 1953

Psychiatric Evaluation of 2nd Lt George C. Schreiber

On 18 June 1953, the Board of Officers established by Special Order No. 164, Headquarters 5th Air Force, conducted a psychiatric evaluation of 2nd Lt George C. Schreiber, AO 2219359, at 5th Air Force Headquarters, Rear.

On the basis of this evaluation and other available pertinent information relating to this officer the following conclusions were established:

(1) That at the time of the psychiatric evaluation, 18 June 1953, Lt Schreiber showed no evidence of existing mental defect, disease or derangement.

(2) That at the time of examination he was considered as capable of recognizing the difference between right and wrong and of adhering to the right.

(3) That at the time of this examination he was considered capable of understanding the nature of any proceedings that might be taken against him and mentally capable of conducting or cooperating in his own defense.

(4) That for the period of time surrounding approximately 27 September 1952, this officer's mental status and behavior revealed evidence of an underlying severe anxiety state, manifested by evidence of excessive worry, constant internal tension, startle reactions, and irritability related to his duty assignment in Korea. This anxiety state could have served within his given combat security assignment to produce a greater than average difficulty in adhering to the right so as to avoid certain offenses against the military code.

(5) This anxiety reaction is not considered severe enough, however, to have prevented him from recognizing the difference between right and wrong.

The conclusions established above concerning the presence of the anxiety reaction were based upon a review and evaluation of the following psychiatric history.

Lt Schreiber arrived in Korea approximately 17 August 1952, to assume his duties as Air Force Officer in charge of a small air police detachment at an Air Force bomb dump, located near K-9. Prior to his Korean assignment, he had served only two months in Spokane, Washington as Air Police Security Officer in charge of a B-36 flight-line. This assignment was not attended by any evidence of external danger.

When Lt Schreiber arrived in Japan and presented with his assignment as security officer for an ammunition depot, the seriousness of the marked dangers surrounding his assignment were drilled into him repeatedly and emphasized over and over. He was told that guerrillas and night intruders were constantly harassing the depot and stole so much valuable equipment and ammunition, that his

Defense Ex E for Ident.
Appellate Ex 2 for Ident. 303

duties as the only Air Police Officer would require a constant alertness on his
part and an unflagging supervision of his small group of security guards. He wa
cautioned to become highly skilled with his .45 revolver because of the many dan
involved and the repeated encounters with snipers who shot to kill. It was evid
that this officer took this orientation very seriously and that upon his arrival
the ammunition dump, that he was in a combat situation in which he was completel
responsible and on call on a moments notice for any situation that might arise.
Although other duty officers for the ammunition depot were available, it was not
their responsibility to take action if bandits, guerrillas or night intruders ma
raids. For the first few weeks following his arrival at this ammunition depot h
was made keenly aware the entire security situation was extremely tenuous and a
"touch and go" situation. The previous Air Police Officer had already departed
so that he was unable to receive any first hand information. Having already bee
quite shaken-up by his original briefing concerning the dangers in his new assi
ment, the fact that he found the security situation quite disorganized, his men
poorly trained and inexperienced in covering the area involved, he felt that a
ebb of morale was present. He was constantly bombarded by a sense of frustrati
and futility in which he could not gain any real control of the situation no ma
how hard he tried or how long he worked. His fears and anxieties over the situ
were even more increased by his knowledge that approximately one month earlier
nearby Army bomb dump had blown-up.

Confronted by all these difficulties this officer found himself constantly
on the move night and day so that he could only sleep irregular hours. At tim
he would have to try to sleep during the day because he was forced to be up al
night. On several occasions he was unable to go to bed for almost twenty-four
He worked incessantly to improve his organization and to assist his airmen in
way that he could, but constantly with a sense of frustration and futility. A
times during the night his security guards would be pinned down by snipers so
he, together with what other available men he could assemble, would have to ge
their assistance. There were frequent repetitions of nightly shooting which h
all of his men under constant tension. All these happenings during this early
of this officer's assignment to the ammunition dump produced a feeling that he
in "one damn nightmare". Although he felt discouraged, he continued to take h
work seriously and carried his responsibilities to the best of his ability. W
night raiders or intruders were caught he turned them over to the National Pol
of Korea, but found that ordinarily little if any action was taken against suc
individuals. There was further frustration because at times individuals could
seen in different parts of the ammunition dump escaping either over the fence
through holes with ammunition or equipment, but could not be pursued or apprel
since the security air police were not allowed to enter the Korean village an
suspects.

In addition to these the constant reality tensions related to his duties
this officer had also been receiving medication for swelling of his hands, fe
and face, which had appeared following an allergic reaction (hives), several
months earlier following treatment with penicillin for an abscess over his up
front teeth. The medication given consisted of ephedrine and benadryl, two
narcotic drugs. The amount taken was not sufficient to indicate that any to
mental reaction could be produced by their use. This reaction does indicate
underlying physical impairment which would have impaired his physical stamin

Def. Ex. E for Ident.
Appellate Ex 2 for Ident

06-30-1953 psych exam report-pg2

and also play a part in increasing his emotional reactions to his entire situation. While the drug, benadryl, had an effect leading to drowsiness, again the amount used cannot be considered as sufficient to cause impairment of mental processes to the point where the recognition of right from wrong and adhering to the right would be influenced. It would be possible that in a drowsy state, an individual's attention to detail or happenings could be inaccurate.

This officer's past history reveals that throughout his life he has always been a stable, well integrated individual. There is no evidence of excessive aggressiveness or underlying emotional instability in any previous period of his life. He has always shown having a keen interest in athletics and social community activities. In his own home town, he played a large part in a community program aimed toward teenagers. There is evidence that in this work with teenagers he was highly regarded. The amount of time he spent helping individuals in this age group reveals that he must have possessed a high sense of moral and ethical values aimed toward the prevention of delinquency by providing wholesome activities for this age group. He also taught the 5th and 6th grades in school at Brookfield, Ill., where again there is evidence that he was highly regarded.

His military history reveals an excellent cooperative attitude at all times. Upon his graduating from OCS, despite his experienced background, which would have made him suitable for other duties, he indicated that he was an "alphabetical choice" for air police officer assignment with no previous law enforcement background.

There is no evidence of instability within his family group, his entire past history from early childhood reveals a normal development in which it was evident that he could make a good adjustment within any group.

A further factor which must be considered important in his anxiety reaction is the history that in 1946, one of his schoolmates from early childhood was killed in Korea while on guard duty. Although this incident did not consciously effect this individual it could easily have been cause for stimulating, unconsciously, further anxiety in relation to the dangers surrounding his assignment as air police officer guarding an ammunition depot which in his mind, during the period described, was a real dangerous combat situation.

The information given above should be recognized as sufficient to cause in this individual who realistically viewed his assignment almost as a combat situation, a severe anxiety state which under certain situations of stress might cause impairment of this officer's ability to adhere fully to the right as is indicated in AFM 160-42, entitled "Psychiatry in Military Law" dated September 1950, page 19, paragraph 16b(2)(b).

BOARD MEMBERS

ALLAN R. SMALL
Capt, USAF(MC)
Member

CLINTON E. TEMPEREAU
1st Lt, USAF(MC)
Member

L. E. GATTO
Col, USAF(MC)
Senior Member

Def. Ex # E for Ident.
Appellate Ex 2 for Ident.

35

06-30-1953 psych exam report-pg3

CHAPTER 16
Motion For Extraordinary Relief

AFTER THE STRAINED events of the previous day and the somewhat hesitant grant of our motion to continue the trial for a day and a half, the mood in the courtroom was one of an expectant battle about to begin. It felt to me what it must feel like if one was an infantryman waiting for the command to begin an attack in battle. It wasn't the usual butterflies in the belly that we all feel when we are about to make a presentation or a speech. Rather, it was like awaiting a hanging with the soon-to-be victim standing beside you waiting for his life to end and you having no control over the events about to unfold in front of you. I guess I was concerned for the welfare of my client, who faced the death penalty, if convicted. I was feeling somewhat helpless against the power of a military general and an entire government, the United States of America.. We were all standing there about to give our best efforts in defending Lieutenant George Schreiber against overwhelming odds. Our anxiety was not derived from any sense that he was guilty. Quite the opposite – we were anxious because we felt that he was innocent of the charges, but knew we were going against the terrible, mighty force of command influence.

The building in which the trial was held was the actual headquarters building for 5th Air Force (Rear). It looked like, and was, an old college building with ivy-covered walls constructed of stone. The temperature during the trial was in the high 80s and low 90s. There was no air conditioning in the courtroom. The court was set up in accordance with the Manual for Courts-Martial, 1951, with the law officer seated on one side of the room, counsel for the defense on the opposite side, and the members and president of the court seated at a long table between counsel for each side. Opposite the defense was the prosecution table. There was room for approximately one hundred spectators, and every seat was filled either with State Department personnel, Korean Foreign Ministry personnel, or reporters from the Associated Press, the *Chicago Daily News*, the *Chicago Tribune*, and *The New York Times*. Within this setting, George's fate would be officially determined. I believe that it had already been unofficially determined by the commander of the 5th Air Force, General Anderson.

The trial day started with Major Farnell, the law officer, beginning as follows:

"The reporter will record these proceedings. Let the record show it is now 0840 hours, 13 August, 1953, and that the accused, counsel for both sides, the law officer, and the reporter are present for a conference outside the hearing of the members of the court. When the defense is ready, they may proceed with the presentation of the various motions that have been mentioned previously."

Mike remained standing. The rest of us sat after Farnell's opening statement. Mike cleared his throat and, in a loud and sturdy voice for the world to hear and record through the words of the press in attendance, he began:

"The first motion the defense will make is addressed to the jurisdiction of this court over the defendant."

He put forth the proposition that the 75th Air Depot Wing was in fact under the chain of command and jurisdiction of the Far East Air Logistic Force, based at Tachikawa Air Base in Japan. He correctly stated that the 5th Air Force had no jurisdiction to try Schreiber, as he was assigned to the 75th Air Depot Wing, which was a part of

FEALOGFOR. In fact, in my duties as Foreign Claims Commission officer number two in Korea, my superior was not attached to the 5th Air Force, but was based at Tachikawa Air Base, near Tokyo, at FEALOGFOR. Mike went on to reference that the only other general courts-martial that arose within the 75th Air Depot Wing were indeed tried at K-10, a FEALOGFOR base. He said that, as I was formerly an assistant staff judge advocate in that wing, I would verify his assertion. I had participated as counsel in two of those trials. He continued on, saying that Schreiber was the first accused to be tried by a general court convened at 5th AF headquarters. The idea was to lay a foundation for our charge that the command was out to convict Schreiber.

The law officer denied that motion out of hand, as he had already been chastised by the command for granting the continuance for a day. General Anderson and his subordinates knew they had to convict, and wanted to do it swiftly.

We were trying the case against what we knew was the preordained finding of guilty, given the circumstances of acrimonious, abrasive, and discourteous treatment inflicted upon the defense team. We weren't even given a space in which to confer or to work as a team. Evidence favorable to our defense efforts was withheld. Requested depositions of witnesses for the defense were not completed and never even left Taegu. We were trying to build a viable appellate record. This is what good lawyers do in such situations – when the trial is stacked against their client, they build and preserve a record of issues to be decided upon an appeal of the case.

Mike then continued, "The defense makes a motion for appropriate relief, in that it desires to have a record of the motions and to submit evidence in that connection indicating the staff judge advocate of the 5th Air Force and the convening authority, General Anderson, are disqualified from further proceedings in this case. And the defense desires to have the record presented to the commander, Far East Air Forces for appropriate relief. If, before presenting the evidence, you desire that we present the main points on which we desire to present evidence, we would be glad to do that."

Farnell suggested that would be helpful. Mike stated that the accused, being a member of the 75th Supply Group, which was part of the 75th Air Depot Wing, was the first person under that command ever to be tried at 5th AF headquarters. He cited three other general court cases by name of the accused in those cases, all of which were tried at K-10 in Chinhae, at the 75th headquarters, by general courts-martial. He flat out charged that there was discrimination against Schreiber.

Mike went on with his second point, that pre-trial press releases emanating from the office of the staff judge advocate and the general command, i.e. the 5th Air Force, indicated their disqualification in connection with this matter. He pointed out that during the voir dire (the means by which the law officer and counsel may question members of the court to determine if they are sufficiently qualified to sit as impartial jurors in a case) of the court members, references were made to pretrial publicity.

Mike went on, "The law officer and all members are aware that there has been some widespread publicity given. The defense became aware late last evening, that yesterday morning General Anderson released a two thousand-word press release in connection with this matter. The press release was stated in a manner indicating there was nothing to be tried. In other words, it was all set, cut, dried, and finished. The defense has not been able to obtain full copies of that press release. We have the heart of the matter, and if the law officer desires, we should be glad to read it to you as it was given to us."

Farnell was willing to listen and, in a nervous voice, told Mike to continue. Mike told him that the authentication of the document was "from an Associated Press correspondent. We received it by telephonic communication."

The prosecution demanded that we read the entire document,

which we didn't have at that time. This was because my friend at the AP had contacted me by telephone to tell me about the press release since he knew that it would be proof that the trial was indeed a sham, just going through the motions to try to look convincing to the world. It was just that the Air Force was going to try and make it look like a fair trial. Try as they could, they couldn't fool the members of the press covering the trial, nor could they fool us. I think the only one in the courtroom who hoped that the proceeding would be fair was Schreiber. We knew better, but kept our counsel to ourselves so as not to diminish all hope of an acquittal, no matter how slim the chances. The assistant prosecutor, Lieutenant Roth, argued that we could be taking words out of context. He submitted that we had gotten it wrong somehow or twisted the words of Lieutenant General Anderson, and that we didn't get the full meaning of the press releases. We not only got it, we got it right. We saw it as a veritable order to the court members that they had better convict Schreiber and do it fast. That ass-kisser Roth was trying to make points with Loewenberg and the brass at 5th Air Force. He was a sleazy guy, and I wanted to get up and punch him. I sat quietly, my stomach churning. Mike went on to say the defense would prefer to have the full statement, then continued, "The defense understands that Colonel Charles Loewenberg refused to grant a continuance of the case yesterday, because he probably knew this was being published and hence the defense would have been precluded from the knowledge of this until the trial was under way."

The fact is that Loewenberg had to have conceived of the idea and had either written the press releases or edited them for the general. Generals didn't do their own press releases. They had staff to do that. Guys like Loewenberg vacated their senses of justice for the sake of their careers, if they ever had such a sense in the first place. There are two kinds of lawyers – the majority, members of which will go to any sacrifice to see to it that an injustice is not perpetrated on anyone, and those who are self-aggrandizing and willing to do anything, including evacuating from their minds any ideas of justice, for what they perceive to be the greater good. In this case, this meant that if the general wanted someone convicted, there would be a conviction.

There are appellate judges on the U.S. Supreme Court today with such a mindset. They were appointed by the president with the consent of the Senate, and they willingly sacrifice the ideals of social justice by interpreting the Constitution and laws to accommodate a particular political belief. Justices Scalia, Alitto, and Thomas, and to an extent Chief Justice Roberts, are politically minded judges loyal to their perceptions of the greater good – the greater good being their political ideas. Colonel Charles Loewenberg and Lieutenant Roth were both of the same ilk. Both would probably be proud that I thought that of them in that way, for such people are blinded to the real ideals of fairness, and they look at the law and their function as jurists as being interpreters of words. They do not consider fairness and coming to righteous decisions as a part of their professional undertakings. A great many prosecutors who later become judges seem to act in that manner. Since the state or government has been their client, they seem to believe that the state can never be wrong when they must adjudicate issues involving their former benefactor. The hope that we as a society have is that President Obama will be able to appoint jurists such as Judge Sotomeyer. We hope that governors will stop making judicial appointments from the ranks of former prosecutors, but will dig deeper into the talent pool available. Because, as I previously stated, the majority of lawyers have a sense of justice and fairness, not a slavish loyalty to the state that spawned them as lawyers.

The assistant trial counsel, First Lieutenant Gerald D. Roth, then started to rehash the proceedings of the day before, interrupting Major Holland, the trial counsel, in the middle of a statement. Roth was a pompous and grandstanding young lawyer, and he continually interrupted whoever was speaking, trying to talk over everyone. It became obvious to me that Major Farnell, the law officer, didn't like him. After that bit of sophistry by Roth, Farnell shut him up whenever he could. Farnell even told Roth that he could be excused from the proceeding, ostensibly "to prepare anything that the prosecution may want to introduce in rebuttal."

Roth, not being quick of mind but nevertheless mouthy, and who was in the habit of listening to himself speak; he was intoxicated by his own verbosity. He remained at the prosecution table. He was one of those people who never quite hears well, but nevertheless has opinions on everything that he thought he heard. I did not like him. As the trial progressed, he tried to take over the prosecution from Major Holland, the senior trial counsel for the government. I despised him as the hours went by, and I played mental games with myself as to how to manifest my feelings toward Roth. On the other hand, Major Holland was a lawyer with a fine sense of justice. It seemed obvious to me that he felt he was doing something odious in prosecuting Schreiber for premeditated murder. He exhibited a melancholy-like countenance when not speaking. All through the trial I had the feeling that Major Holland was unhappy in his job.

Mike then read out loud the notes that I had taken from the phone call. "The incident occurred at approximately 2100 hours, at the 543rd Ammunition Supply Squadron, at Korea. The incident involved a man by the name of Kinder, who apprehended the Korean at the bomb dump. After apprehension of the Korean, Toth arrived and took Kinder to Air Police operations. Toth summoned Schreiber; Schreiber discusses it with Toth; and Schreiber arrived at the decision that the Korean should be shot. Since the Kinder case is disposed of, Kinder is no longer involved. A decision was made by Schreiber to take the Korean out and shoot him. The Korean was placed on a 6x6 truck and driven to the bomb dump to an area near K-14. After shooting the Korean and firing one shot into the air to summon the sergeant of the guard, the sergeant of the guard arrived at the scene with Lieutenant Schreiber. After that, Lieutenant Schreiber summoned an ambulance, and the Korean was taken to the K-9 hospital shortly afterwards. The record of the incident was falsified. No higher headquarters was made aware of the incident. As the defense indicated, this statement, the entire release, was released by General Anderson in the evening of August 11th from the Seoul press billets."

Mike continued, "The third reason the defense advances is that the staff judge advocate failed to forward depositions turned over by the defense. These depositions were returned unopened to the defense yesterday after adjournment of the court."

"The fourth item: The staff judge advocate failed to make available to the defense material information in the case as was his duty. For the first time, one document was received at 11:30 yesterday after the defense found out it existed and further received a second document at approximately 1900 hours yesterday after the same procedure had to be used."

He did not reference my and Jesse's examination of the last document in Loewenberg's office. I held my breath when he started down this path. My heart throbbing as I saw myself being an accused, and then I relaxed and exhaled when there was no allusion to the matter of Jesse and I seeking out the document he referenced. In the Air Force, such doings were often referred to as "midnight requisitions."

Mike went on to present our fifth item. "The staff judge advocate has failed, and still has failed, to turn over documents received in the full OSI investigation. Only such essentials as the trial counsel has seen fit to make available were released to the defense."

Roth would later testify that it was his understanding that we were only entitled to documents that the prosecutors would use to convict Schreiber, and that any items helpful to the defense could be kept a secret and not disclosed to us. This guy had an unfailing habit of not understanding justice or due process. In a way, I could forgive him because he was too dumb to get it. But the commander and his staff judge advocate did get it, and they intentionally disregarded any efforts to be fair. In the final analysis, that is what the law is supposed to be about – a system of fundamental fairness to protect the innocent and convict the guilty with a fair system of rules, fairly implemented.

Mike then presented our sixth item. "Despite the fact that the defense was to interview a Korean doctor, a material witness to the case, who was here yesterday to testify, said witness was released to leave. Despite the fact that we made efforts to locate said witness for an interview, he was not available."

They didn't want us to talk to the doctor. As would become evident at trial, he had never examined the body. He had been out of a Korean medical school for less than two weeks, and had entered the cause of death in the death certificate. We were sure they had told him to get the hell back to Pusan before we could talk to him. Roth said that they couldn't find us. Everybody else at 5th Air Force knew we sat at a table in the officers' club, as no other venue was made available to us. Schreiber had no club privileges. That had to be part of the game – make the defense prepare in a space where they could not confer with Schreiber. I invited George into the club, and no one dared to bring it up.

Mike moved on to our seventh item. "The staff judge advocate assigned trial counsel long before referral of this case. It is in the record that this case went to him on July 31st. In other words, before any pretrial investigation, this case had already been assigned to trial counsel. The trial counsel did go to work on this case as investigating officer."

In presenting our eighth item, Mike said, "Certain assigned personnel thereupon entered into actual and full investigation long before said referral. [This was] contrary to court-martial procedures, in that before any pretrial investigation of this case, the trial counsel was already examining witnesses and obtaining statements from them. Such duties as the trial counsel [are] usually performed after appointment, thereby becoming an investigating officer."

It was illegal under the UCMJ for one to serve as an investigating officer and prosecutor. The investigating officer was supposed to be impartial. Major John Webb was anything but impartial.

Regarding our ninth item, Mike said, "Failure of the staff judge advocate to designate an impartial investigating officer, as required." Major Webb was given 48 hours to complete his "impartial investigation" and to make his recommendation to the general. What bullshit. A lot of our witnesses were in the United States or stationed elsewhere other than in Korea. We had no chance to get the investigating officer to talk with them. He only dealt with those whom the commanding general wanted him to interview.

We requested the right to present evidence on these issues and asked that the record be forwarded to the commander of Far East Air Forces for review along with the request that we have a trial in another place where no such discrimination would be tolerated. Not likely, since the entire case was going forward on instructions from Air Force headquarters in Washington.

After that, Lieutenant Roth said that we "should have made our motion to the commander of the Far East Air Forces." He evidently was not listening again, as that was precisely what we sought to accomplish. The law officer, looking sneeringly at Roth for his stupid remarks, then told us to proceed and to put on whatever evidence we had to back up our positions.

Mike stated that I would testify as to three prior general courts held at K-10. Holland agreed to so stipulate. (A stipulation is an agreement. In a trial, it is usually an agreement as to what a particular witness would say if called to the witness stand or an agreement as to a fact or a set of facts.) As to the press releases, we didn't present anything further, other than to refer to them. There was a stipulation that the scene of the events in the case took place at or near K-9 Air Base.

We then called Master Sergeant Hebert E. Fensler to the stand. Fensler was the chief clerk at the 5th Air Force JAG office, assigned to the military justice section. The term "military justice" seemed like an oxymoron to me at that point in time. When he said that, I rolled it over in my head. If there was to be justice in the military, I thought, why in hell were we all assembled? What were we all doing there, and why were we trying to eradicate Schreiber? I was having a difficult time understanding all of the events that were rapidly happening in Schreiber's life. I recall that I didn't quite know how to figure it all out. At the time, it just did not make sense to me. I was an Eagle Scout. I loved my country and all it was supposed to represent, including a blind justice system. Seated beside me was an All-American basketball player, a grammar school teacher, a religious person, a patriotic American boy, a mild-mannered person by nature, and by reputation a very good officer. How was it that he was on trial for his life? Normally, a guy like George Schreiber would be believed by the chief of staff, the commander of the 5th Air Force, Lieutenant General Anderson, Colonel Loewenberg, or even by Major Billy Holland. But here we were going through the motions of performing a trial by court-martial prior to sentencing him. The conviction was a foregone conclusion according to General Anderson's report to the world press. I did later learn from Billy Holland that he never doubted Schreiber's testimony and that he truly believed that he was innocent of the crimes for which he was convicted.

Sergeant Fensler testified that Major Bryan had sent several depositions of defense witnesses to the 5th Air Force JAG Office for transmission to the United States in order for us to obtain evidence of George's good character and propensity for truthfulness. It was intended that these testimonies under oath would be evidence favorable to George Schreiber. The depositions, instead of being forwarded to the United States for the testimony to be obtained by military lawyers, never left the office. Someone put them into the safe, and there they remained. Fensler testified that his boss told him to give them to trial counsel Major Holland. The chief clerk, Fensler, said that he had given the depositions to the trial counsel, then had seen them again on the previous morning, when he gave them back to Major Bryan before court started. He said that they were in the safe. He said that Major Bryan had come to the office and asked him if he knew where the depositions were, and Fensler said that so far as he knew they were still in the safe. "I went to the safe, and there they were," Fensler said. No one from the prosecution saw fit to do what was required of them – namely, to review the deposition questions, add their own cross-examination questions if desired, and forward them to JAG officers in the areas where the witnesses resided. The JAG officers, who never received the deposition questions, were then to obtain the answers to the questions under oath, write down the answers, administer an oath to the witnesses, and return them to the prosecutors so that the testimony could be placed before the court. Those documents were marked as appellate exhibits.

But we still didn't have the testimony under oath from those who knew George best and could have testified that murder was something that George would have never conceived, let alone have ordered. It would have been completely out of character. We had intended to obtain depositions from the president of Valparaiso University, his basketball coach, the superintendent of schools where he had worked, the athletic director at the university, a man who was a director on the board of General Motors Corporation who knew George well, and others. We had none of these depositions because the government didn't want us to have them. In a murder case, the character of the accused is always an issue, particularly when he is to testify that he didn't do it and is innocent of the charges. This evidence could at a minimum sway court members to vote for conviction of a lesser offense, one that would conceivably avoid the risk of the death penalty. Lawyers must consider the life of their client in such a case and do everything possible to avoid the harshest penalties available. This we tried to do.

Again, Roth had a suggestion. The law officer had just suggested that some of the proposed testimony could be stipulated. Everyone was in a rush to convict Schreiber, it seemed. I asked myself, "What's the hurry?" Then Roth said, "As each of these points are brought up, do you think it would be appropriate if trial counsel answers them in their legal concepts at that particular time . . . rather than waiting until it is dulled in the counsel's memory?"

I again thought the only dulled memory among counsel would be Roth's. If he couldn't remember our issues, he could have written them down as Mike stated them to all of us. Major Farnell responded, "No, I don't think so." He was again interrupted by Roth trying to force his point. Farnell let us proceed in the order that Mike had presented.

Our next witness was Major Jesse O. Bryan IV. He testified that he had started his duties as defense counsel for Schreiber on or about the 21st or 22nd of July, that he had prepared deposition questions for the proposed defense witnesses, and that around the 28th of July he had sent them to Major Holland as required. He said that he had next seen them on the previous day. He said that Holland had told him on the phone that they hadn't been forwarded to the United States as required, and asked Jesse if he would stipulate the testimony of the witnesses. Jesse said he told Holland that it was up to Mike as individual counsel. Mike asked Jesse if he was aware of the difference between stipulations and depositions. Jesse responded that he was "most certainly" aware.

Jesse then testified, "Well, in my experience, the court will believe what they want to believe about any witness, but a stipulation is not necessarily proof that something is false or true. It is just something stipulated. Later on, it can be attacked just like any other piece of evidence can be attacked. I do know, so far as depositions are concerned – in my experience, they carry much more weight than a stipulation would carry, and that was the reason I prepared them. Because, in my experience, in my studies, the law says a reasonable doubt can be created by proof of character alone, and that is why I wanted the depositions to reach the various people of the United States, such as the president of the university, the athletic director of the university, besides the board of directors of General Motors, and things of that kind."

Jesse told how on the previous morning he had been at the window in Loewenberg's office, and the colonel had told him that there wasn't enough time to obtain the depositions. So it was again evident that it was Loewenberg who was calling the shots. There was a Dutch door on Loewenberg's office, so that it opened in halves, and when the bottom was closed and the top was open, it was like looking into the office through an open window.

Mike then asked, "This is a very serious case?"

Jesse responded, "It is the most serious case I have been associated with in my life."

Both Holland and Roth were permitted by the law officer to cross-examine Jesse. This was something that I had never seen before, nor have I seen since, in my years of trial practice. It now makes me reflect on the question of how much actual trial experience Major Farnell had. The usual rule is that only one lawyer to a side gets to question a witness, unless there is an agreement to the contrary. Mike objected to the procedure of allowing both of them to cross-examine Jesse, and he was overruled.

Roth bumbled on with a misconception of how the deposition process was supposed to work, and Farnell finally shut him off. I thought to myself, "What a pompous know-it-all that guy seems to be." I disliked him more and more. On re-cross by Holland, there was an attempt to get Jesse to admit that he knew the depositions would not be returned to Taegu by the time of the trial. Jesse responded, "I knew no such thing."

Billy Holland kept trying to ask questions by testifying himself, and Jesse would not bite. Holland was on the spot. Roth tried to come to the rescue of his senior, both by asking and telling Jesse that the depositions would not have been back in time for the trial even if they had been sent to the United States and other places as required. Jesse said he considered the depositions "would be here on the 12th." Roth kept pressing, and Mike objected.

Roth said, "But he has not answered the question."

Farnell responded, "Objection sustained. I believe the witness has answered the question."

The next witness was me – First Lieutenant Robert A. Shaines, 8th Fighter Bomber Wing, K-13, Korea. At this stage of the trial and all that preceded it, I was too angry within to be nervous about anything that would or could be asked of me. I answered in response to Mike's questions that I was the assistant defense counsel. He showed me the psychiatric report and asked if I had seen it before. I said I had seen it on the previous afternoon.

He asked me, "Did you know that such a document existed?"

I replied, "I didn't know such a document existed for a fact, no sir. I suspected that such a document should have existed, but I had no actual knowledge it was in existence."

I further responded that the withheld document was of great significance to the case and could definitely affect the outcome of the trial.

Mike then asked me, "After receipt of this document, did you suspect another document existed?"

A. "I did, sir."

Q. "Did you take any steps in connection with that?"

A. "Yes, sir. I asked Major Holland, and he said he did not know if such a document did exist or not and that he would make a search for it."

Q. "Did anything happen after that?"

A. "Yes, sir. Late in the afternoon, I learned this other document which I suspected was in existence was actually in existence, and I did see a copy of it."

I said that I saw a copy of it late in the afternoon. I identified it and said that I later received a typewritten copy of it. We moved to mark it as an exhibit, and Holland objected because it wasn't signed and he didn't know if it was something the psychiatrist prepared for his own files or not. Upon this, Farnell said that he assumed we would withdraw the psychiatric report.

Mike responded, "No sir, I did not withdraw it. I intend to put on another witness."

I was then cross-examined:

Q. "Were you present during the original psychiatric interview of Lieutenant Schreiber?"

A. "What do you mean by original?"

Q. "The one the document Defense Appellate Exhibit No. 3 relates to. The last document."

A. "Yes sir, I was present."

Q. "You knew the answer?"

A. "I did, sir."

Q. "Did you at any time request of me the second psychiatric interview a copy of the second report?

A. "I did, sir."

Q. "When?"

A. "On 18 June, 1953, at approximately 1100 hours, I think, sir."

Q. "This document is dated 30 June, 1953?"

A. "That is right, sir."

I went on to testify that Major Holland told me on that day that a report would be prepared and that I would receive a copy it.

Q. "Weren't you furnished a copy?"

A. "We were not, sir."

Q. "Did you make any further request for a copy?"

A. "I believe, sir, I made a further request after that board was over that afternoon. I made a request of the board and another request of you."

I went on to reiterate in response to questioning that Schreiber asked me to accompany him to the psychiatric board review, which I did. I added that, after the board's inquiry of Schreiber, I talked with Major Holland. I added that Holland was the one who had advised me of the board being convened in the first place, and that he had told me that when a report was issued, I would get it. I then explained that I had never seen the report until late in the day on the day preceding. I did not go into any detail as to how I had first seen the report on the preceding day, as that matter was closed by the intervention of higher authority.

I was then cross-examined for a second time by Lieutenant Roth, who asked me when I was assigned as assistant defense counsel in the case. I said that I had been informed of the expected assignment in early June, but that my orders officially came on July 31. He again asked me the same question, at which point Farnell said the question was already answered. "It provides no worthwhile point," he said.

I smiled – another gaff by the goof.

We then called Lieutenant Roth as a witness. He identified himself as First Lieutenant Gerald D. Roth, U.S. Air Force, Headquarters, 5th Air Force. Mike showed him Appellate Exhibit No. 2. Roth said that he had seen it about one week after "it was compiled." He was then shown Appellate Exhibit No. 3 – the psychiatric report. He testified that he had given a copy to Schreiber late in the morning on the previous day. He said that he looked for a copy and couldn't find one, so he went to the doctor who conducted the examination, "and I found in his files this report. At that time, I looked for the defense counsel to get in touch with the defense counsel. And I believe I spoke with the accused and said we had it ready, but believe the defense counsel was not in this area. And the next time I saw defense counsel, I told him about it and said we would give it to him any time he wanted it."

Mike continued questioning Roth.

Q. "When you were asked yesterday, by myself and possibly Major Bryan, whether such a document existed, did you answer at that time that you are not sure whether or not there was a document; that you would search the records?"

A. "I may have said I am not sure I have one. If I was asked directly whether such a report was compiled by Lieutenant Tempereau, I most certainly would have said yes, there was such a report. I may have said I don't think we have one and that I would look."

Q. "Did you indicate to us that a written report did exist at that time?"

A. "I believe I must have. I don't recall the conversation, but if I knew it existed, I certainly would not have told you that it did not exist. I don't remember the conversation specifically."

The conversation about which he was being questioned had been held the day before. The answers were patently false as far as I was concerned. Mike continued with his questioning.

Q. "Did you see the original of this document?"

A. "At one time, I did see the original. I can't recall exactly when or where. I believe it may have been when I spoke to Lieutenant Tempereau at one time."

Q. "Did you have copies prepared of this document yesterday?"

A. "I did not prepare them, but I heard they were being prepared by the trial counsel."

Roth was next asked if the exhibit was a true copy of the original, and he said he couldn't swear to it. Farnell then let it be marked as authentic. Holland did not object any longer.

Mike continued.

Q. "Have you now turned over, or is the defense in possession of, all documents pertaining to this case?"

A. "I don't know what documents the defense has, so I could not answer your question."

This was not a very astute question on Mike's part, but as he became agitated by Roth's answers, he seemed a bit unnerved. This was not good for us, as Roth was a smart aleck and fended off Mike's questions by claiming he did not recall the answers Mike sought – basically lying, but in a protective way. If a witness doesn't recall something, there is nothing that can be done other than to keep pressing until that witness looks and sounds preposterous.

Q. "Is it your duty, or part of your duty, as assistant trial counsel to see that the defense is informed and has full copies of all material furnished to it?"

This was another bad question by Mike. I knew what he meant, namely that the prosecution must turn over to the defense all reports and statements concerning the accused and obtained in the investigation of the offenses. This would include psychiatric reports and statements of witnesses and experts, whether or not the prosecution intended to use them at trial or not.

A. "What I understand of the Manual {the Manual For Courts-Martial} that defense counsel will be supplied all statements and all evidence that the prosecution uses on trial, and I believe to understand completely why these reports were not turned over to you prior to today. The records should reveal they were psychiatric reports, and that the conclusion of the reports was that the accused was sane."

Mike then said the reports would speak for themselves and that he wasn't asking Roth to interpret them. Farnell then started discussing the Manual. Mike responded, "I don't want to question on the basis of the Manual," and he continued to question Roth.

Q. "Did I understand you to say, Lieutenant Roth, you believe the trial counsel's duties are to turn over only those documents which the trial counsel intends to use at the trial?"

A. "I believe that is what the manual says."

Unbelievably, the law officer, Farnell, then broke in with the statement, "I believe it is an immaterial question. I am going to . . . "

Mike countered, "Well, sir, give me an opportunity to go further."

Farnell then says, "All right."

Q. "Then, in the conduct of your duties as trial counsel, you do not turn over to the defense those documents made available to the defense because the trial counsel will not use them. Is that right?"

A. "As I understand it, every statement, whether favorable or unfavorable, made by any witness in the course of the many investigations in this matter has been turned over to the defense."

Mike then asked if Sergeant Addleman was a material witness, and Farnell stepped in to tell him we were discussing the two psychiatric reports. Mike said he was addressing our point five. He asked if he could show Roth the manual and ask him about it. Farnell dismissed the issue of what the manual provided, although it was the most important issue of due process. Due process said another way amounts to a fair trial. But Farnell was having none of it. Having been chewed out, reprimanded, and threatened by Loewenberg, he was taking the route of fair trial be damned. His approach seemed to be, "If it's a conviction they want, I will let them have it."

My mind was made up. If this was the way the Air Force determined justice, I wanted no further part of it. Roth's corrupted interpretation of what was required sickened me, and the fact that the supposed impartial judge, the law officer, couldn't or wouldn't recognize this as a serious problem was a signal to me that we were doomed. This was true unless, that is, someone at higher authority, to whom we were appealing, woke up to what was happening in Taegu and in this trial. Mike said, "Very well. I am discussing operations of the duties, and whether the staff judge advocate failed to furnish all material copies. And the question was if he considered Sergeant Addleman a material witness."

Q. "Did you turn over to the defense the interview of Sergeant Addleman by the OSI investigator on March 18th?"

A. "I did not, myself, individually, turn over any documents to the defense in this particular case. I do remember at one time when, answering your question, sir, I do remember when Major Bryan first came down, I showed and gave him the whole file – every single statement."

Q. "Did you turn over the OSI investigation in this case?"

A. "I was never asked to. No one ever asked me. I did not turn it over."

Trial counsel Major Holland interjected, "They are not entitled to it, anyway."

The law officer responded, "This is a matter of argument."

Mike continued, "We contend this staff judge advocate is prejudiced, discriminatory, and the accused cannot get a fair trial here. And I would like them to have the trial counsel state so."

Mike asked Roth if the OSI file contained information harmful to the interests of the United States or if it contained material that could aid the enemy. Roth said, "It is marked 'confidential.'"

Roth admitted that the prosecution had complete copies of the entire OSI investigation. Mike told Farnell that the defense had made a written request to the staff judge advocate for the complete file, and that we had never received it. "The defense again repeats its demand that this important document, containing material which will be of material value to the defense in the trial of this case, be turned over to the defense, and charges that failure to turn that over indicates such prejudice and discrimination as to justify the actual request."

Responding to questions from Major Holland, Roth then stated that he had told Major Webb about the psychiatric report and asked him if he wanted it. He said that he told Webb that unless the defense asked for the psychiatric reports that Webb didn't need them. It got worse with this fool testifying.

Q. "The defense counsel didn't know it existed. Is that right?" Roth was asked in reference to the psychiatric reports.

A. "The accused went through a number of psychiatric examinations. Each time, he was accompanied by the defense counsel, so that I imagine that the defense counsel did know the existence of the report, that the examination did not lead to a dead end, and further, therefore, I assume the defense counsel did know of the existence of the report."

Q. "But you had never turned it over to the defense counsel until yesterday. Is that right?"

A. "Yes, that is right. I never turned it over to defense counsel."

Roth was asked more questions, including whether or not he turned over the entire copies of statements taken by OSI agents. He said he didn't know. He also made a particularly peculiar statement. "From a legal standpoint, it is immaterial completely . . . " to identify a dead person in a murder investigation.

Things got worse.

Q. Referring to the OSI's inability to trace the identity of the deceased, Roth was asked, "And is that the reason you did not turn that over to the defense?".

A. "No, I did not turn any papers over in this case, and I wish the record to reveal this. I, in the office, am a minor participant. I am only a lieutenant in the office of the staff judge advocate of 5th Air Force, and I can't answer all of the questions you asked. I do not do the actual handling of the material."

Q. "Who does have the responsibility in your office, the office of the staff judge advocate, of turning over to the defense material documents in a case?"

A. "I imagine it would be the trial counsel and assistant trial counsel."

Q. "Which includes yourself?"

A. "Yes, it does."

This last repartee thereby exposed the stupidity of the assistant trial counsel.

We next called Major Holland to the witness stand. He very much kept to the same party line as Roth had. It was obvious that he had started working on the Kinder, Toth, and Schreiber cases in mid-May, as he knew he would be trial counsel if they came to trial. He said that he thought Lieutenant Penabaker and Sergeant Addleman were withholding information. He was ultimately asked the following questions.

Q. "Didn't you threaten the witnesses at that time unless they gave you testimony as to certain facts?"

A. "No sir, I did not. I was asked by Penabaker 'What can they do to me?' and I said, 'Well, Penabaker, I don't know.' I opened the manual, pointed to the portion there about poor memory under perjury and dereliction of duty. Now, on Addleman, I couldn't answer truthfully whether Addleman was told anything about perjury or not. He asked me, 'Major, I want to know my legal rights," or something to that effect. Whether or not they could do anything with me or not, I don't know truthfully whether I said anything about perjury or not."

Q. "You get the statement you desired when you interviewed them?"

A. "No, as a matter of fact, I didn't."

Holland testified that Colonel Charles Loewenberg told him to start working on the cases in May. The significance of this is that the Article 32 investigations were a sham and, all along, he knew the case would come to trial, no matter what the investigating officer found or recommended.

Q. "I show you Appellate Exhibit No. 4 for identification and ask you whether you interrogated Lieutenant Penabaker or not?"

A. "Not when the statement was made, I did not interrogate Lieutenant Penabaker."

Q. "Is that statement incorrect?"

A. "That statement, insofar as the time he signed it, saying that I interrogated him – I interrogated Lieutenant Penabaker the day before, and he gave some of the information, but not the part about the agreement between Lieutenant Schreiber and Kinder and Toth. That part was gotten from Lieutenant Penabaker by Lieutenant Roth."

Getting down to facts, Penabaker was Schreiber's roommate at K-9. On the night of the killing, he was also the duty officer. If he heard Schreiber give an unlawful order, i.e., to take the man out and kill him, he had a duty to intervene, countermand the order, and stop it all. He also had the authority and the duty to arrest and place in custody anyone, including Schreiber, if he believed there had been a violation of military law. Thus, if he overheard an agreement to murder the Oriental victim, he had an obligation to stop it. He was an Air Police officer and, as the duty officer, stood in the stead of the squadron commander. He was either a co-conspirator, or he was out of it and overheard nothing. He was like a cat on a hot tin roof, and he ultimately concocted his story to say what was in his best interest. Major Holland was in a deal-making mood after making his threats to key witnesses such as Penabaker and Sergeant Addleman. The fact is that Penabaker could well have been prosecuted as an accomplice, if not a conspirator, but was allowed to go home in exchange for his testimony. Charlie Weir made the same deal for Kinder – tell them what they want to hear, and we will let you plead to manslaughter and go free.

After a bit of wrangling, and after Roth insinuated that Jesse was lying about when he was assigned as defense counsel, Jesse testified that he was told he would defend Schreiber around June 18 or 19.

Major Farnell then asked the most important question.

Q. "When did you receive the majority of papers accompanying the charges in this case?"

A. "I received them on, I would say, to the best of my recollection, I received them on or about the 26th or 27th of July."

Roth made an attempt to continue to questioning Jesse, but he was cut off. We then called Major Webb, the Article 32 investigating officer, as a witness. He identified himself as Major John A. Webb, U.S. Air Force, Station K-9 Air Force Base, Legal Office, 75th Bombardment Wing, Light.

He said that he had originally received some OSI reports concerning this case, but that he was told that the 75th Air Depot Wing would handle it and all of the reports following that were sent to Major Weir at K-10. He testified that he had served as investigating officer on only two cases, Kinder's and Schreiber's. Major Webb testified as to his lack of experience with military justice. He said that he had been a JAG officer for only two years, but was certified as counsel in general courts-martial.

It was clear upon questioning that Major Webb was not an unbiased investigating officer as required by the UCMJ. He had served as investigating officer in the Kinder case and had read OSI files concerning Schreiber. He knew he was acting contrary to the provisions of the new Code of Justice, but didn't bring the matter to the attention of anyone. He sat as spectator during some of Kinder's trial. He admitted that he compiled his report in the Schreiber case before actually conducting the investigation pursuant to Article 32. He testified that he delayed the formal investigation of Schreiber's case for "the convenience of Mike Braun," probably because the colonel suggested to him that Mike would stay on after Webb's investigation for the trial. In other words, this guy admits that the Article 32 was nothing more than going through the motions, and there never was any intent to have an impartial review of the circumstances involving Lieutenant Schreiber.

Mike asked about the psychiatric reports.

Q. "I would like to show you this document marked Appellate Exhibit No. 2 and ask you whether you have seen that document before, or a copy thereof?"

A. "I don't remember seeing it before. It seems to me that a document with a similar title, and that this document was handed to me, entitled 'Psychiatric Report of Second Lieutenant Schreiber.' It seems to me it was a one-page document rather than a three-sheet affair, and I had that particular document a matter of a few minutes. Lieutenant Roth handed it to me, and shortly after that took it back."

Q. "I read to you the final paragraph:

'The information given above should be recognized as sufficient to cause this individual, who realistically viewed his assignment almost as a combat situation, a severe anxiety state which under certain circumstances of stress . . . '"

The assistant trial counsel Roth objected in the middle of the reading by Mike and was again overruled.

Mike continued, " . . . might cause impairment of this officer's ability to adhere fully to the right as is indicated in AFM (Air Force Manual) 160-42, entitled 'Psychiatry in Military Law,' dated September 1950, page 19, paragraph 16b (2) 9b)."

This was the defense that every lawyer representing one charged with premeditated murder would hope for, as it set up a complete defense as to the premeditation of the accused and could act as a complete defense to the charges against Schreiber. This is the document for which we had to search and inspect by any means available. This why Colonel Gatto was so upset that he had flown to Korea the night before the trial began. He, like us, smelled a rat and was beside himself that the railroading of Schreiber to trial on these charges was so blatantly wrong. The command did not want us to know such a report existed, and we had to use extraordinary means to discover it.

Mike continued with his questioning.

Q. "If you had that document as investigating officer, would you have conducted your duties as investigating officer differently than what you conducted them?"

A. "I don't know. You never know exactly what you would do if you had different circumstances, but I don't think I would. Now, as I got through with that hearing, there was no objection made there to the Kinder investigation, nor in the present 32 investigation on Schreiber, as to anything referred to here. Now I did bring it up very briefly in examining Airman Toth. As a matter of fact, he didn't bring it up."

The answer was not only unintelligible, it was completely stupid since it was clear that we didn't know the document existed and it was kept from us at every turn. Since he had now changed the subject to Toth, Mike began a line of questioning on this subject.

Q. "It was raised by the voluntary statement by Airman Toth?"

A. "After he was fully warned of his rights."

Q. "What was the voluntary statement?'

A. "It is in the Article 32 investigation, and you saw it. I have a copy of it."

Q. "And what did it say?"

A. "It said that he was a very fine officer. It said he pulled the organization together when he got there and made it into something, and that he was always cool and collected and that he never showed any nervousness under strain – at least, that he never acted queerly."

Q. "At least that they could tell?"

A. "Well, you see, I read all those statements, and from these statements I gathered quite a bit that Toth was being either acting sergeant of the guard or corporal of the guard, or some such, for a period of time, and from his own statement that he was there before Lieutenant Schreiber was there, and that Lieutenant Schreiber was a wonderful officer and had a good record, and the fact that I got it in another statement from Major Vanderhoven, his commanding officer, who said he was an excellent officer. He was definitely above the average. I thought Robert Toth was a very material witness on any particular issue of facts."

Q. "You didn't consider that civilian Toth was a qualified psychiatrist?"

A. "No, of course not."

Q. "You knew there had been a psychiatric report?"

A. "Yes, I knew it. As I . . . "

Q. "I refer again to the original question I asked."

A. "Just a moment. After I read all these statements over, before I began the hearing, I am referring to – you asked me about this Kinder case?"

Q. "No, you are not an experienced psychiatrist are you?"

A. "No sir, I am not."

Q. "As a trained officer and a legal officer . . . "

A. "The Article 32 on the Schreiber case, I also examined all these documents and I made a determination at the time that Schreiber was sane at the time of the alleged commission of the alleged offense and at that time I was beginning the investigation, now, then during the period of this investigation, as I mentioned, Toth volunteered a statement and I questioned on it at some length to bring out any possible indication that we should make a possible investigation into that particular fact of the case. Now, no questions were offered and made, and no suggestions were made by the counsel for time to have a separate investigation made by any doctors or psychiatrists, so we continued on."

The law officer asked him who was present at the Article 32 investigation, and he said that Jesse, Mike, and I were present. After a bit of thought, he recanted and said that I was not there. I was not there, having been reassigned to the 8th Fighter Bomber Wing, a long distance away in Suwon. There, I was overwhelmed with responsibilities as the sole legal officer for the wing, and I had to perform a variety of duties, as my wing commander and the deputy wing commander were combat pilots and left the administration of the legal affairs solely up to me, with the authority to sign their names to any matters which I deemed appropriate. It is too bad that I couldn't have been there, as I was the one who had the conversations with the psychiatrist Colonel Gatto and whom he told he could be helpful to the defense.

Webb continued on and volunteered the following statements.

" . . . Now, at the end of that hearing, I thought about it again. I don't know whether they received it or not, but somewhere along there I made a decision and there was no issue raised on the question of sanity. And I think that is what you have reference to in the excerpt you read to me. Then again, after all these, we had a verbatim report made of this hearing at your request. And we complied with that request and, after writing that out, proofread the testimony. And then you were furnished with a copy, and a considerable period of time has elapsed since that afternoon and this trial we are now in. When I was collecting this material to forward to the convening authority in accordance with instructions, I had a form to fill out, an investigating officer's form, which had certain boxes with reference to sanity. And I marked those 'no' and, at that time, I had to make a decision as to what I said, and I put it down and I made the determination there to the best of my knowledge and conscience."

Q. "And you didn't receive that document at the time you conducted the investigation?"

A. "It might have been in my hands, but I am sure I didn't read it."

Q. "I believe you are aware that the defense did not receive this document until yesterday?"

A. "I don't know when they received it, if they did receive it. But I know I didn't give it to them."

Q. "If you had seen this document, would you have sent it to the defense?"

A. "I don't know whether I would or not, because I made my determination. It might have been wrong, but I was appointed to make the investigation and make certain answers in my report, and I didn't feel that on everything I had. Now, this is just one report purportedly by some doctors. And assuming they are the best and fully qualified, still in all, I had a voluminous amount of testimony that I had carefully read and testimony from witnesses they had given us answers on certain parts of whether they thought the individual was sane. Now, I can go on to other things, besides the medical reports, and that is on what I made most of my decision on."

There was some discussion that he had attached a psychiatric report on Kinder as a part of his investigation on Kinder. Major Holland interjected at this point that the psychiatric report on Schreiber was missing. Major Farnell then interjected, "I don't think the trial counsel would accuse the defense counsel of stealing."

The argument continued, and Webb then amazingly testified, "I didn't think it was important, or I would have put it in. I didn't think the man was insane, or there wasn't any issue raised on that point, and that is why I didn't go to any great length on that."

Mike continued with his questioning.

Q. "Isn't that a point of judgment you were making before conducting the pre-trial?"

A. "No. I wouldn't think you would put it that way. No, at least three different times I drew up and considered this question. One was when we started the hearing and the second was one was during the hearing. And then Toth brought out about Lieutenant Schreiber being such an excellent officer, and I think he was telling the truth. And I did bring out any possible suggestion along that line, and if you will look at the testimony of Toth in that investigation, he gave a completely negative report on this issue. He is one of the men that knew a great deal about Lieutenant Schreiber and had worked with him, and I consider Toth one of the best witnesses on this point which was at issue."

Farnell, after some back and forth among counsel as to why he attached the psychiatric report on Kinder, but not on Schreiber, questioned Webb.

Q. "After your investigation was prepared, the hearings were over, the typing completed, and you signed your report and forwarded it – did it contain all the information that you had obtained during your investigation? All of the material?"

A. "With the possible exception of the psychiatric evaluation, which seems to the best of my recollection that it came into my possession for a period of a few minutes."

Major Webb was then asked if the accused and his counsel were furnished with a copy of Webb's report. Webb replied, "And the answer is I don't know, sir. The manual calls for three copies to be prepared and forwarded to the convening authority. However, the answer is no. But even though the answer is no, many of these statements were furnished to Major Bryan many, many days before the Article 32 investigation occurred. And even before I was appointed, he had these statements and was given them, a very complete set, and he was studying them when I first saw him." He then added that he didn't know if the defense got a complete copy of all of the statements of witnesses.

My less than brilliant colleague Roth then said, "Before we recessed, I asked the defense counsel to clarify the motions he made at this time. I do not understand specifically what the motions are – what relief is requested?" If he didn't know by now, no one would be able to amplify on the motions. We were raising the issue that the most important document and proposed testimony to keep our client from the death penalty had been obfuscated by him, Major Holland, and Colonel Loewenberg, and that we had to go to extreme lengths to even find it. Apparently, Major Webb was too ignorant of the law to understand the significance and extreme importance of the psychiatric opinions given. As I said earlier, Webb was described to me as a Harvard Law School graduate and an "intellectual idiot" who couldn't answer a straightforward question. On the one major defense item, all of them played stupid. Major Holland was not being stupid, just covering his ass for the sake of his position. The other two, Webb and Roth, were just plain stupid or at least devious, in my opinion. After Roth spoke, Mike said, "I think we better recess before we get into an argument."

Roth, not to be silenced, said, "At this time, we have no idea what the legal context is. We have a lot of motions that do not request relief so far as I know. I do not understand what relief is being requested by the defense counsel."

Major Farnell then gave us a forty-minute recess. Upon our return from recess, we called Colonel Charles L. Loewenberg to the witness stand. He identified himself as the staff judge advocate of headquarters, 5th Air Force. He was asked the following questions.

Q. "Are you aware, sir, that a release was made by General Anderson on the night of August 11th or the morning of August 12th at the Seoul Press Billets concerning this case?"

A. "No."

Q. "You have no knowledge at all of that, sir?"

A. "I answered the question."

Q. "Are you aware at this time that such a release has been made?"

A. "No."

Q. "In other words, prior to this interrogation, you have received no information of any such release?"

A. "Is that a new question?"

Q. "Sir, it is a new question I wish you would answer."

A. "Read the question back."

Q. "Sir, do you know whether such a release has been made?"

A. "I don't know if such release has been made."

Q. "Do you know if such release has been prepared?"

A. "I know that PIO at headquarters was working on a release in this case. I will change that to say, another release on this case – there have been many, many releases on this and Kinder's case."

Q. "Do you know of any one which has been prepared and was complete by the evening of August 11th?

A. "No."

Q. "Did you have anything to do with the preparation of this release you mentioned, as being prepared by the PIO office?" [PIO stands for Public Information Officer.]

A. "I furnish information to the PIO office as requested by them."

Q. "Have you furnished the PIO in connection with this, for this pending releases or a release which has been made, but not made as to your knowledge as yet?"

A. "I don't know what release you are talking about."

Q. "Did you know that General Anderson was contemplating making a release in connection with this release?"

A. "I know he was not preparing to make a release in connection with this case."

The sparring continued. It was obvious that the information

in General Anderson's press release about Schreiber came from Loewenberg. He avoided saying as much by saying he gave all of the information for a release about the Kinder case. He was then asked the following questions.

Q. "In furnishing that information, did you mention the name of Lieutenant Schreiber in any way?"

A. "Did I mention it?"

Q. "In the information which you furnished the PIO?"

A. "The information was prepared in my office, and I forwarded it to the PIO. And I am quite sure that in that information, the name of Lieutenant Schreiber was mentioned."

Q. "That is the only release within the past one week which you know has been pending. Is that correct?"

A. "I am the staff judge advocate, not the public information officer. The public information officer is one hundred fifty miles away, and I am not competent to testify to what releases he made."

Mike pressed on and didn't get a straight answer to his questions. The trial counsel objected, and Farnell ruled the issue was "immaterial" and sustained the objections, neither wanting to incur the wrath of the colonel.

Mike nevertheless pressed on.

Q. "I know it hasn't been answered. I know you said you helped prepare many releases on this case."

A. "I didn't say that at all. I never prepared or helped prepare any release. I told you that I am the staff judge advocate. The PIO has a staff officer, and I answer questions of the staff agency, including the PIO. I did prepare releases or assist in the preparation of releases."

Interestingly, the transcript of the trial was amended so that the last sentence was made to say, "I do not prepare releases, etc." This could have been a Freudian slip of the tongue. Who knows? – but I doubt it. We suspected and believed that the commanding general of the 5th Air Force was not so dense that he would release information on this trial without first running it by his staff judge advocate. Besides, the PIO only can write what he was told to write by Loewenberg and his staff. Loewenberg's staff didn't do anything regarding these notable cases without him knowing it. We knew enough to know that. He ran a tight office. He was universally hated by his subordinates. He had a nasty disposition and showed it constantly. One did not question Colonel Charles Loewenberg and get away with it. You took it from him and shut up as he could and would make life difficult for you if he thought you were disloyal to him. Like others of his personality type, he was oblivious to the controversy that surrounded him. What he took as respect was in fact fear. Loewenberg finally admitted that he had furnished information about this case many times.

Mike then asked when he assigned trial counsel in this case. He responded that the general assigned trial counsel, not him. That, of course, is a fiction, since he made the assignments in the name of the general. Mike continued with his questioning.

Q. "Have you recommended any persons to act in the capacity of trial counsel prior to 31 July, 1953?"

A. "I don't understand your question."

Q. "Did anybody have the right to act as trial counsel in this case before 31 July, 1953?"

A. "No."

Mike pressed him, asking if he told Major Holland that he would be trial counsel in this case in May. He avoided answering by saying that he had many conversations with Holland, and he couldn't recall. The game with the colonel went on.

Q. "Did Major Holland have authority after that to proceed in this case, interview witnesses, to continue psychiatric examinations, and perform other duties which the trial counsel would ordinarily perform?"

A. "The question is not clear to the witness."

Q. "To this conversation in May . . . "

A. "That conversation in May is something that exists in your mind. There has been no testimony on my part that there was a conversation in May."

Loewenberg then said he did tell Holland that he would be trial counsel in all three cases – those of Kinder, Schreiber, and Toth.

Mike continued with his next question.

Q. "Sir, may I ask you to try to recall which date, or approximately which date, you first told Major Holland that he would probably be trial counsel in all three cases?"

A. "I don't recall."

Q. "Could it have been in May?"

A. "I have answered the question."

He never would answer the questions, as he knew what the law required and that he had violated it by making up his own rules in his jurisdiction. He also knew that he wasn't going to be criticized for it on appeal. Farnell protected him by making us move on.

The subject of Major Al Nice was brought up. Al Nice had been stationed at 5th Air Force headquarters as a JAG officer. He had investigated the case, believed Schreiber, and closed the file. He was transferred to K-13 on the same date that I was, June 8, 1953. He was the SJA for the 51st Fighter Interceptor Wing across the base from my headquarters at the 8th Fighter Bomber Wing. Al always felt that his transfer was a punishment because it put us in some danger, and K-13 was the favorite target of "Bed Check Charlie." The North Koreans would have a plane fly over our base – an old biplane that flew so slow that we had nothing available to shoot it down. The pilot would drop five-pound bombs, causing everyone to get up in the night and go to slit trenches to avoid these missiles. If he happened to hit a fuel dump, it was chaos. We all lost sleep and were in jeopardy. Al figured that Loewenberg must have been out to get him. I didn't feel that way, but was rather pleased that 5th Air Force thought that I was capable of filling a slot normally held by a major or a lieutenant colonel.

The parrying between Mike and the colonel was getting us nowhere. Loewenberg said he arrived in Korea in March of 1953 to assume his job. He said that that he was not knowledgeable as to where the various bases were. He said that the commanding general decides where a particular case will be tried, but then admitted that it is upon his recommendation. He was then asked about the psychiatric reports and the OSI reports. He said the OSI report is a classified document and is not available to the defense. He claimed no knowledge of the psychiatric report, but it got to his desk drawer somehow. He didn't know who said the OSI reports were not available to the defense. Mike kept pressing. The trial counsel objected, saying Mike was asking leading questions calling for yes or no answers. Mike said that the witness was a hostile witness, so that he had the right to ask leading questions. Farnell ruled that the witness was not hostile. The fact that he kept sneering at every question, talking down to Mike, and not answering questions was enough to have him declared a hostile witness in most any forum in the civilized world, but not in Farnell's courtroom. Loewenberg was asked if he knew about the depositions not being sent on. He said he did know and that he regarded the filing of the depositions as a dilatory tactic on our part.

Mike tried to reason with Loewenberg. "I am a rather simple person. I am not accustomed to the language linguistics and do not attempt to indulge in it. I am attempting to make clear in my mind as defense counsel what your answer is. I would like to have whatever material there is, in order that a full case may be presented to enable justice to be done. Are you, as staff judge advocate, willing to help in that or not?"

A. "I would suggest that you make demands to the proper people for anything you wish and that, any time a request is made, it will be properly cleared. When you request in general terms everything that is material, your ideas of materiality may differ with someone else's ideas of materiality."

We never obtained a straight answer to any question concerning the reason documents were not provided and why the psychiatric reports were hidden in Loewenberg's desk. He revealed and admitted nothing. I was ashamed that he was a lawyer and that, in a sense, I worked for him. In my opinion, he was sleazy. He was the reason I wouldn't remain on active duty in the Air Force for a minute longer than I was required to do so. I had, up to this time, loved the Air Force and the work that was assigned to me. It is unfortunate because it was a career that I would have otherwise loved.

Mike finished by telling Loewenberg that he wasn't answering the questions. Major Holland accused him of "badgering the witness." Farnell said that the line of questioning was getting us nowhere. He was wrong – it wasn't the questioning, but the failure of Loewenberg to tell the truth and answer the questions.

He finally said that he talked with me before assigning trial counsel, because Schreiber was in the same location as I was. He did say he talked to Major Bryan about serving as defense counsel during the trial of another case. After a few more questions and objections by trial counsel, we concluded. At the request of the law officer, Mike summed up our motions.

All of our motions and the issues raised were denied by the law officer, and the trial itself commenced with the members of the court coming back to the courtroom at 3:15 in the afternoon.

IMMEDIATE RELEASE

STATEMENT TO PRESS CORRESPONDENTS

From Lt. Gen. S. E. Anderson
Commander, Fifth Air Force

In response to a formal request for a factual review of the Toth-Kinder-Schreiber case by national news agencies I am presenting the following facts surrounding this case.

I have undertaken to document this statement so that the press may have the same information that is available to me.

I must point out, however, that this statement in no way touches upon any evidence pertaining to the innocence or guilt of the individuals concerned. That evidence has been assembled by investigating agencies and will be presented before a Court Martial in the event Toth is required to stand trial for the offense from which this case stems.

The Toth case had its inception in an incident which occurred at approximately 11 p.m. on Sept. 26, 1952, in the bomb dump of the 543d Ammunition Supply Squadron, an enclosed area adjacent to a Fifth Air Force Base at K-9 in Korea. This incident terminated with the shooting and killing of a Korean National. Airman First Class Thomas Kinder, Cleveland, Tenn., was performing guard duty at the bomb dump on the night of 26-27 September and was on sentry duty at Guard Post 13. Kinder saw a Korean walk into the bomb dump, in the vicinity of his post. Kinder challenged the Korean and when the Korean turned and ran, Kinder fired one shot over the Korean's head and then overtook and apprehended the Korean.

Airman First Class Robert W. Toth, also a member of the 543 Squadron, and sergeant of the guard on the night of Sept. 26-27, arrived at Kinder's post in a jeep in response to rifle shots which were fired from the area of Kinder's post. Toth placed the Korean in the back of his jeep and, with Toth driving the jeep and two other airmen, one riding the front with Toth and one riding in the back with the Korean, drove the Korean to the office used by the officer of the guard. After driving 100 to 150 yards from the post on which Kinder was stationed, Toth stopped the jeep and pistol whipped the Korean.

Upon arriving at the office, Toth summoned 2nd Lt. George Schreiber, Hollywood, Ill., who was officer in charge of the security force, and he, Toth,

MORE

and Schreiber discussed the incident.

Investigation disclosed that these two arrived at the decision that the Korean was so badly injured by the pistol whipping that he should be shot. The shooting was to conceal the pistol whipping and to serve as an object lesson to other Korean Nationals. Schreiber directed Kinder who had been relieved from guard duty and who had arrived at the guard house during the discussion between Toth and Schreiber to shoot the Korean.

The Korean was placed on a 6x6 truck by Toth and Kinder and they, together with two other airmen, drove out to a revetment, Revetment B-14, where the Korean was put off, along with Kinder, and Toth and the two other airmen drove off. After firing one shot into the Korean, Kinder fired three shots into the air and Toth returned with the vehicle. Lt. Schreiber also arrived on the scene at this time and when it was found that the Korean was not yet dead, Lt. Schreiber ordered an ambulance and had the Korean taken to the K-9 dispensary.

Following the Korean's death, Lt. Schreiber advised all who had knowledge of the incident not to speak of it to anyone. The record of the incident was falsified to show Kinder on guard duty at the time of the killing so that no higher headquarters was made aware of the killing.

The incident came to light again early this spring when Kinder, home on an emergency leave, told the story to his mother. The first time a higher headquarters of the Air Force became aware that a murder had been committed was when this information was made known to Hq. USAF.

Airman Kinder, who had been rotated to the United States and was then stationed at the 674th Aircraft Control and Warning Squadron, Osceola, Wis., was questioned by the Air Force Office of Special Investigation and in a statement Kinder admitted the shooting. The statement was taken on 10 March 1953 by a special agent of the OSI.

Kinder was returned to Korea where he stood trial before a General Court Martial on charges of premeditated murder and conspiracy to commit murder. The trial opened on July 14, 1953, and ended on the evening of July 16, 1953. The court sentenced Kinder to life imprisonment.

Upon determination by the investigating agencies that Toth, who also had rotated to the United States and been honorably discharged from the Air Force, was implicated in the crime, the Air Force invoked the provisions of Article 3a of the Uniform Code of Military Justice, enacted by Congress on May 5, 1950,

MORE

to regain custody of Toth and make him amenable to trial by a military court.

For the benefit of the press, Article 3a, entitled, "Jurisdiction to try certain personnel," is quoted:

"Subject to the provisions of Article 43, any person charged with having committed, while in a status in which he was subject to this code, an offense against this code, punishable by confinement of five years or more and for which the person cannot be tried in the courts of the United States or any state or territory thereof or of the District of Columbia, shall not be relieved from amenability to trial by courts-martial by reason of the termination of said status."

(The provisions of Article 43, which establishes Statue of Limitations for certain crimes and offenses, are not applicable in this case since the crime of murder is exempted from statues of limitations.)

Toth, whose home is at 220 Dunseith St., Pittsburgh, Pa., was located working in a steel plant in Pittsburgh.

On May 13th, 1953, at 4 p.m., Toth was arrested at the steel plant by Maj. George S. Owen, assistant Provost Marshal of the Continental Air Command.

Major Owen identified himself to Toth, who was in the office of the plant police, and after Toth, in response to inquiry as to his name and former Air Force serial number, had given his correct serial number, Major Owen told Toth he was under arrest by direction of the Secretary of the Air Force.

Present at the time were two officers of the steel plant police force, three airmen, Air Policemen, an agent of the OSI and Major Owen.

With Toth in custody the Air Force personnel departed the steel plant premises and proceeded to the Greater Pittsburgh airport, arriving there at 4:40 p.m.

Before leaving the steel plant office Major Owen read to Toth the charges and specifications, the Air Force secretary's letter ordering his apprehension and return to Korea for trial by court martial and then advised Toth of his rights under Article 31 of the Uniform Code of Military Justice.

At the airport Major Owen again read the charges and specifications, the Secretary's letter and advised him of his rights under Article 31. When Toth said he could not understand how he could be returned to Air Force control since he was a civilian, Major Owen read to him Article 3a of the code and asked Toth if he wanted a more simple explanation. Toth said no, that he

MORE

08-11-1953 press release-pg3

completely understood it.

Toth, at this time, was advised by Major Owen that he would have an opportunity to telephone his parents and to contact a civilian lawyer if he so desired before departure from Pittsburgh.

At 5:15 p.m., Toth was taken to the base dispensary where he was given a physical examination by the Flight Surgeon. Toth entered no objections to the examination. At the conclusion of the examination the Flight Surgeon executed a certificate attesting that Toth was physically able to travel by any means.

After the physical, Major Owen again read the secretary's letter, the charges and specifications, and Articles 31 and 3a to Toth and again asked Toth if he desired to contact a civilian lawyer. Toth said he did not and would wait to have defense counsel appointed in Korea.

After eating the evening meal in the 500th Air Defense Group mess at the Greater Pittsburgh Airport, at 6 p.m., Toth was again advised he could made a call to his parents if he so desired. At 7:20 p.m., Toth telephoned his home from the base Provost Marshal's office. His mother answered the telephone and he asked to speak to his step-father. He told his step-father he had been arrested at work and was being returned to Korea under Military escort for trial and that he did not want the press to have any knowledge of what happened. He was asked if he wished to telephone anyone else and he said no.

From Pittsburgh he was flown to Andrews Air Force Base, Washington, D.C., arriving there at 11:40 p.m., after an hour and fifteen minute flight.

On the following day Toth wrote a letter to his mother, which Major Owen posted for him. At Andrews Toth was issued Air Force clothing, given a second physical check, received necessary immunization shots, and afforded an opportunity to see an officer of the Judge Advocate General's Department or a Chaplain, both of which he declined. During the night he was confined at the Base Guardhouse.

On May 15th, Toth was flown by military aircraft to Washington National Airport, arriving there at 8:15 a.m. He was taken to the VIP waiting room where he remained until flight time. He was flown next to Travis Air Force Base for the final air journey to Korea.

At Travis, Major Owen relinquished his escort duties to Capt. Edwin A. Jerore, an Air Police officer, who escorted Toth on the trans-oceanic flight.

MORE

08-11-1953 press release-pg4

On 16 May Toth was flown to Hawaii aboard a Pan American Airways flight and arrived at Honolulu International Airport at 11 a.m. The flight took 11½ hours.

After lunch at the Airport restaurant, Toth wrote two postcards and commented on the fine treatment he was receiving. At 2 p.m. that day the flight to Wake Island was begun. They arrived at Wake at 10:50 p.m., and after a light meal took off again at 1:15 a.m.

On arrival at Haneda airport in Tokyo, Toth was lodged in the base Air Police detention facility until a flight to Korea could be arranged. He was flown to Korea the same day, arriving at K-2 air base near Taegu at 3:10 p.m. on May 18th.

Toth was turned over to the Fifth Air Force Correction Center authorities by Captain Jerome.

Upon his arrival at the correction center, Toth was processed in the same manner as other personnel confined at the Center. He was first quartered in the Orientation Tent, under maximum confinement, but after an interview by the Commandant of the Correction Center he was recommended for elevation to Medium Custody.

On May 29, ten days after his arrival, Toth was released from confinement and placed in a "restricted status" to K-2 Air Base. The Correction Center staff was advised that Toth was to be allowed full privileges of the Airman's Service Club, Post Exchange, library, and base theater. He was to live within the Correction Center but to be allowed to come and go as he pleased. However, as this was considered unsuitable from a custodial viewpoint with relation to the other occupants of the Center, Toth was moved to the Supervisors living quarters. There he was quartered with the NCO's who supervise the Correction Center. His comforts and conveniences in the Supervisors' quarters were the same as those of the NCO residing there.

Since his release from confinement on May 29th, Toth has enjoyed full and complete freedom of movement about the air base.

With Toth's arrival in Korea a pre-trial investigation was directed and Toth was assigned a military defense counsel. Lt. Col. James F. Rood, staff judge advocate of the 315th Air Division, Fuchu, Japan, was named chief defense counsel, and Maj. C. H. Shirley, legal officer of the 58th Fighter Bomber Wing, Korea, was named assistant defense counsel.

MORE

08-11-1953 press release-pg5

Colonel Reed is a lawyer of 25 years experience, ten in civilian practice and fifteen in the military.

Major Shirley was admitted to the Georgia Bar in 1950 and had served, prior to his admission to the Bar, as Court Officer for the Civilian Court of Fulton County, Georgia. He has practiced military law for over two years.

Toth's civilian counsel, John McGrath of Pittsburgh, has recently requested that Lt. Col. Reed be relieved as defense counsel and this action was taken after the Judge Advocate General was advised by Toth that he desired that Colonel Reed be relieved as defense counsel.

The pre-trial investigation, however, never was conducted as Toth's civilian counsel initiated action in the Federal Courts of the United States and the Pre-trial was halted pending outcome of the action in the U. S. courts.

Toth's civilian counsel sought and successfully obtained a writ of habeas corpus in the United States District Court for the District of Columbia. At the time of the granting of the writ, which normally would require that Toth be produced in Washington by the Air Force, the Federal Judge granted a stay permitting the Air Force to retain custody of Toth in Korea until an appeal could be made to the United States Court of Appeals, District of Columbia, providing that the Air Force ceased court martial proceedings against Toth until the appeal was decided. Accordingly the Air Force stopped the court martial proceedings against Toth until the appeal was decided.

The Air Force commenced their appeal to the Court of Appeals but the appeal was dismissed on the ground that the judgement of the District Court was not final and therefore could not be appealed from at that time.

It is expected that Toth will be ordered returned to Washington, and there be released. At that time the Air Force will be able to pursue its appeal to have the legality of its action in this case determined by the Court of Appeals.

Since his arrival in Korea, Toth's physical and mental condition have been the subject of continuing attention.

On July 5th, Toth was given a physical examination by the Surgeon of the 58th Fighter Bomber Group at K-2 Air Base. The medical examiner reported that Toth "is in good physical condition with exception of a chronic ear infection (for which he is receiving treatment) which apparently existed prior to his entry into military service. He is not concerned about his physical condition and seems to be adjusting himself very well to the present situation in which he finds himself."

MORE

08-11-1953 press release-pg6

The medical examiner says that Toth denies press stories that he is troubled by "dreaming, headaches and nervousness." The medical report shows that Toth's pre-service weight was 147 pounds average. At the time of discharge from service he weighed 160 pounds and at the time of the medical examination in July he weighed 153 pounds.

Major Fred D. Ownby of the Air Force Medical Corps was the examining surgeon.

Throughout Toth's entire custody by the Air Force since this case caused his return to Air Force control, he (Toth) has been the sole individual to determine what, if any, publicity would be given his case. Initially, at the time of his apprehension in Pittsburgh, Toth expressed a desire that his arrest not be made public and this desire was carried out by the Air Force.

However, the day after his arrival in Korea, elements of the press in Seoul sought permission through the Fifth Air Force Public Information Office to go to Taegu and interview Toth. This request was passed on to Toth and he was told the decision rested entirely with him. Toth elected to meet the press and was interviewed first by an Associated Press correspondent. Subsequently, he granted other interviews and had continually been free to meet and talk with the representatives of the press at any time.

In some press reports there has been reference to a "mystery man" in the case. The complete facts about this individual are as follows:

He was a member of the security force of the 543d Squadron and was assigned to B Flight for guard duty that night. His name is S/Sgt. Kenneth A. Bouchard. He reported for duty at 11:30 hours the night of September 26th. This was half an hour after the Korean had been apprehended, and when Bouchard arrived at the guard office Toth and others were loading the Korean aboard

MORE

08-11-1953 press release-pg7

Bouchard was told by Schreiber to go with Toth on the truck. He got into the front of the truck with Toth, who was driving, and the Korean and Kinder got in the back. Bouchard was not present when the Korean was apprehended and had no knowledge of the decision to kill him. Bouchard, however, said he saw the Korean lying on the ground, a wound in his back, when he returned to the scene with Toth. Both Toth and Bouchard left the area in which the shooting occurred after depositing Kinder and the Korean at a revetment near Kinder's guard post.

(Documents attesting these facts are available at the Fifth Air Force Public Information Office.)

In conclusion, I wish to state that an impartial investigation has disclosed that there is no truth whatsoever to certain press reports alleging intimidation of Toth by "goon squads."

END

CHAPTER 17

Start of the Trial

AT 3:15 P.M. on the afternoon of August 13, 1953, in a dank and sultry courtroom, the trial of Lieutenant George C. Schreiber began. The room was full, and smells of sweat, cigarette smoke, and fear filled the air. There was no air-conditioning system in the large and high-ceilinged courtroom. I thought of an old movie about the Bengal Lancers in the Punjab region of India in which there was a large, sheet-like appliance with a boy pulling on a rope to move a sheet back and forth to cool the room. But that was only imagination and wishful thinking on my part. We had no local boy pulling the sheet and no fans in the ceiling slowly twirling. We had only our own thoughts as to what was about to transpire in this place at this time. We tried to stay cool and collected, but our summer khakis that darkened readily with a bit of moisture gave us away. Our armpits and backs reflected our nervousness, as well as that of everyone else so attired in the room.

Major Farnell, the law officer, called the court to order and went through the brief but required ceremony of announcing who was present in the courtroom. Of course, this did not include the spectators, who had filled all of the seats. Some even stood without seats. The courtroom was now standing room only. As they say on Broadway, "the house was sold out."

Major Billy Holland, the trial counsel, stood and was recognized by the law officer, who was the military judge. He asked Holland if he wanted to make an opening statement. He did, and it took all of one and a half minutes – the briefest opening that I ever heard before or since in any trial. He reiterated what Schreiber was charged with doing, namely committing premeditated murder. He then referred to the Manual For Courts Martial and quoting it, saying, "When a person has not himself directly committed an offense, but is liable for its commission as a principal under Article 77, he may be charged as though he himself committed the acts which constitute the offense." He went on, "Any person punishable under the Code is one who commits an offense, or aids, abets, counsels, commands, or procures its commission. That is the conclusion of my opening statement."

Nothing was related about the facts or how Schreiber was connected to Kinder and Toth. Nothing was mentioned about the death of the "Oriental male, Bang Soon Kil" – who or where he was, where he was killed, the cause of death, the results of any autopsy, or the qualification any Air Force witnesses. Kinder's prior plea of guilty went unmentioned, as did anything else that a jury would want to know in a capital-murder trial. The reason was apparent to me, and I know to members of the press in attendance, because we discussed it at the many recesses during the trial. Despite all of the statements that the court members knew nothing of the case during their voir dire, we were convinced that they all knew all about it, so no opening explanations were necessary. Indeed, their commanding general two days previous had announced to the press of the world the details of Schreiber's guilt. Thus, the "full and fair" military trial commenced. In my opinion, we could have gone directly to the sentencing at that point, saving us all the discomfort of sitting in that hot, damp, and drab place listening to the evidence for the next several days. The outcome was a foregone conclusion. Here I was, a newly minted lawyer and officer, and I could see through the charade. You can bet that the press in attendance did as well, and the stories they relayed to their respective papers reflected just that. This was supposed to be a trial under the new brand of military justice conducted in accordance with the newly presented Uniform Code of Military Justice. If it was, I feel a great deal of pity for those tried under the old rules that the UCMJ had replaced. I did learn one thing well, and that is if a commanding general, no matter how stupid or how jaded, wants something done his way, it will be done. The service was filled with ass kissers, or, said in a polite way, "apple polishers." I hope that things have changed since then. As I tried many courts-martial as a civilian defense counsel after my release from active duty, I really saw some improvement in the system. Those improvements would not benefit Schreiber in his trial, however.

The first witness was Leroy D. Gillette of the 3525th Medical Group, Williams AFB, Arizona. He said that on the night of September 27, 1952, he was stationed at the 17th Medical Group at K-9, Pusan. He was a medical technician on call. He told how he went to the dispensary and saw "a Korean found with a gunshot wound on the right side of the chest and lacerations to the lower right eye and scalp." He told them that he tried to administer plasma, but couldn't. He opined that he could not because of the "collapsing of the blood vessels of the patient, the loss of blood." He said he applied pressure dressings, and then the patient died. He continued that an Air Police investigator had come and photographed the body, then it was transported to a Korean hospital.

There you have it all. This guy was never asked about his training, education, qualifications, or experience, but gave testimony and opinions that only a trained physician would be allowed to give in a civilian court, particularly in a capital case. He identified photos of the deceased. That was it. His testimony on direct examination was thereby concluded. He knew the deceased was a Korean, how he had died, and the cause of death. Maybe he was not a trained medic and didn't know how to insert the catheter to administer plasma. No matter that other causes of death may have existed, such as a subdural hematoma, as a result of Toth's beating or was the cause of death the bullet hole? He was the expert witness as to the cause of death of the victim.

The defense counsel proceeded. Mike Braun asked him if his memory was better on August 13, 1953, or on March 31, 1953, as to the events of September 26 and 27, 1952. The witness said that it was better today – August 13, 1953. He said that his memory of the events in March was poor and that he had no recall of the events until interviewed by an OSI agent in Arizona. At that time, he said he could not identify the photograph of the individual who was dead. Once prompted by the OSI agent, his memory improved. The law officer found the photo to be admissible, as memories do get better over time, especially when they are obtained through coaching, intimidation, or veiled threats, however subtle.

Each witness was read his rights against self-incrimination by the OSI investigators, automatically putting the interviewee on alert to be careful and to tell them what they wanted to hear. Every cop in America and elsewhere knows the routine. I don't want to single out the OSI, because, for the most part, they were good investigators, even in the old days. But intimidation of witnesses in capital-murder investigations puts everyone on guard, as they have no idea where they stand. The same witnesses who gave statements in the original investigation by Lieutenant Colonel Al Nice constantly changed their stories once confronted by the OSI or the prosecutors, almost to a man.

The prosecution then showed the witness several more photos, all of which he identified, as his memory improved after March 31st, because "he had been thinking about it." He was the first of many witnesses with the same story and the same revival of memories with changed testimony.

On further cross-examination after identifying more photos, he agreed he could not identify them on March 31, 1953, because he remembered no details of the event. He then said this was because, on that night in September, "I didn't pay much attention." The prosecution broke in with a question – highly unusual procedure in such a trial – and was allowed to ask, "What time of day or night was the person administered treatment to in March of 1952 in the dispensary?" Boy, what a screw-up – where did the March of 1952 come from? It was a sign of either the nervousness or the impending mental breakdown of Major Billy Holland. It came from nowhere. The witness obliged him and said it was, "About 7 or 8 o'clock in the evening." Of course, it wasn't – it was in the wee hours of the morning of September 27, 1952. But the charade continued. Whatever the prosecutor wanted, the prosecutor got, no matter how much it deviated from reality or from prior statements in writing and under oath. He said that no photos were taken in 1952, so what were they talking about? Major Farnell, the judge, then broke in, "Why was there any doubt in your mind when the photographs were shown to you?"

"I don't know, sir. I couldn't remember at the time."

The poor witness then answered more questions all about the pictures already admitted into evidence, finally stating that by June of 1953, his memory had improved and he could recognize the photos.

In answer to questions by the law officer, he opined that the man was a Korean. He was then qualified to again render his opinion that the Korean was dead, which he had gathered by considering the appearance of the victim's eyes, his lack of pulse, and his lack of heartbeat. Mike then cross-examined him as to his study of genetics or anthropology. He said he did not have such a background. Mike next asked him if he had testified in the recent Kinder trial, and he said that he had. He was then asked if, in that case, he was asked if the dead "Korean" was a man or a woman. His answer was, "I am not qualified for that, sir." He then changed his testimony and admitted in so many words that he did not check the genitalia of the deceased "Professionally I am not qualified, sir," he said.

He went on to say that there was no American doctor present when he viewed the body, but that an Airman Stoops was present with the corporal of the guard and a Korean doctor. On March 13, 1953, he had written a statement saying that said that another physician – a Doctor Stokey or a Captain Smith – had been present. His report said that Doctor Stokey, an Air Force physician, was present. In March of 1953, he didn't know if it was Smith or Stokey, but at trial, when his memory had "improved," he admitted that his report and statement to the OSI were erroneous. He was then asked to describe the three-and-a-half- inch wound to the back of the man's head, which he did. Again, Major Farnell stepped in and asked about the man's condition when he first saw him. He opined that the man was in shock, that he had a weak pulse, a weak blood pressure, and that he was breathing. He said that the man died over period of fifteen to twenty minutes. This was probably more than enough time for a trained medic or a physician to have treated him for shock, administered oxygen and plasma, and applied pressure dressings in order to keep him alive. But no such treatment was offered. He died, I believe, due to lack of proper treatment. The technician got much of it right, but was obviously not qualified to treat a seriously injured person, let alone to make a medical diagnosis or render any medical opinions as to the cause of death.

The next witness was Airman Stoops. He said he was with the 301st Medical Group, Barksdale AFB, Louisiana. He recalled rendering medical treatment to a wounded Korean on the night of September 26-27, 1952. He said he was at the dispensary at Pusan when the man was brought in, and that he had started to treat him by bandaging him. He said that, sometime later, Airman Gillette came into the dispensary, and then he, Stoops, was: " . . . in and out quite a bit." He testified that, later on, "they took him out," referring to the corpse. He said that he suctioned blood from the man's mouth in addition to applying bandages, and that it had been two days later when he made out his report of the events of September 26 and 27. As to the report, Stoops said that he had written it up in longhand and that it was later typed up, but was worded differently than what he had written. He said he never knew the name of the individual mentioned in his report, but that someone told him it was Bang Soon Kil. He said that he learned this from either the Korean interpreter or the Korean doctor. After further questioning, he then said he got the name from an Air Police report and not from the interpreter or the doctor. And so, back and forth, it went. He was not sure of anything, but he was certain of the facts when it fit the prosecution's case. He admitted that if the Air Police had named the man "John Doe," it would have gone into his report. He said he usually would never make up a report concerning a Korean, but this was an exception. Stoops said that he was in and out of surgery all that night and that he hadn't known if the Korean was a male or a female, as his trousers were never lowered while at the dispensary. He said that he had attended medical school. He opined that the wound to the Korean's head was "very bad" and it could have caused his death.

He was asked if he knew who shot the Korean, and he responded that Kinder had. He said that Kinder had told him the following day and that Kinder was always in and about the dispensary, "joking around." He also said that Kinder said nothing about being ordered to shoot the Korean. He said that this treatment was to clean and dress wounds and to suction out the mouth. The president of the court then questioned Stoops, who said that he was assisting the "new man" in cleaning up the dispensary that evening and that the new man didn't know much about the job, referring to Gillette, who had rendered all the medical opinions in his testimony. Stoops also said that the report had misstated the time of the events, missing by about twelve hours.

The law officer then adjourned the court until 8:15 a.m. the next morning.

The next day, August 14, started with the usual announcing that all persons present the day before were again present in court. That is, all of the official players were present.

The next witness was Airman Frank E. Zappulla of the 3450th

Motor Vehicle Squadron, Cheyenne, Wyoming. Zappulla said that he had been assigned to the 17th Medical Group about twelve or fifteen miles from Pusan, Korea, in September of 1952. He was an ambulance driver. He said that he and another medic went to the 543rd bomb dump and found the Korean lying on the ground. He said that they took him to the dispensary, about 500 yards away, to get treatment for him. He said the other medics had "tried some medicine, something of the sort, and after he died. I was the driver who took him to the Pusan CAC, civilian something –I don't know what the CAC stands for – but we did take him to the CAC Hospital at Pusan. From there, we made out a death certificate and proceeded to the morgue, where we left the body and came back to K-9 again."

He said that, when he had come to the dispensary from the bomb dump, there were three or four medics at the dispensary. He continued that Stoops and Gillette didn't arrive until he was there for a half hour. This meant that if the man died within fifteen or twenty minutes of Stoops' and Gillette's arrival, as Gillette had testified, he was alive for close to an hour while no one with sound medical knowledge treated him. In the real world, this would have been a great opening for a medical-malpractice case, as it is clear that there were at least two physicians on duty there at the same time and a bunch of medics who really didn't know what to do other than to apply bandages and suction out the man's mouth. It is apparent from all of the testimony that, had the victim been properly treated for shock and blood loss, he would have had a better chance of survival.

Now it was our turn to question Zappulla. At Kinder's trial just a few weeks earlier, Zappulla had testified completely differently as to events and to his non-recollection of events than he had this day. He was then asked if there was a hole in the man's jacket and if the hole matched the hole in the man's chest. He said there was a hole in the jacket and a hole in the man's chest, but that they didn't match and couldn't be made to match.

After Zappulla was cross-examined, my old friend Lieutenant G.D. Roth, the assistant trial counsel, resumed with the exposition of his complete lack of legal knowledge or of the rules of evidence. Roth asked the witness if he made a written statement on February 4, 1953. Now, it is a basic rule of evidence that a prior statement of the witness can be used on cross-examination to impeach a witness by showing to the jury that that, at another time, the witness said something different. Every first-year law student who paid attention in class knows that you cannot use a prior statement of the witness to validate for the jury that the witness was telling his or her story correctly. If a witness says he has no independent memory or recollection of the events, the witness can view the statement to refresh his recollection under certain circumstances. But it is the witness' recollection of events that is elicited and which is admissible in court – not the prior statement, unless the witness has no memory at all, in which case the writing can be admitted as a past recollection recorded in some trials.

When Mike brought out this basic rule of evidence in his objection, the learned assistant prosecutor, Roth, started to argue about it with him, as did Major Holland, the senior prosecutor. Mike then requested that anything they had to say should be addressed to the law officer and not to defense counsel. The law officer asked the trial counsel if he had any authority for his position, and he cited page 290 of the Manual for Courts-Martial. Mike said "precisely," and the law officer sustained Mike's objection. As usual, Roth had gotten it wrong, and so did Major Holland.

The Rule as set out on page 290 said, "If his impeachment is sought on the ground of collusion or corruption, consistent statements made prior to the imputed or admitted collusion or corruption may have such evidential value as to make them admissible. And if his testimony is attacked on the ground that such testimony was a fabrication of recent date, evidence that he had made a consistent statement before there was a motive to misrepresent, and before any imputed or admitted inconsistent statement, may be received." In short, if a witness is known to be corrupt or in collusion about his testimony, the prior statement can be used in an effort as it were to impeach the witness.

The effort here was for us to show that the witness had a poor recollection of events since months earlier and then, even a few weeks earlier, he did not recall events that he was now testifying about in this case. Faulty memories are common, but to have made a couple of inconsistent out-of-court and in-court statements does not entitle the prosecution to rehabilitate their own witness by putting a former statement in the form of a document before the jury in the instance involved here. The Lieutenant exhibited little by way of style or class, coupled with an incomplete knowledge of the rules of evidence. There are certain rules of what I will term "trial etiquette" to which good lawyers adhere. Roth did not know how to do so, or he was unable to exhibit basic behavior and etiquette during the trial.

Mike brought out that Zappulla had only been in the presence of the man "on and off" for maybe ten minutes during all of the nearly two hours that the deceased was at the dispensary. Then Jesse took over the questioning of Zappulla. Inasmuch as Farnell had allowed the two prosecutors to play as a tag team, the defense went along with it, and we played as a tag team as well. Jesse brought out that Zappulla had no knowledge that the man was a Korean, but simply adopted what everyone else had told him. He said he didn't even know if the victim was a male or a female. He testified that when he had taken the body to the CAC hospital, the Korean doctor looked at the body "from two to five minutes" and then made out the death certificate. There was no autopsy to determine a cause of death. He then said that the he couldn't swear that the person that he had taken to the CAC hospital was the same person he picked up in the bomb dump. He said that he had based his knowledge of the case on what some medic told him. The law officer then questioned him, and he said that he picked up the person at the bomb dump, drove about 500 yards to the dispensary at about midnight, and left the dispensary with the body two hours later. After a few nondescript questions from the president of the court, the witness was excused.

The next witness called was Warrant Officer Junior Grade Paul Langgle. A warrant officer was a hybrid – an enlisted man with officer status. He was entitled to a salute from a person of lower rank. He could avail himself of the officers' club, but in those days rarely did so because he could use the NCO club, which most usually did as they felt more at ease in so doing. That is a brief but concise description of what a warrant officer used to be. Now I understand that there are commissioned and non-commissioned warrant officers in some service branches. The Air Force has done away with the rank of warrant officer.

The witness said that he was Warrant Officer Paul Langgle, Headquarters, Second Logistical Command, APO 59, U.S. Army, Civil Affairs Section. He said that he was the assistant civil affairs officer in charge of civil affairs at the hospital, and that his duties included being in charge of the hospital records. He was the one who found the death certificate. He authenticated the certificate – that is, he attested to the copy that the prosecutor had in court and signed it. On cross-examination, he said he didn't originate the document and knew nothing about the truth or the accuracy of it. He said the doctor who wrote it was unavailable, and that this would be the person who could testify as to its validity.

CHAPTER 18

Trial Continues With Penabaker

LIEUTENANT EDWARD G. Penabaker had been Schreiber's room-mate at Pusan. He was present with Schreiber at all critical times on the night of September 26-27, 1952. He was the OD, that is, the duty officer. He was in a position to take command of any situation that was deemed to be an emergency, and he was charged with maintaining good order and discipline as a part of his responsibilities both as the senior officer present in the AP operations office and as the duty officer. He testified that he was the "Officer of the Day" and that he went to the Air Police operations shack at 2400 hours. He said, "There was a Korean lying on the floor, and there were several airmen present there, Lieutenant Schreiber and Sergeant Addleman."

Major Holland proceeded:

Q. "What was the drift of the conversation?"

A. "While they were deciding what to do with the Korean, and I believe they decided to take him out and kill him, sir."

Q. "Why?"

A. "I believe because he was so badly hurt."

Penabaker said that he spoke to Schreiber the following day and asked him what had happened on the previous night.

Q. "What did he tell you?"

A. "I can't remember all that he told me. I can't remember what we were talking about."

Q. "Can you remember the gist of what he told you?"

A. "I formed an opinion, sir."

There was a proper objection by Mike, which Farnell sustained. But unbelievably, determined to get a conviction, Major Farnell interjects with a question to Penabaker.

Q. "Was this an opinion that you based solely on your conversation with Lieutenant Schreiber?"

A. "I don't know, sir, how it was formed, but I formed an opinion from his answers that he told the boy to go out and shoot him."

Then, after eliciting the objectionable answer from Penabaker, Farnell told the court to disregard the answer of the witness. Very cute strategy – the impartial judge interjecting himself into the examination after sustaining the objection to the very harmful opinion of the witness, eliciting the opinion, and then telling the court members to disregard it. The damage was done at the behest of the judge.

Penabaker was then asked about a telephone call with Schreiber in February of 1953, but he could not remember the conversation. Not wanting to give in, Major Holland questioned Penabaker.

Q. "How did you happen to get an indication that the Korean had been shot on his orders?"

While asked in another form, this was the same question that the law officer had found objectionable before and still let it in, with a caution, of course, to disregard it. Such things happen in every trial, and any experienced trial lawyer will tell you that the fact that the judge says to disregard something merely highlights the objectionable testimony. It is never erased from the memories of the jurors. It is a slick way of getting the inadmissible evidence before the jury. Penabaker never answered the last question because Mike objected to it as leading the witness, and the objection was sustained.

Mike started his cross-examination of Penabaker by asking about an interview in which he had participated in June, producing a statement

Penabaker had signed at that time. There was a skirmish, and the law officer said he needed to study the issue. The president of the court objected, overruled Farnell, and ordered that trial proceed. This is just the kind of command influence at all stages of a trial that the code was designed to prevent. But, with rank still having its privilege, Farnell submitted instead of exercising his judicial prerogative. He was a wimp and feared for his advancement. Any judge worth his salt should have and would have told the president that, with all due respect, he was not running the trial, but that Farnell was. Such was the state of the art of a court-martial in 1953.

Ultimately, Farnell let the statement be marked with the following instruction. "This prior inconsistent statement, Defense Exhibit D, made by the witness is admissible in evidence for the limited purpose of impeaching his credibility. The court is, therefore, instructed that this prior statement may be considered by the court only in determining the credibility of this witness. The court may not consider this prior statement, or any part of it, for establishing the truth of the matters asserted therein."

The witness stated that, at the time he made the statement, he had been interrogated by Major Holland and Lieutenant Roth, the prosecutors. He admitted that Mike had told him that he wanted the truth and to state "all the concrete facts."

Mike then questioned him.

Q. "And that is the only part of the conversation that you heard in the office, the only conversation in which you heard Lieutenant Schreiber say 'take him out'?"

A. "I heard him speaking before that."

Q. "Did you hear what he said before that?"

A. "I can't remember."

Penabaker then responded that he didn't hear anything said by Toth or Kinder. He did say he recalled Addleman telling him what had happened. And then the critical question came.

Q. "You were the duty officer that day, or officer of the day?"

A. "That's right, sir."

Q. "As OD, you had some responsibility with regard to any offenses taking place in the camp that day?"

A. "That's right, sir." Penabaker went on to say that he knew Schreiber was on medication that day in September.

The law officer, Farnell, then questioned him. He asked about what he had heard once again. Was Farnell acting impartially, or was he trying to get a conviction? His behavior was, at the least, bizarre in my judgment. I was only the assistant defense counsel, but if I had been defending George, I would have objected loudly to such conduct. It was such impressions that led me to curtail my active military lawyering. It was a nasty business trying to have a fair trial.

Colonel Perry, a member of the court then tried again to ask the same questions – "What did you hear?" etc. He then hit the jackpot without objection from anyone. He asked, "Would you repeat that part which you overheard, the context or the substance of what you heard?"

A. "The gist of what I heard, they were trying to decide what to do with the Korean, and then I believe they decided to take him out and shoot him, sir."

Q. "That was based on what you overheard?"

A. "I believe so."

Colonel Perry was persistent. Despite Farnell saying, "I must stop the witness at this point," Perry disregarded him. Perry then continued asking, "You stated in your testimony that the gist of the conversation in the APO shack led you to conclude that they were going to kill the Korean?"

A. "Yes, sir."

This is the very testimony that Farnell had told the court to disregard earlier before again bringing it out himself and, adding insult, allowing Colonel Perry to bring out yet again. In my mind, this represented unbelievable idiocy or sheer incompetence. It acknowledged the foregone conclusion that I had before we started – that George Schreiber was doomed.

The law officer then reinforced the errors with more questions for the witness.

Q. "Is your testimony then, Lieutenant, that this conclusion you stated was based on your observations and the conversation you overheard that night – but because of the time element involved, you weren't able to repeat any conversation or any particular words? Does that pretty well state your position?"

A. "That's right."

He told Captain McClain, a court member, that he had reached that conclusion before leaving the guard shack that night. He then contradicted himself and made a 180-degree turn in response to Mike who then asked him if his conclusion was formed much later, pointing out that, when interviewed in February of 1953 as a part of the investigation, he said he had not reached this conclusion before leaving the guard shack. He then testified that he lied when questioned in February of 1953.

Holland questioned him.

Q. "Why were you lying?"

A. "Because of what is going on right now, sir."

Q. "What do you mean?

A. "I don't think the boy should be prosecuted."

Colonel Perry then asked if he was concealing information, and he said that he was not.

Let's assess what Penabaker's situation really was. If he had any inkling that the Korean was to be harmed or killed, he had a sworn duty to take command, intervene, countermand any such orders, and to prevent the killing. Further, he should have made an arrest and taken into custody anyone who disobeyed him. Was he complicit in the killing, or was nothing said about killing that night? I believe that he was threatened with being charged as a conspirator if he didn't change his story and help convict Schreiber.

The next witness called by the prosecution was Airman Second Class Eddie Mullins, an Air Policeman now stationed in Amarillo, Texas. He was in the AP shack and rode with Kinder in the 6x6 truck carrying the Korean back to the bomb dump. He said he did not know what was to be done with the Korean, but did hear Toth say, "Do you want us to take him back up on the hill, like we used to?" He did add some pertinent information for the defense on cross-examination. He testified as to the active guerrilla activity at the bomb dump. He told of two guards who were killed "two weeks ago" and "two miles away." He spoke of the nightly firing of weapons, and the sabotage and theft as a daily occurrence. He told of the poor morale and discipline in the guard detachment before Schreiber came, and how things sparked with much better morale and training after Schreiber took over. He told of how Schreiber introduced the use of sentry dogs, and how the loss and destruction of materiel in the bomb depot was reduced when Schreiber was in charge. He said that he never knew of Schreiber giving anyone an illegal order. He did think one of Schreiber's orders, which involved him going to the LST area and digging up some lumber, was unreasonable. Mullins testified that he made entry No. 23 in the logbook as to events that occurred on the night in question and that his entry into the logbook was correct. The court members had some questions about the truck ride, including who was driving and the whereabouts of Toth, Kinder, Borchardt, and the Korean in the truck. He answered all of the questions, but all were immaterial and a waste of time, as far as I could determine.

Sergeant Borchardt was the next witness. He had joined the 543rd the day before the killing, and was told by Schreiber to report to the guard shack at 11:30 p.m. on the September 26 to learn procedures. He said that when he arrived, they were loading the Korean into the back of a 6x6 truck and Schreiber told him to go with Toth. He said that Toth was driving. Mullins had said that Kinder was driving and that Toth was in the back with Borchardt and the Korean. Borchardt said the opposite – that he was in the front of the truck, that it drove up a hill, and that Toth got out and said something to Kinder. He testified that he didn't get out of the truck and didn't hear what was said. As he started to get out of the truck, he said, Toth told him to get back in, as they were leaving. As they drove by another guard post some miles away, the guard there stopped them and told them that he had heard shots from a distance. He said that they returned to where Kinder alighted from the truck, and he saw the Korean lying on the ground with what appeared to be a hole in his chest. Just then, he testified, Sergeant Rumpf drove up in a Jeep. He said that Rumpf drove off, and that was when Schreiber arrived in a Jeep followed by an ambulance. He then returned to AP operations, and Toth asked him if he still had to clear the base the next day. He said that he did have to do so, and that Toth then told him to take the rest of the night off. Mike then asked him about the standard operating procedure after he arrived to handle a Korean apprehended in the bomb dump.

He testified that Schreiber had always counseled him to tell the truth about his knowledge of the events of September 26-27. He said that Schreiber was one of the best officers with whom he had ever worked. He said Schreiber always took care of his men and never gave an illegal or unreasonable order. The court members questioned him, and he admitted that he didn't know the identities of the men that night, and particularly that he didn't know Toth. His identifications of who was where in the 6x6 were questionable, but not very critical to anything in the case.

Airman Kinder was the next witness. It was 5:00 p.m. We had been going since 8:00 a.m. Jesse told the law officer that he was tired and did not want to proceed with Kinder at that late hour. He wanted to recess until the next day. Despite Holland's objection, Farnell gave in, and we recessed until the next morning.

Unless you are engaged in trials at any level, it is difficult to understand just how taxing it is on the participants. I have had clients tell me over and over how much of an ordeal it is to participate in a trial, no matter how minor their role in the proceeding. I can attest to this. A trial is a draining experience, both mentally and physically, even though it looks like everyone is calm and reasonably settled in. It is anything but a calming experience, no matter what role one plays in a trial. Counsel, particularly, are on stage all of the time. Any performer will relate that an hour or so on stage is exhausting. At this point in my career, after trying thousands of matters at all levels of trial and administrative proceedings, I can tell you that your feet ache, your back hurts, and your head hurts from constantly trying to keep up with the process. The memory one must have is surprising. You must know every word of every evidentiary document, as well as what each witness has said and might say in giving testimony. There is a certain strategy in every well-planned trial. It is necessary to try and keep to the strategy developed in advance of the trial. A profound knowledge of the many rules of evidence is critical, and one must be ready to meet objections of opposing counsel or to explain briefly objections that you make to someone else's questions or proffers at trial. It is exhausting, and to go for nine hours in a capital-murder trial is astounding. Many courts in the United States now go for four hours of testimony a day. Trials are marked with objections, issues of law, and legal rulings that can emasculate a case or a position in an instant. I wonder how we do it and how we continue to do it sometimes.

Remember the old adage, "Fools rush in where wise men fear to tread." I am one of the fools, but I still love the challenge of it all, despite the butterflies in one's belly, the exhaustion, and, at times, the confusion. Incidentally, a good trial lawyer never shows this confusion or lets on about it to the opposition, the jury, or the judge. One's apprehension or the setback of a witness testifying to something unexpected can be a life-altering experience. "Never let them see you sweat" is the adage of trial lawyers. I have a private saying – that if your shoes are not filled with water at the end of the trial day, you have not done your best. Only those who walk through the valley can know this.

CHAPTER 19
Thomas Kinder the Killer

TO REFRESH ONE'S recollection of events, it was Thomas Kinder who actually shot the Korean and put the bullet hole in his chest. It was Kinder who cried to his mother about his having shot the Korean. It was Kinder's mother who talked to her congressman about her son's story and who got to the secretary of the Air Force and then to the chief of staff of the Air Force, who ordered the commander of the Far East Air Forces to reopen the investigation. Considering the origin of such an order, most with any prior service in the military would consider the trial and conviction of Schreiber and Toth to be a command, not a simple request to reopen the investigation of those events.

Thomas Kinder was the ultimate perpetrator of the murder and the only witness who could convincingly convict Schreiber and Toth. He was at times an admitted liar, both in his own trial and in Schreiber's. He excused his lies by stating that he was on trial for his life. This was the true act of a coward and one with no moral scruples. He was willing to condemn both Schreiber and Toth for his own actions and was willing to do so with egregious perfidy. In short, he was both a physical and a moral coward. There was no redeeming quality about Thomas Kinder in my mind, then or now.

From his testimony at Schreiber's trial, it was obvious that Kinder had, together with the prosecution or the OSI, concocted a story that differed from everyone else who had knowledge of the events of September 26-27, 1952. The pat way in which he told his story belied the obvious rehearsal for his play-acting at Schreiber's trial. His story differed in almost every aspect from those of other witnesses who were there. Toth would later testify that Kinder said to him, "To hell with Schreiber, let's look out for ourselves," or words to that effect. Toth took his attitude as evidencing a willingness to lie and perjure himself to save himself. He did it, and he did it with a deal brokered by my old boss, Major Charlie Weir. Charlie was a great guy and a person for whom I had the utmost respect. I regarded Charlie as completely ethical. I never had cause to change that thought. Charlie came to me at some point after the deal had been struck on Kinder's behalf and told me that he was sorry, that he had done it for what he regarded as his duty to his client, Thomas Kinder. He said that he hoped that I would not disrespect him for that, as he knew that I was a friend of George Schreiber and that I believed in Schreiber's innocence. I was too new at the business of representing people accused of crimes. Most experienced criminal-defense lawyers have told me that they don't want to know if their client performed the acts or said what was attributed to them. They say never question the client regarding his ultimate guilt or innocence, but assess all of the evidence available and advise the accused accordingly. They have told me that it interferes with their judgment to have to take the moral high ground if they are convinced of the client's innocence or guilt, and that it interferes with their performance either in cutting a deal or handling the trial of the case. From Charlie's demeanor and his words, I knew that Kinder would say anything to save himself, and it was a part of his deal that he had to be a key witness at Schreiber's trial. Kinder did as he was directed by both Charlie and the prosecution. I knew what Charlie was telling me was that Kinder would lie to save himself – and lie he did, even admitting at Schreiber's trial to telling conflicting stories in his own defense.

He testified as follows.

"Yes, sir, at approximately 2330 hours I was released from my position. I spotted a Korean on the bomb dump. I hollered 'halt' to the Korean, and he started to run. I fired one shot over his head and still he didn't stop, so I ran and apprehended him. Sergeant Toth, sergeant of the guard, came up in the Jeep and asked me what had happened. I explained to him what had happened. I explained to him how I apprehended a Korean and he said he would take him to Air Police operations."

There was an inquiry and a statement that Toth had asked Kinder if he told his dog to attack the Korean. Kinder said he didn't. He said Toth told him to "sic the dog on him now." He said that he did, but that the dog would not attack. His story then continued in a narrative.

"Toth put the Korean in the Jeep and drove away, and shortly after I was relieved from my post by another airman on the shift coming on."

Q. "Who was that?"

A. "Airman Second Class Forelock. So I got a ride to the Air Police operations on an ambulance truck. When I got there, I believe Sergeant Rumpf was there and was standing in the doorway, and he said Schreiber wanted to see me inside. I went inside and Lieutenant Schreiber asked me to explain to him in detail how I apprehended the Korean. So I explained to him and then proceeded into the gun room to clean my weapon. I was in there cleaning my weapon, and just finished putting it back together, and to the best of my recollection, sir, Lieutenant Schreiber and Airman Toth were standing out by the desk talking. I heard something to the effect that, I believe Lieutenant Schreiber asked Toth where would be a good place to take the Korean, and I think Toth answers, 'B-14, sir.' Then I started out of the gun room."

"When I started out, Lieutenant Schreiber said, 'Hey, Red, come here. Do you think you could take this Korean up on the hill and shoot him?'"

"I said, 'No sir, I don't think I could and I would rather not.' He said, 'Don't you think it would help the morale of the troops and Korean natives if one of our boys shot a Korean in the bomb dump?' I said I guess it would, and then he said, 'Do you think you could take the Korean up in the hills and shoot him?' And I said, 'No, sir, I don't think I could and I would rather not.' He said something to the effect that, 'If I gave you an order, you could.' And I said, 'Yes, sir, I guess I would have to.' I believe Lieutenant Schreiber turned around to Toth and told him to put the Korean in the truck, and he said to me, 'Get your carbine and clips and go with Toth.' I said, 'Is that an order, sir?' And he said, 'Yes, that is an order.' And I asked Lieutenant Schreiber if the higher authorities investigated this, would he take full responsibility. And he said yes. So I proceeded to the truck, and Toth told me to get in the driver's seat and drove the truck up to B-14."

"Now, when we got up to the Area B-14, Toth told me to stop, and I stopped. I believe Toth took the Korean off the truck and helped him up the hill. He told me, 'I will drive around to the bomb dump and, when I hear shots, I will come back.' So I fired one shot at the Korean after the truck left, and a few seconds later the truck came back, and Toth jumped out and asked me, 'Did you get him?' And I said, 'I don't think so.' I only fired one shot at him. At that time, Sergeant Rumpf came up in the Jeep. I don't recall him saying anything to anyone. He walked over and looked at the Korean and got back in the Jeep and drove off. I believe the ambulance came up next. Lieutenant Schreiber and another airman came in a Jeep. There was some conversation. I don't remember what it was. Anyway, the Korean was put in the ambulance and I got in the Jeep with Lieutenant Schreiber and went down to the Air Police operations."

Q. "Did Lieutenant Schreiber say anything to you at Air Police operations after you went back?"

A. "I believe I told Lieutenant Schreiber I was nervous and didn't like the incident. And he said, 'Don't worry about it. Probably nothing will ever be said.'"

Kinder said that he gave a false statement to the Air Police the following day. He stated that his reason for lying was, "Prior to going to the Air Police investigator's, Lieutenant Schreiber and myself made up the story of how the Korean was apprehended, sir."

Q. "Did he say you would coordinate the statement?"

A. "Yes, sir. Before we went to K-9, Lieutenant Schreiber said that the Korean had been shot in the stomach and we would have to coordinate our story to that effect."

Kinder then admitted that, while he was at the K-9 dispensary, he told Airman Stoops that he had shot the Korean. He told how, months later while he was in Wisconsin, he had received a letter from Schreiber telling him of his rights under Article 31 and to remain silent if investigated about any incident. Kinder was then further questioned.

Q. "In the conversation in the Air Police operations, was everybody in agreement as to what to do with the Korean?"

Mike objected to this question, but was overruled by Farnell.

Q. "The conversation between Schreiber and Toth and yourself, was everybody in agreement as to what to do with the Korean?"

A. "Sir, I wasn't part of the conversation as to the disposition of the Korean."

Q. "How about Sergeant Toth and Lieutenant Schreiber?"

There was an objection to this question because it called for the witness to give the mental processes of other people. The objection was overruled, and Kinder answered, "What I seen and overheard, sir, they seemed to be in the mood."

Q. "When did you have the intent to kill the Korean?"

A. "From the time Lieutenant Schreiber gave me the order, sir."

Before we get into the cross-examination of Kinder, let's take an assessment of what he said. He said that he didn't want to kill the Korean, but did so based on Schreiber's order. He obviously knew that such an order was inherently wrong if it was ever given. The officer of the day, Penabaker, was there. Why was there no appeal to him? He was the ranking authority on the scene. Kinder admitted he lied to the Air Police investigator the next day. He blamed it on Schreiber. Kinder was an Air Policeman for three years and had an eleventh-grade education. His story didn't jive with anyone else's who had testified or was to testify.

The first issue on cross-examination was a glaring inconsistency. At his own trial some three weeks earlier, Kinder had testified that, at the time he left Air Police operations accompanying the Korean back into the hills, he had no intention of shooting the Korean. He said that when he returned to Air Police operations after Toth took the Korean from him, Toth told him about the pistol-whipping of the Korean. Mike then continued with his questions.

Q. "Did Lieutenant Schreiber ever give you an order to shoot the Korean?"

A. "I understood it to be an order, yes, sir."

Q. "Just your understanding. Is that right?"

A. "I questioned him concerning the order."

Q. "Will you answer the question? It was your understanding. Is that right?"

A. "Yes, sir, that's right."

Q. "Did he give you an order, 'Airman Kinder, shoot the Korean'?"

A. "Not in those exact words, sir."

Q. "He did not give you any such order, is that right? The order he gave you was, 'Get your carbine and clips and go with Toth.' Is that right?"

A. "That wasn't what I understood as the order, no, sir."

Q. "Will you please answer the question? Was that the order he gave you? Were those the words he used?"

A. "Yes, sir, those were the words he used."

Q. "And that was the order you received? Because after that you asked, 'Is that an order, sir?' Isn't that right?"

A. "I asked if that is an order, sir, because I understood . . . "

There was an objection by Holland, who claimed that Mike was badgering the witness and that he was trying to "scare the witness." Mike responded that he was twelve or fifteen feet from the witness and requested that Farnell direct the witness to answer his questions. The last question was then withdrawn, and Mike continued with his questioning.

Q. "After you received the order, 'Get your carbine and clips and go with Toth,' you asked the question, 'Is that an order?' Is that correct?"

A. "That is correct, sir."

Q. "And you received an answer, 'Yes, it is,' or 'Yes, that is an order.' Is that right?"

A. "Yes, sir."

Q. "You never received any other order besides that. Isn't that correct?"

Trial counsel: "Any other order?"

Law officer: "I believe it is perfectly apparent to the witness what order the question concerns. Objection overruled."

A. "Not in any exact words, no, sir."

Q. "Now, you made a statement today that after Lieutenant Schreiber said, 'That is an order,' or 'Yes, it is an order,' that you further inquired would Lieutenant Schreiber take the full responsibility if higher authorities investigated, or something to that effect. You testified to that today?"

A. "Yes, sir."

Q. "I show you your record of trial, consisting of forty pages on your part, and ask you to point out any place where you said that at that time?"

A. "I don't believe I made that statement at my trial, sir."

Q. "You mean this is a different case? This is no longer Airman Kinder on trial?"

A. "I was on trial for my life, sir."

Kinder was then asked if he had a conversation with Toth in which he said, "Why should we care about Schreiber? We got to take care of ourselves." He didn't deny it. He said he didn't remember. Mike continued pressing him.

Q. "I refer you to your testimony, page 178, question, 'What did he . . . referring to Schreiber . . . tell you to do?' The answer, 'He told me to get my carbine and go with Toth. He told Toth to get the Korean out of the truck.' Is that question and answer correct?"

A. "Yes, sir."

Q. "Question, 'What did you answer?' You say, 'I said to Lieutenant Schreiber is that an order, sir?' And he said, 'Yes, that is an order.' Is that correct?"

A. "That's right."

Q. "Was there any other order given at that time? Was there any further statement made at that time?"

A. "Yes, sir. I asked Lieutenant Schreiber if he would take full responsibility."

Q. "Did you say that so at that time in your trial?"

A. "No, sir, I didn't. My defense counsel instructed me not to."

Q. "What instructions are you under now by the defense or anyone else?"

There was an objection by Major Holland, and Mike inextricably withdrew the question. Mike then continued.

Q. "Are you under any instructions as to your testimony right now?"

A. "Yes, I am."

Mike didn't follow on with questions regarding who told him what to say and what not to say. He continued with his questioning.

Q. "Now, you made a statement to the OSI on March 10th?"

A. "That's right, sir."

Q. "Now I refer you to your testimony, page 184, 'Why wasn't there something about an order in that statement?' Answer, 'I don't know why it wasn't in there, sir.' Is that question and answer correct?"

A. "Yes, sir, it is."

Q. "Now I refer you to your testimony, page 188, in your record of trial, 'From what Schreiber told me, I presumed that he meant for me to shoot the Korean. So, I asked him if that was an order.' Did you so testify?"

A. "I did, sir."

Q. "You testified that was the presumption on your part. Is that correct?"

A. "Yes, sir."

Q. "And did you further testify in that case that it was your opinion that you received an order to shoot the Korean?"

A. "I don't remember, sir."

There was an interruption and objection by trial counsel that was overruled, so Mike continued.

Q. "Did that refresh your recollection?" (Mike asked this in reference to Kinder's trial record, which Mike had shown to him.)

A. "Yes, sir."

Q. "Now, do you recall stating in your opinion, you stated, 'Did you receive an order to that effect? And in your opinion, did you receive an order to shoot the Korean?' Answer, 'Yes, sir.' Was that your testimony in that case?"

A. "Yes, sir, it was."

Mike then elicited that Kinder thought the Korean was a dangerous person and that he had to use force to apprehend him. Further, Kinder said that he knew that Toth had to subdue him with force. He said that he feared the Korean. He said he didn't remember standing over the Korean after he shot him, saying, "Die, you son of a bitch, die." He testified that there was heavy guerrilla activity in the area of the bomb dump.

There was heavy guerrilla activity in every part of South Korea, from my knowledge. The place proliferated with bandit gangs, North

Korean and Chinese irregulars, South Koreans who hated the Rhee dictatorship, and those whose relatives had died at the hands of the American and UN Forces while trying to flee the battlefields. In truth, all of the kids like Kinder had good cause to be scared in going about their sentry duties. Death and destruction were close at hand. Death was the end result of relaxed vigilance for all of the forces in the south.

Mike then asked him if he recalled discussing the case with Mike and Lieutenant Schreiber in the corridor a few days previous. He said that he did. Mike asked him if he had said that it was possible that he misunderstood Schreiber's order that night. He responded, "Anything is possible."

Q. "Did you say it is possible you misunderstood his order, and your answer was, 'Yes, it is possible,' on the morning of that day?"

A. "Sir, if I hadn't been sure of what Lieutenant Schreiber was talking about, I would have questioned his order."

Q. "I am asking about the question in the corridor that morning [with] Lieutenant Schreiber and myself, and was your answer to us, 'Yes, it was possible'?"

A. "I believe it was."

Billy Holland then tried to rehabilitate the witness by dealing with the inconsistencies between his sworn testimony and statements previously made. An argument between counsel ensued, with Mike insisting that Holland was trying to impeach his own witness. Colonel Mathews, the president, intervened. He had no right to do so, as he was in effect a member of the jury and not the presiding judicial officer. He could not get accustomed to the new rules, where trials were conducted by judicial officers and he had a duty to leave the trial management to Major Farnell, the law officer. It was another indication that the old "drumhead justice rules" were alive and well in 1953 in Korea and the 5th Air Force.

Mathews said, "I would ask counsel to refrain from speaking when the other counsel speaks. It is only politeness to do so. If you render an objection and argue when the other is speaking, it is very improper, and I ask you to refrain from it."

There was nothing really bad about what he said. In reality, it was our old nemesis, Roth, interrupting and trying to talk over Mike that triggered the statement. But, nevertheless, it was Farnell's job to maintain order in the trial, not Colonel Mathews' job.

Mike said, "The objection of the defense is that, in cross-examination, there is a right to show that any witness, or attempt to show, that inconsistent statements of some kind were made at a previous time. That the defense has attempted and believes that it has shown inconsistent statements were made. On re-direct, the witness can be asked what the testimony is now. That is a proper question. When the witness is here to testify on direct examination, that is not the time to testify from documents, sir."

Again, Roth refers to page 290 of the manual. Mike was correct in his legal analysis of the rule of evidence as it then existed and still exists today. A prior statement of the witness cannot be used on direct examination to corroborate what the witness has been sworn to do — tell the truth under oath. However, Farnell allowed Roth to proceed.

Trial counsel: "May I show the record to the witness?"

Law officer: "Very well."

IDC: (individual defense counsel refers to Mike Braun): "We are going to object to that. There is no showing that the witness' memory needs refreshing. The is no showing that the witness does not remember."

What Mike was referring to were two exceptions to the general rule of evidence — namely, past recollection recorded and recollection refreshed. In so many words, if a witness says he doesn't remember the events or statements, but that he recovered a contemporaneous memo in writing at the time or close to the time of a happening, it can be used to assist the witness with refreshing his memory or recalling what happened or what was said. That does not amount to validating testimony, as it is a case of the past being refreshed in one's memory or assisting in the recall of one's memory. A proper evidentiary foundation must first be laid to do this. Here, trial counsel had not done this, and Farnell was in error. Kinder then said that he intended to kill the Korean when he left the operations office. Farnell allowed the prosecution to review with the witness all of the very same questions that had been asked of Kinder in the direct examination. Mike objected on the grounds that this was repetitious, which it was, and he was overruled.

It is easy to discern that Farnell was anything but neutral as I review the trial records. He was tasked with overseeing a conviction, or felt bullied by Colonel Loewenberg, and he was not about to blemish his career by conducting a fair and balanced trial. He allowed the prosecution to once again let Kinder testify to his soliloquy of Schreiber and his conjuring up the murder of the Korean.

Mike continued with his questioning.

Q. "Kinder, let us go back on that hill. Do you remember talking to Major Bryan and myself on July 22nd at K-2?"

A. "I don't think I remember the exact date, no, sir."

Q. "Do you remember at that time telling us you saw the Korean moving? You thought he was going to go at you and you got scared, and that is when you shot at him?"

A. "I don't remember saying those exact words, no, sir. I believe I said the Korean started moving, I was scared, and so I shot him."

The members of the court had a right to ask questions of witnesses, and they did so. Colonel Mathews asked him if the Korean was even capable of attacking him, and Kinder said that it was improbable. Kinder then drifted to high ground and said he was scared of what he had to do, as he was concerned about the morality of it, and that frightened him. He ended with, "I was just a little bit scared." He then answered Captain McClain's questions about the original apprehension of the Korean. Colonel Mathews then asked him about the ride back in the Jeep with Toth. Kinder had said he wasn't in the Jeep. Perry forgot such testimony.

The impartial law officer then asked a couple of questions.

Q. "What was the purpose of the trip from Air Police Operations up to B-14?"

A. "To take the Korean up and shoot him."

Q. "No other purpose for the 6x6 going up there at that time?"

A. "Not to my knowledge, no, sir."

Farnell didn't want to leave any doubt as to Schreiber's guilt so far as Kinder was concerned, or, for that matter, so far as he was concerned.

The next witness was a clerk who came to the 543rd on September 27, 1952. He told of mailing a letter for Schreiber to Kinder. He was a clerk-typist and said that Schreiber was a very fine officer.

CHAPTER 20
Addleman Cross-A Critical Point Made

DR. CHAIN CHAN Yo was called as a witness for the prosecution, but first his interpreter, Chai Jin Woo, was sworn to faithfully translate the doctor's testimony. The doctor said he examined the deceased, Bang Soon Kil, on the night of September 26-27, 1952. The man was already dead when the doctor saw him. The doctor was asked the cause of death, and we objected on the grounds that he didn't really examine the body. He testified that, "The man died because he had a gunshot wound at a place in right chest." He then allowed that there were other places of injury, " . . . but that place was the main cause of death."

On cross-examination, he said that the body was at the Korean hospital for about five minutes. He got a history from the typist in the hospital, who had talked with the driver who brought the body to the hospital. He had no memory of clothing on the body, just a memory of the hole in the right chest. He made out a death certificate, and the body was then taken away. At the time of his viewing the body, the witness had been practicing as a doctor for three months. He remembered no wounds to the head, just the "gunshot wound." He could not identify the photograph of Bang Soon Kil, which had been in evidence and shown to him by the defense. The witness was excused, and Farnell told the court that he was an expert witness and that they could give his opinion such weight as they deemed appropriate.

I can say with all sincerity and clarity, given the lack of an autopsy, the inexperience of the doctor, and his lack of notes or any memory save for the "gunshot wound," he would not have been qualified as an expert as to the cause of death in any courtroom in any civilized country in the world, even at that time. However, this was a military court convened by indirect order of the Air Force Chief of Staff and directly by the Commanding General of the 5th Air Force. Even Major Farnell knew what was in his interest, and he so ruled that the opinion was admissible evidence. He allowed this neophyte Korean doctor, who did nothing more than to look at the body, make out a death certificate, and be done with it, to testify as to the cause of death of the deceased in a capital-murder case. There was no autopsy, no probe of the "hole" in the chest, no history. He didn't even turn the body over to examine the back, the head, or the extremities of the deceased.

The next witness was an Air Police guard at the ammo depot at Wong Dong on the night of the killing. He said he heard a shot and went with Sergeant Holcomb to investigate. He told of how he saw Kinder with a Korean in his custody and that they put the Korean in the Jeep. He said that Sergeant Toth took the Korean to operations. The witness said that he had remained in operations for five to seven minutes and then left when Sergeants Addleman and Borchardt relieved him from his post. He heard no conversation while at operations. The Korean was lying on the floor when he left. On cross-examination, he said he rode in the Jeep with the Korean on the way to operations.

Mike then questioned the witness.

Q. "Did anything happen during the course of this ride?"

A. "Yes, sir."

Q. "What happened?"

A. "About 100 yards from the entrance to the Air Police Operations, Sergeant Toth stopped the Jeep and took the clips out of his gun and went behind the Jeep and pistol-whipped the Korean."

Q. "Now you say he pistol-whipped the Korean?"

A. "Yes, sir."

Q. "Will you tell the court just what he did?"

A. "He went behind the Jeep first, took the clip out of his gun when he got out, went behind him, and with the butt of his gun he hit the Korean in the head, on the side of the head."

Q. "How many times did he hit him?"

A. "Approximately, maybe three or four times."

Mike then brought out a discrepancy between his testimonies at the Kinder trial and at this trial, but it was not material in my mind – just a little satisfaction of a defense lawyer showing the jury the inconsistency of the witness' testimony. The Air Policeman told how the Korean slumped to the floor of the Jeep after being struck. He was bleeding and staggering, and Toth assisted him into operations and placed him on the floor.

He was then asked how the AP squadron functioned before Schreiber arrived in August of 1952. He said that it was in "very bad shape." He testified that Schreiber was a good officer who had really shaped up the squadron and the protection of the bomb dump. The witness added that Schreiber "did a good job."

Q. "Did he ever give an illegal order of any kind?"

A. "No, he did not."

Q. "Did he ever give an unreasonable order whatsoever?"

A. "No."

Q. "To your knowledge, to any other person, did Lieutenant Schreiber give an illegal or unreasonable order?"

A. "No, sir."

Q. "If someone told you that Lieutenant Schreiber gave such an order, would you believe it?"

A. "No, I would not."

The president of the court then asked questions, and the witness said that Kinder had his guard dog with him, that Toth guided the Korean into the Jeep, and that Toth, Holcomb, the Korean, and he were riding in the Jeep, with Toth driving. He said the Jeep had no top, that he rode in front, and, most importantly, that before and as Toth was in the act of pistol-whipping, no one made any effort to stop Toth. And finally he asked, "As far as you know, there was no cause for Sergeant Toth's action?"

"No, sir."

He then testified that he never heard Toth give any explanation as to why he beat the Korean. He said the Korean made no effort to escape and didn't evade the beating. He said that when they came to the operations office, Lieutenant Schreiber was there and instructed them to just lay the Korean on the floor. Of course, Schreiber was not there at that time, but this goes to show how eye witnesses to events often lose recall or are coached on statements, responses, and memories – a situation that was endemic in this trial. A few questions later, he testified, "I never saw Lieutenant Schreiber that night." So it goes – the nerves of the witness often erase what was just said under oath. And if one is an airman second class, the appearance of a general, all those colonels, and other ranking officers can be devastating to one's nerves and memory of events. It is the same with lay witnesses at trials – the adrenaline pumps and the innate desire to flee overcomes conscious thought and memory.

The next witness was Sergeant Eugene Lewis Rumpf. He was the sergeant of the guard between 1800 and 0400 hours on the night in question – that is, from 6:00 p.m. to 4:00 a.m. the next morning. He was asked to state what was unusual about that night.

"At approximately 2330 hours that night," he responded, "Sergeant Toth and Sergeant Carpenter brought a Korean national to the office, and he was bleeding. And Sergeant Toth said that the Korean went for his gun. We called for Lieutenant Schreiber. Lieutenant Penabaker came down to the office – he was duty officer. Then, three to five minutes later, Lieutenant Schreiber came down, and they were talking in there, Sergeant Toth and Lieutenant Schreiber. I started to write a letter, and around a quarter to twelve or twelve o'clock Master Sergeant Addleman asked me to go outside and pick up the clips and tell the men to go to bed. I went outside, and the relief came in. I took the clips off of them and told them to go to bed. I don't know for sure – I think it was Lieutenant Schreiber and Kinder were in there. I believe that Lieutenant Schreiber said that he wanted me to . . . "

At this point, an objection was raised by Mike on the grounds that the witness was speculating, when he said "I believe" and the objection was overruled.

"Kinder went into the office. When he came out, I went and took the clips and put them in the gun room and sat down and finished writing my letter. It was approximately 1220 hours, and Lieutenant Schreiber had called on the telephone to the main gate on the base phone and asked the gate guard to clear the Air Police 6x6 through the gate. I asked Lieutenant Schreiber if he was going to turn the Korean over to the national police, and he informed me that the Korean was going to be taken to the bomb dump to be shot, or words to that effect. Maybe three to five minutes later, I heard three shots. Lieutenant Schreiber told me to go the dump to investigate, and I went out and took the Jeep, went up to the bomb dump, and as I approached Post 12, I met the 6x6 coming out of Post 12. So I turned up into Post 12 and I got up alongside of Revetment B-12 and saw the Korean laying on the ground, laying on his stomach. And then I saw Airman Renteria with his dog, Airman Kinder, and Sergeant Borchardt. I got out of the vehicle, talked with them. I don't know what all was said. I believe that Sergeant Borchardt told me that a man had been shot, and Airman Kinder rolled him over on his side, and I went back to the APO and informed them at the office that a man was shot. Lieutenant Schreiber and Sergeant Addleman were in the office."

He said that when Schreiber told him that the man was going to be shot, that he said he would have to notify the OSI. He then told how, in January, Lieutenant Schreiber called a meeting of the Air Policemen and advised them of their rights under Article 31 of the UCMJ – that they did not have to make any statements in the investigation. He had dismissed all of the new guys from the meeting and asked only those who were there on the September dates to stay. Some of the men had already given statements, including Sergeant Rumpf.

On cross-examination by Mike Rumpf testified that it was possible that Schreiber told him that the Korean was to be "shot at" and not "taken out to be shot." He then testified that, in his statement to the OSI in January, he said, "At this time I asked the Lieutenant if they were taking the Korean to the Korean National Police. . . . I was told no, but instead he was trespassing in the dump and would be shot at." This represented quite a distinction in a few words and quite a distinction in memory. He allowed that he again made a statement in February and probably said the same thing, "shot at." He also said that at no time did Schreiber ever ask him to lie about the events. He said he saw Toth's gun after the Korean was brought to operations, and that the stock was "busted clean through. A triangle piece was chipped out of it, and it was full of blood."

The next witness was Master Sergeant Raymond F. Addleman, probably the most crucial witness for both sides in the trial. He was asked on direct examination to testify as to what Schreiber said to Kinder and to describe the events of the night. He said that he was the senior NCO at operations during the night of September 26-27. On direct examination, he said the following under oath.

"After we completed talking, I turned to leave the gun room, and as I reached the gun room door, Lieutenant Schreiber told Kinder, to the effect, 'take him out; take the Korean out to the bomb dump and shoot him. Kinder, you do the job.' Kinder asked if that was an order, and Lieutenant Schreiber said, 'That was an order,' at which time I believe Toth got the Korean off the floor and left the office."

He then testified that he had closed out the logbook early because he normally closed it out at the end of the shift and that Schreiber had told him that he would take care of the logbook entries. He identified the copy of the logbook and the entries. It was obvious that he was concerned about his involvement with the logbook, and the prosecution concentrated its questions on the entries. His direct testimony was damaging and probably fatal to Schreiber at this point in the trial. Here was a senior NCO, a career Air Policeman, and he ratified the damning words of Sergeant Rumpf, making clear Schreiber's part in the killing.

Major Jesse O. Bryan IV, the appointed military defense counsel, commenced with the cross-examination of Addleman. He started by asking about the logbook and comforted Addleman by getting him to agree that there were no false entries in the log, but simply some additions after it was closed out to reflect the shots in the dump and that Rumpf was sent to investigate them. He said that Schreiber never told him what to say or what to enter in the logbook. Jesse then questioned him as to what Toth had said about the appearance of the Korean in operations – that his head was bloody and that he tried to sit up but couldn't. He recalled Schreiber and Penabaker coming to the operations office that night. He was asked to describe Schreiber, and he said that he looked "like a man getting out of bed in the middle of the night." He said that he was present all of the time, but heard no conversation between Rumpf and Schreiber. He testified as to "bad feeling between Rumpf and Lieutenant Schreiber." They didn't like one another. He said Rumpf was not a good NCO and didn't know how to get along with the men. Jesse said that neither Schreiber nor he had much regard for Rumpf. He said that Rumpf was known to him to be a liar.

Next was a masterful cross-examination by Jesse. It is difficult to describe the facial expressions of the questioner and the witness, let alone the voice intonations and sheer anguish of the witness in trying to remember and so state his memory. As for the defense counsel, Jesse was at a crossroads in the trial, and he knew it. The sheer effort and strain showed on him as he defended George's life.

Q. "Now you have testified with regard to the conversation you heard, statements Lieutenant Schreiber made to Kinder, is that right?"

A. "Right, sir."

Q. "And, in part of your testimony, you said Kinder asked, 'Is that an order?' And Lieutenant Schreiber said, 'Yes, it is,' or 'Yes, it is an order.' Is that right?"

A. "Yes, sir."

Q. "Did that conclude their conversation?"

A. "If I recall it, sir, 'Yes, that is an order.' Kinder then left the office."

Q. "That was the end of their conversation?"

A. "Yes, sir."

Q. "Now, Sergeant Addleman, has your testimony always been the same with regard to this conversation in the office?"

A. "How do you mean, sir?"

Q. "Were you questioned by Agent Grindstaff, special agent of the OSI?"

A. "I have been questioned by Agent Grindstaff on numerous occasions. The actual dates I am not sure of."

He was asked if he told the truth each time he was so questioned, and he said that he told "what I believe to be the truth as I know it."

He said that when first questioned, he had forgotten the incident and had no recollection of it.

Q. "On 12 February, 1953 – you knew about the incident at that time, didn't you? You learned about it on January 31, and actually the investigation was started on 27 January, but the statement was taken on 31 January. Isn't that right?"

A. "Approximately that time it started, sir."

He said again in February he was not positive about what was said and that they told him, "that I had been talking to Lieutenant

Penabaker in the office."

Q. "They tried to refresh your recollection, sergeant. Did they read to you a lot of things that were said?"

A. "They said that Lieutenant Penabaker said he had been talking to me. They used what they said were statements. They read parts out of it and said this happened and that happened."

Q. "Did they let you see those statements?"

A. "No, sir."

Jesse then asked if a lot of "stuff was thrown at you," and if he gave another statement on March 18. The cross-examination was going too well to suit the prosecution, so there was an objection and a request for a bench conference. By that time, both the interrogator and the witness passed on the question. Score a point for Billy Holland.

Q. "At that time, your recollection started to change, isn't that right? You had a lot of statements made to you, said to be statements which weren't shown to you. And at this time, sergeant, what was your recollection as to the conversation?"

A. "As stated in that, sir, Sergeant Toth had brought the Korean in and told me about Kinder making the apprehension, that the Korean tried to get his weapon, that he used it on the Korean, and that Lieutenant Schreiber and Lieutenant Penabaker had been summoned and arrived, and that Lieutenant Penabaker and I had a talk in the gun room, where I explained what Sergeant Toth told me. At that time, Lieutenant Schreiber had told Kinder to take the Korean out and get rid of him, and Kinder asked if that was an order."

He then reiterated that, on March 18, "I was of the opinion that Lieutenant. Schreiber said, 'Take the Korean out and get rid of him.'"

Q. "That was the language used at that time, is that right?"

A. "I believe it was."

Q. "Do you have any recollection of that talk with Kinder at any time?"

A. "Apparently I do not, sir."

Q. "Did you have any recollection of using the word 'shoot' at that time?"

A. "Apparently not, sir."

Jesse then had him recount the normal procedure upon apprehension of Koreans in the dump. Addleman said that it was normal procedure to take them out to the gate, "turn them loose, get them off the base."

Jesse then asked about another interrogation in early June of the year 1953.

Q. "At that time, sergeant, you had no recollection of any order being given by Lieutenant Schreiber to Kinder. Isn't that right? When they were interrogating you at K-10?"

A. "At that time, yes sir. I was not positive of any order."

Addleman agreed that he had always been telling the truth during the numerous interviews with the investigators of the OSI.

Q. "When did you finally say there was an order?"

A. "The first time that I made that statement about the order was to Major Holland and Lieutenant Roth when I was called up for an interview, sir."

Q. "When was that? Was it around June 6th of this year?"

A. "I believe in the beginning of June. I can't recall the exact date."

After a few more questions, the testimony continued as follows.

Q. "Didn't they tell you anything about your getting involved in this case?"

A. "I asked them whether I was being accused, or rather if I was being charged in the case, or where I stood – what my position was."

He said that they didn't tell him he would not be charged. Rather, he said, they told him "that as long as he told the truth, they didn't think he would be charged with an unlawful logbook entry," thereby leaving him guessing and afraid not to cooperate with them.

Q. "And the truth to them was that you had to say it was an order. Is that right? And you told them there was an order?"

A. "I told them there was an order."

Q. "I am going to ask you to do something. I am going to ask you to forget every one of these interrogations, to throw out of your mind every statement written or oral that you have ever given. You made them all sorts of ways. What this court wants, and I believe what Major Holland and Lieutenant Roth want, and the defense wants, is your own recollection of what happened on September 26th – nothing induced by any fear or thoughts. The man is on trial for his life, and your recollection depends on it. Get rid of all these previous interviews and put yourself back in the Air Police operations on the night of September 26th. You are in the gun room with Lieutenant Penabaker. You come out of that gun room, and you hear Lieutenant Schreiber's voice. And what does it say, sergeant?"

The record shows that the witness paused, placed his head in hand, and, after about a minute of silence, answered.

A. "I am sure, sir, hearing Kinder asking if that is an order, and Lieutenant Schreiber saying, 'Yes, it is an order.'"

Q. "Of that you are sure, sergeant? All we want is your own recollection. All we want is what you are sure of. Forget about all of us and go back into that shack and try to recall."

The witness again paused for approximately a minute and then answered, "What comes to my mind first is, 'Take him out and get rid of him.'"

That cross-examination should have been enough to turn the case in favor of the defense. It showed that most of the witnesses had been subtly but surely guided into making statements that were not necessarily true. But, in an abundance of self-preservation, they acceded to making the statements. The prosecutors seemed to turn the tide when the witness asked about being charged. Their ambivalent responses oftentimes was sufficient to coerce these enlisted men into saying what they thought was required of them.

My own recollection is that Major Jesse Bryan asked Sergeant

Addleman to step into a phone booth, shut the door, shut out the world, and recall the truth. In the record, it is a "shack." The court president, as usual, had some questions about the logbook, and there was a redirect to examination to again get Addleman to say, "Shoot him." But, in my view, any fair-minded juror would not have believed that he ever heard that order. Addleman, in the final analysis, said that Schreiber never said the words "shoot him." Would members of the court find reasonable doubt based upon that cross-examination testimony? It certainly would permit such a finding.

At the end of that witness' testimony, the prosecution rested its case, which meant that it had no further evidence to present.

Mike then moved to dismiss one of the two inconsistent charges against Schreiber. He said, taking everything the prosecution had claimed as true for the purpose of the motion, that we were entitled to have one of the charges dismissed. The Code gave the power to the law officer to make such rulings. The issue was that Schreiber was charged with issuing an order to Kinder to kill the Korean and also with entering into a conspiracy with him to kill the Korean. Kinder said there was no agreement, just an order to do so. The motion was denied.

Mike then made a motion that the prosecution had not proved a prima facie case of conspiracy. That is, he argued that the evidence produced by the government failed in all respects to prove that there was an agreement to murder the Korean. He said that there was no corpus delicti of a conspiracy by a meeting of the minds. He continued, "There has to be an agreement on the part of the parties alleged to be conspirators to do and perform an illegal act, and the burden of the prosecution is to prove that such an agreement existed." Mike argued well that there was no direct evidence of a conspiracy and no circumstantial evidence of a conspiracy. Although Mike was profoundly correct in his recitation of the evidence and the law, his argument fell on deaf ears. Major Farnell denied the motion.

Mike then moved to dismiss the charge of premeditated murder on the basis that there had been no competent testimony as to a cause of death of the Korean, whether it was from Toth's beating or Kinder's gunshot. This was not a good argument, and it was denied. The law says that if either event caused or contributed to hasten death or did contribute to the death, the result is the same. We tried to argue, in effect, that the Korean was already virtually dead when Kinder shot him. It was now the defense's turn to put on a defense of Lieutenant George C. Schreiber.

CHAPTER 21

Doctor Ralph Robbins at the Trial

AS SOMETIMES HAPPENS in a battle or in a trial, events are shaped by unforeseen advantages and disadvantages. One of the interested spectators to show up to watch the trial unfold was an Army surgeon, Dr. Ralph Robbins, MC, U.S. Army, 930th Engineers Aviation Group. He chatted with me during the few recesses of the trial and commented on the sloppiness of both the prosecution and the so-called Korean doctor testifying as to the cause of death of the victim, Bang Soon Kil. He was, in fact, dismayed and appalled that, in a capital-murder case, the evidence pertaining to the cause of death could be so callow. He likewise was critical of the defense team for not protesting in a more vehement way about allowing incompetent witnesses who were not trained physicians to testify as to the cause of death, particularly without an autopsy. Doctor Robbins told me that in his opinion allowing such testimony was outrageous. He not only volunteered to be a defense witness, he insisted upon it to comport with his sense of propriety and an effort to add justice to the trial.

Dr. Robbins was sworn in and said that he received his medical degree from the University of Virginia Medical School, graduating in 1945. He said that his specialty was internal medicine and that he had sat through the testimony of the Korean doctor. He was then questioned.

Q. "Doctor, I would like to ask you a hypothetical question as a doctor of internal medicine. If a patient is brought to you and he is D.O.A., dead on arrival, and that patient has suffered wounds about the head and gunshot wounds to the chest, would it be possible to for you to determine the cause of death without performing an autopsy?"

A. "It is my opinion that conclusive evidence as to the direct cause of death of an injured individual must be determined by an autopsy finding."

Q. "Now, is it possible that blows on the head could cause death?"

A. "Yes, it is possible."

Q. "How is that so, please?"

A. "Blows of an extensive nature on the head, any extensive injury to the head, can cause a respiratory death by injuring the breathing centers, the cortex of the medulla and the hypothalamic, which is the breathing center. Death could be caused from internal hemorrhaging due to the blow on the head."

Q. "Is it possible, have you seen it, or do you know, if a person received a blow on the head, would that also cause blood to come up in the mouth?"

A. "Yes."

Q. "Doctor, were you present in this courtroom when the testimony was given as to the violent nature of which a person was hit about the head with a pistol?"

A. "I believe I was."

Q. "From hearing that testimony, would it be your official opinion that blows of that nature would be sufficient to cause death?"

A. "I could not give my opinion without ever having seen the individual and the circumstances at that particular time you are talking about. I could say it is possible that death could have been caused by an injury to the head, from the testimony I have heard since I have been in this court."

On cross-examination, the doctor was asked how much of the

testimony he had heard. He said he had heard all of it since the trial started, except for an hour on that morning. He was asked a hypothetical question as to what organs could have been hit by bullets from the holes described in the victim.

He responded: as follows.

A. "There is no way of determining that unless you find out the exact pathway of the bullet on autopsy findings to tell what organs have been injured."

Q. "As I understand in your testimony, that possibly no organs were hit?"

A. "Possibly none that I know of. I don't know what other organs it could hit."

He was then asked, if a bullet hit the lung, if it would cause a hemorrhage as a result of a collapsed lung. He responded that it could possibly cause a hemorrhage. He was then questioned as follows.

Q. "Collapsed lung – how long could a person normally live?"

A. "You do not have to die from a collapsed lung."

Q. "Supposing a bullet . . . – Did you hear the testimony about the bullet hole being in the back under the right shoulder blade?"

A. "The testimony I remembered, I heard the bullet entered the right side of the chest and exited through then left side of the back, beside the spinal column. That is all I remember."

Q. "Supposing the bullet entered the right, here, and gone out over here What organs would it hit?"(Mike pointed first to his chest and then to an area on his back)

A. "On the right side?"

Q. "Yes."

A. "It would hit the lung or the liver."

Q. "Would that cause a hemorrhage?"

A. "Yes."

Q. "Which would be most likely to be the main cause of death in the event the victim dies – blows on the head or the bullet?"

A. "I can't answer that because I don't know the exact pathway of that bullet."

Q. "Assuming it went in where I told you?"

A. "I could not answer that."

Q. "Do you know how hard the blows were?"

A. "No, that is why I can't answer the question."

Not satisfied, the eloquent Lieutenant Roth then chimed in with a question.

Q. "If a person was beaten about the head and thereafter, about an hour later, was shot, as has been described in the courtroom, would the bullet wound probably accelerate the death?"

A. "I can't answer that question."

Mike then questioned the doctor.

Q. "Doctor, is it true that people are walking the streets today that have collapsed lung?"

A. "Yes."

Billy Holland then asked a question.

Q. "It is also possible to be shot in the heart and live too – isn't that true?"

A. "Yes."

The president of the court then asked about the condition of a victim's eyes after receiving a blow to the head. The doctor responded as follows.

A. "It depends on the extent of the injury. If there is a brain concussion, there can be what we call a subdural hematoma. There are various injuries to the head. The pupils on either side can be dilated; one can be dilated and the other constricted; and both may be dilated and both can be constricted, depending on the extent of the injury."

Q. "And the fact that . . . whether a man's eyes are dilated or constricted bears no particular relation to the blow on the head?"

A. "Not as to the cause of death."

Q. "I am not saying as to the cause of death."

A. "It may determine the exact diagnosis of the injury to the head."

Q. "If a man's eyes were dilated, can you tell what effect that would have, or what would they tell you it would be?"

A. "It would help me in making a diagnosis together with other clinical evidence. It is just one of the signs that we notice."

Q. "Does it indicate anything in itself?"

A. "It is not conclusive in itself, no."

Q. "Does it indicate there has been a brain injury?"

A. "If there is history of an injury and one pupil is dilated and the other constricted, it would indicate a possible brain injury."

Q. "If both were dilated, would it indicate a brain injury?"

A. "It is possible, yes."

Colonel Mathews, the president and a court member, then pressed on with questions as to whether any bullet passing through a body would cause hemorrhage and accelerate death. (The transcript refers to Colonel Perry, but it is evident it was Mathews who asked the following questions.) Dr. Robbins responded that that this is not always the case, saying, "I have seen cases with penetrating bullet wounds, without hemorrhage, enough to cause death."

Colonel Mathews, obviously trying to make a point for the prosecution, asked the following questions.

Q. "In your official opinion, did this bullet going through this individual accelerate his death?"

A. "I have no way of telling unless I knew the exact pathway of the bullet. A person can be hit on the leg and get shot on the leg without any hemorrhage – it may just be a superficial wound. You would have to know the exact pathway to make a judgment and find out what organs were damaged. It is the same in the autopsy finding – you have to find out if the blow on the head caused the damage."

Q. "Would the blood loss from the leg wound help a man die?"

A. "If there was enough hemorrhage to produce shock from that cause alone, yes."

Q. "If a man who is shot in the chest suffered some degree of shock?"

A. "Yes."

Q. "Would shock be a contributing factor to his death?"

A. "A contributing factor, yes."

Q. "Thus, if a man was shot in the chest, shock would have contributed to his death – is that proper?"

A. "Yes."

Q. "Would a blow on the head cause severe hemorrhaging enough to fill a man's throat to a point where you have to put a suction pump for the blood to be drawn out?"

A. "Yes, definitely."

Q. "How soon after a blow on the head is suffered would blood appear in a man's mouth, if he is going to hemorrhage from a blow on the head?"

A. "Possibly immediately."

Q. "Would it be delayed in any case?"

A. "It could be."

The two colonels, Perry and Mathews, thus satisfied themselves that the lack of an autopsy did not really impact the prosecution's case. This was so, because if the two injuries contributed to hasten death, that was all the prosecution needed to prove. The counsel were somewhat timid in asking the questions, and it took both colonels to diffuse Dr. Robbins' efforts to assist Schreiber's defense. (Note: the court reporters often confused who was speaking, Colonel Mathews or Colonel Perry, as they were not familiar with the members of the court.)

All was not lost, however, as Major McCain tried to resurrect some helpful opinions from Captain Robbins He asked the following questions.

Q. "Concerning your answer to Colonel Mathews' question

concerning shock from a shot through the chest, would the same condition result from severe blows inflicting injury on the head?"

A. "Yes."

Q. "Could shock resulting from those blows be delayed?"

A. "Yes."

Q. "Captain Robbins, since you have been in Korea, have you had any association with the physicians, hospitals, or medical societies of the Korean medical profession?"

A. "Yes."

Q. "Do you know whether it is a practice of theirs to perform autopsies on persons who were delivered to their hospital D.O.A., or those who died in the hospital?"

A. "I cannot answer that."

Dr. Robbins was then excused as a witness.

At least we knew that we had one friend on the court, Major McCain. What we hoped to show through the doctor was that the cause of death was really not known without a properly conducted autopsy. For instance, what if the guy had died from an overdose of drugs, or bad whiskey, poisoning, or disease? The point is that we can't presume a cause of death without a proper autopsy, correctly performed by one trained to perform autopsies. However, since only a lowly lieutenant's life was at stake, the colonels didn't care. They had their duty to perform in going through the motions of a fair trial, but their bias against Schreiber was open and notorious. This fact was not lost on the members of the press covering the trial. Their reports home magnified their concern and stirred up many high officials in Illinois, including Governor William Stratton, the Attorney General of Illinois, the U.S. Senators Dirksen and Douglas from Illinois, numerous congressmen, officials of veterans' groups such as the American Legion, and the labor unions. All was not lost on these folks as the press reports flowed to Schreiber's home state. The Air Force looked bad then and, as time played out, it would look much worse. The new Code was more of a showpiece than a protection of the rights of an accused in a military trial of this type where orders for the trial emanated from Washington and the Air Force Chief of Staff, a four-star general.

CHAPTER 22
Defense Continues its Case

THE NEXT WITNESS was Airman Rodolfo Rentaria. He said that he was in the bomb dump after Kinder shot the Korean, and claims he heard him say to the Korean on the ground, "Die you son-of-a-bitching gook, die."

Our purpose in getting that evidence in was to show that Kinder intended to kill the Korean and that his pious, choir-boy-like demeanor was a colossal act. It was our position that Kinder and probably Toth acted on their own. We felt that Kinder, once he was accused of an unlawful killing, came up with the story that the Lieutenant made him do it. The same could be said for Penabaker, who heard everything in the shack, as did Addleman. If either of these guys felt that Schreiber was giving Kinder and Toth an illegal order, e.g., to commit a murder, it was their duty under military law and common sense to stop it at any cost. However, the interrogators had a neat way of making veiled threats to witnesses and actors in their investigation of the case. That is, they scared the hell out of these guys by suggesting that if they didn't tell a tale that incriminated Schreiber, they would be charged with conspiracy or, even better, being accomplices to a case of premeditated murder as abettors.

The members of the court all seemed to have questions for this kid. While these questions seemed to be nothing more than efforts to get into the game in some meaningful way, they were not especially meaningful to either side of the case. A military trial is different from a civilian trial in that everyone is not equal. Most of these young airmen rarely saw a colonel, let alone were quizzed by one. In a military trial, there is an intimidation factor involving rank. The witnesses are already hyper-nervous, and to be questioned by a higher-ranking commissioned officer about the minute details of an event that they wanted to forget was intimidating, bringing responses that were often what the witness thought the officer wanted to hear from him.

The next witness was Airman Second Class Bobby Holcomb. He said that he spoke with Kinder the morning after the shooting and that Kinder told him that he had killed a Korean. But Holcomb said that Kinder never said anything about being ordered to do so. He also testified that he rode in with Toth and the Korean in the Jeep after Kinder had apprehended the man. He told how Toth stopped the Jeep and went around to the back of the vehicle. He said, "Toth drew his .45 and leaned over the back of the Jeep and hit the Korean several times. Then he got back in the driver's side of the Jeep [and] drove down to Post 8, which was my post that night. I got out of the Jeep, and he proceeded towards Air Police operations." Holcomb was asked what he did since the beating was taking place almost in his lap, where the Korean was lying in the back of the Jeep with him. He replied, "I just kept still."

He said he kept still and watched the unprovoked assault "because my superior NCO was on duty."

Here was another incredulous story of ignorant depravity on the part of Toth and Holcomb. Holcomb was either just plain stupid, as he denied being afraid of Toth, or he was complicit in the beating, although he denied this also.

After the lessons of the Second World War, one would have thought that the military would have been teaching its personnel, particularly its Air Police personnel, how to behave toward captives, innocents, and even one another. But this entire case was a showcase of ignorance and stupidity as well as depraved indifference on the part of most of the actors. It began with the murder of streams of refugees by the 5th Air Force under orders from high command. These came after 5th Air Force pilots had the good sense to protest such killings, but to no avail. Holcomb testified that Kinder never mentioned to him that he was ordered to shoot the Korean.

The next witness called was Airman Second Class Forelock, another of Kinder's buddies. He said that Kinder, in telling about the killing, never said anything about an order to kill the Korean. He had given a statement previously that Kinder had told him that he had taken the Korean to the AP shack, although all of the other evidence indicated that Toth and Holcomb did that. He said that Schreiber had instructed him to tell the truth at all times.

What we were trying to establish through these witnesses was that Kinder was bragging to his peers about his killing of the Korean, which Kinder felt would elevate his stature among these fellows. The detail of being ordered to kill the Korean came many months later, when an official investigation got started. At this point, many of the participants began to reinvent history, while others began to forget it. There is no question that Schreiber tried to help his men, including Kinder and Toth, and to shield them from harm – to his detriment as it turned out.

Our next witness for the defense was Mister Robert Toth, formerly known as Sergeant Toth. Toth would ultimately make legal history as a result of his sister's persistence in appealing his abduction by OSI agents after he had been honorably discharged from the Air Force. After my interview with Toth I had misgivings about using him as a witness, since he made no bones about hating the Air Force and that he was forced to be in Korea against his will.. Nevertheless, my personal feelings aside, we enlisted him to assist in Schreiber's defense. He said that Schreiber was a fine officer, and he told how Schreiber pulled the guards together at the 543rd to make it a fine defense force. Obviously, though, Schreiber didn't teach manners and common sense. Give a scared person a weapon, and he just might use it. This is particularly true when the armed person is a poorly trained teenager in fear for his life, and he tries to mask his fear with bravado, which is exactly what I think happened to Thomas Kinder on September 26 and 27, 1952.

Toth was warned of his right not to incriminate himself under the Fifth Amendment to the U.S. Constitution, a nice touch by Farnell since Toth was now a civilian and was contesting in federal court the right of the military to try him. He had brought suit against the Secretary of the Air Force in the U.S. District Court in Pittsburgh. The judge had issued an injunction against the Secretary stating that the military had no right to hold him or to try Toth. The Air Force appealed, and it was agreed by the judge that Toth would stay in Korea, but not remain in pre-trial confinement, pending the outcome of the appeal in his case. He couldn't go anywhere anyway, as Korea was not a choice place during the war or even after the cessation of hostilities in July of 1953. It was filled with lost humanity, thieves, recently freed prisoners of war from the North and China and deserters of all shades from all forces. In June of 1953, Syngman Rhee decided in a fit of pique at the United States to turn open the gates of several Prisoner of War camps around Pusan and let thousands of North Korean and Chinese prisoners loose into the South Korean countryside. In my opinion, he was a bit of a madman and should not be considered the father of modern South Korea. He was our paid lunatic, and Kim Il Sung was Russia's paid crazy man in the north. Both hated one another, and each saw himself as the strongman and ruler of all of Korea. To that end, neither wanted to have an armistice, even though the United Nations and the United States insisted on having such talks. Rhee said he would not participate and would keep on killing with his forces even if the United States and United Nations left the place. He would have lasted about a week or less had that occurred. He was also loaded with bravado.

After Law Officer Farnell went overboard to caution Toth about his rights, Toth told of a conversation he had with Kinder as he was about to leave Korea. He said that Kinder said to him, "We should stick together on this and don't worry about Schreiber." He didn't recall the exact words. He was then asked by Mike to do his best to recall, and he said, "He said you and I shouldn't worry about Schreiber, and fuck Schreiber. I told Kinder to leave my name out of it. I was going home and didn't want to say anything more about it."

Roth, the assistant trial counsel, then asked him if Kinder had said anything about telling the truth. Toth testified, "He said let us worry about ourselves." The president of the court started asking questions and was cautioned by Major Farnell to stick to the conversation that Mike had asked about. Toth just said that the only other thing Kinder said was that Senator Kefauver of Tennessee was helping him and that there were articles in the paper in the United States about the case.

Our next witness was Major Westland. He was from Far East Air Materiel Command, the outfit to which the 75th was assigned, and it was in turn a part of Far East Air Logistics Force. He told how he met George Schreiber on several staff and field visits to the 543rd Ammo Supply Depot.

Major Westland testified that when he was the commander of the 542nd Ammunition Supply Squadron, stationed in Japan. that he had visited the 543rd in Korea, that as he was leaving the 543rd one night to return to Japan he had asked for a vehicle and a weapon to "protect himself." No one at the AP station could find a weapon for him to use. As noted, we were ill equipped. Those of us stationed in Korea were mandated to wear or carry our weapons loaded at all times as a general order. He told of how Major Vanderhoven told him about the lackadaisical officer in charge of the AP squadron at the 543rd at that time, and how things changed for the better when George came to town. He said everything looked real sharp on his later visits with the new Lieutenant Schreiber in charge – better discipline, better uniforms, better morale, etc. – and he heaped considerable praise upon George for making a really good unit out of a really bad unit. He went on to talk about his knowledge of the AP guards being fired upon at night and how he could hear shots. He told of "rampant guerrilla raids" and how a small radar station in the area was raided and the personnel were killed by the guerrillas. He testified that the 543rd and the 547th were the two major bomb dumps in Korea and both were under the command of the 75th Air Depot Wing. He told of how the Army bomb depot at the other side of the "mountain" from the 543rd was blown up in the summer of 1952.

There is no doubt that the guards in the 543rd AP squadron were in constant danger of being attacked and that Schreiber had a very crucial post in safeguarding one of the two major bomb depots that we possessed in South Korea. He summed up his testimony by saying that Schreiber was an exemplary officer, or words to that effect. In reality, he hardly knew George and wanted to help his friend Major Vanderhoven help George's cause.

We next called Chief Warrant Officer Thomas A. Reagan. He had been the officer in charge at the Bachelor Officers' Quarters at the 543rd when Schreiber arrived in Korea. Just a reminder, the Air Force no longer has the rank of warrant officer, unlike other branches of the service. The Air Force created senior non-commissioned officer ranks above master sergeant and did away with the hybrid ranks of warrant officers. As Mike was about to question Reagan, Major Farnell came up with a really cheap shot at Mike. He said, "Mister Braun, in the examination of these witnesses, would you phrase your questions so as to exclude as much objectionable material as possible?" Hit with that, poor Mike responded, "Yes, sir." A remark like that from the presiding officer indicated to me what an inexperienced trial lawyer we had running the trial. He was fearful of his position from the time we made our motion for Extraordinary Relief and for the continuance right through the trial. If we kept score, our objections sustained from the prosecution's questions numbered one, versus about twenty-five of theirs. And the military judge, Major Farnell came up with this cheap shot – unbelievable! It was an indication to me that his patience was waning, as it became apparent to me that he was under the gun, so to speak, to not let the defense have too much leeway in presenting a defense of Schreiber..A conviction was almost a command by forces we could not control..

Reagan told of George Schreiber's arrival and how he inspected his troops the following day. Reagan told of how unhappy George was with their appearance. He set out to get some uniforms for the men. Remember, when the Air Force arrived in Korea, it came as a "rag-tag army." We had no consistent uniforms or winter clothing, so everyone, airman and officer alike, dressed in what they had or what they could buy before embarking or on any black market in Korea, since ammunition and weapons weren't the only thing being stolen. At the 75th, we had Marine Corps fatigue uniforms courtesy of the First Marine Combat Service Group at Masan. In Pusan, uniforms apparently consisted of whatever you had available or could scrounge. This all probably sounds quite unreal, since all of the movies depicting World War II and even Korea show all military personnel in the same branch of service dressed in some uniform manner. But, in reality, the Air Force was not well equipped, well clothed, well armed, or well fed. Our quarters would have made a Russian peasant's hut look lavish. We had torn tents for the enlisted men, weathered and not waterproof. Some huts of tin were available for the officers, but these had roofs held down with sandbags or used tires and no furniture except for what we could steal or requisition from bombed-out buildings. We did build much furniture from packing cases. Reagan said George kept at him for sixty days to get clothing for his men, and it took at least that long to get his men properly clothed. He told of George saying that, if we could not get clothing through requisition, he would buy it somewhere. When he did finally get the clothes, there were not enough to go around, so he initiated a swap that allowed those on duty to wear the uniforms. There were not enough uniforms to clothe all of his men at the same time. He told of how Schreiber finally got whistles for his guards to blow to attract attention instead of having to fire their weapons. He told of George's high moral standards and how he counseled his men and insisted on getting them vehicular transportation to the infirmary when they needed it. He said Schreiber was often up all night making the rounds of his guards in the bomb dump as they were being shot at on a regular basis during the night, and how George would not get any rest until 3:00 a.m. on many days. He was a very good witness and portrayed George as the kindly, school-teacher type that he was. He also got across in some detail George's concern for the well-being of his men.

Our next witness was an airman who knew Sergeant Rumpf, one of the most hostile witnesses against Schreiber. He told us what a lousy NCO Sergeant Rumpf was and how he hated Schreiber for not promoting him and putting Airman First Class Toth in charge of his shift instead of him.

He also told how Kinder had told him a story of how he shot toward the Korean to "scare him." He added that Kinder told him that the Korean came at him, and Kinder got scared and shot him down out of fear of being attacked.

Our next witness was a giant of a Dutchman, Major Leo F. Vanderhoven. He was a large, bulky man, and could have been the model for any of the storybooks with pictures of Dutchmen that we had as kids. He was not smoking a pipe, however. I swear he spoke with a Dutch accent, although it was probably my imagination. He was my idea of the perfect Dutchman building a dike and saving his cattle from the encroaching sea. He was the commander of the 6414th Ammunition Supply Squadron Depot in Kosoji, Japan. He had commanded the 543rd Ammunition Supply Squadron when Schreiber had arrived in Korea in June of 1952. He told of how the

Air Police unit at that time was comprised of seventy-five indigenous guards along with twenty-four Air Policemen. He said pilfering amounted to about fifty-thousand dollars' worth of materiel a month, and that the unit was under constant pressure from guerrillas and bandits. He alluded to attacks on his depot every night. He told of how the adjoining Army depot was blown up and, shortly thereafter, how the 547th depot was blown up. That made the 543rd the only functioning supply depot in South Korea to supply the entire Air Force mission in Korea. He told of the disorganization of the four inexperienced officers running the Air Police at the depot. He said that it became so bad that he asked General Hewitt to relieve all of them, and immediately thereafter Lieutenant Schreiber arrived to replace the four of them. He said Schreiber immediately took over the task of building an Air Police organization. He told how Schreiber let all of the indigenous guards go because they were mostly thieves. He assigned more personnel from the organization for Schreiber to train. He told of how most of the forty-three men that he gave Schreiber had been court-martialed one to three times and that they were just GIs with no police training. He said that, because of Schreiber's superior training program, forty-two out of the forty-three turned out to be exemplary airmen. He told of how Schreiber taught most of the day and then stayed up with his men on guard duty most of the nights. He told of two of his generals coming through to inspect and how impressed they were with Schreiber, his organization, and his training skills. These generals, Hewitt and Rustow, were "highly pleased" with Schreiber's efforts, and he was promoted by spot promotion to first lieutenant. The losses diminished from fifty-thousand dollars a month to less than one-hundred dollars per month. Schreiber had changed an outfit with "a very bad morale problem" to an outfit with "superior morale." Schreiber accomplished all of this in sixty to seventy-five days. It certainly showed that Schreiber was an exceptional Air Force officer and, had he remained one, he would have prospered and advanced rapidly. He was the type of officer who any commander would love to have in his organization, as the better the organization and its component parts look, the better the commander looks, and so forth.

One thing that should be pointed out is that the ammunition-supply organizations of the Air Force required a lot of manpower, as just plain stevedores and lumpers were needed to offload ships and rail cars, sort the materiel, and reload it on trucks and rail cars for trans-shipment to the combat air bases.

On cross-examination, Major Vanderhoven was asked if Schreiber ever lied to him. He replied that Schreiber had not. Major Holland then showed Vanderhoven the logbook entry of September 26-27, and asked Vanderhoven if that was a lie. He said that Schreiber was truthful with him in making his report of the event. He agreed that he said upon learning of the shooting that "maybe this will teach them a lesson." On redirect, he was asked if anyone else besides the man who was shot was ever apprehended without identification. He answered that, on prior occasions, two Chinese were apprehended, and they had no identification and couldn't speak Korean. In fact, Bang Soon Kil was identified in all of the pleading as an Oriental male because there was never any evidence that he was in fact a Korean, nor was there any evidence as to what language or dialect he spoke. He was believed by the defense team to have been a Chinese infiltrator, but we could not prove that any more than the prosecution could prove that he was a Korean or what his name was. He was, for all purposes, a man without a country who spoke a language to which no one could swear. We all referred to him as a "Korean" only for the sake of convenience during the trial.

Our next witness was Captain Delmar Bartlett, 75th Supply Group, Headquarters Squadron at K-10, the headquarters of the 75th Air Depot Wing to which Schreiber was transferred when charged. I worked at the time in the JAG office at 75th ADW Headquarters

K-10 in Chinhae, Korea. Bartlett was now Schreiber's commanding officer. He said that George had a good reputation and that he was a "peaceful" person. He said that, while Schreiber didn't work directly for him, he knew from Major Breitnick (who will be properly introduced shortly) that Schreiber was doing a good job. We had not summoned the captain, but he said that he liked Schreiber and wanted to help him in his trial. He came to Taegu of his own volition to testify on George's behalf. He said that he first met Schreiber at K-9 in January and that Schreiber was transferred to his unit in April of 1953. He told of how George had set up a training program for the airmen in the supply group and that it was the best training program that he had seen since being in the Air Force.

Major Lawrence Breitnick was our next witness. He said that he was chief of the Management Procedures Division, Director of Supply. While these jobs sound mundane, there is no way the Air Force could carry out a mission or even a single strike if this organization was not properly functioning. An army does not fight in the modern era with what they can steal or find in the area. It takes a very well trained cadre of officers, NCOs, and men to track all of the needs of a functioning air force in combat. It was a monumental task carried out by a few very well-trained people with a staff of misfits, in many instances, to load and unload the materiel of war. It took very well-trained NCOs to directly manage the movement of materiel of war, and the 75th was equal to the task, even though it consisted of reservists from the Southwest augmented by some of us from other parts of the country. Major Breitnick spoke of the excellent training program run by Schreiber. He testified as to Schreiber's good character and reputation, and said that he would believe Schreiber under oath. He said he would like to retain Schreiber in his job.

Because the prosecution and Colonel Loewenberg's staff failed to or refused to transmit our depositions to the United States so we could obtain the testimony of various witnesses who knew George before he embarked on his Air Force career, we had arranged to stipulate with the prosecution as to what these people would have said had they been properly deposed in the United States. These witnesses were Harry Howard; George D. Horne Jr. (who was with the Atomic Energy Commission at Sandia, New Mexico), Frank J. Kessel, president of the Board of Education, District No. 95, State of Illinois; Jesse Swanson Dickey, a professor at Valparaiso University; Harry Von Huber, an engineer for the State of Illinois; Dr. Otto P. Kretzman, the president of Valparaiso University; Carl M. Henrichs, the athletic director at Valparaiso University; and Henry Bauer, the head football coach at Valparaiso University. All of these people would testify as to George Schreiber's outstanding reputation, both as a scholar and an athlete, during his college career. George was an All-American basketball player. All of these witnesses were prepared to testify as to George's high moral standards, his excellent reputation as a person, and most of all his veracity. Since George's testimony was critical to his defense, we felt that it was incumbent upon us to be able to show the court members that George was not mean or evil. This way, the court members would have ample grounds upon which to accept and believe his sworn testimony. We were duped by it all. Since the conviction was preordained, we'd have had no luck even if we had the Pope testify as to George's good character and behavior. We believed that, since he had lived an exemplary life, it would appear highly evident to the court members who did not know Lieutenant Schreiber that he was a man of excellent character and that he could be believed when he testified. Most criminal defense lawyers do not have their clients testify in such cases as this, particularly when charged with premeditated murder. However, most defense lawyers do not have a client of such outstanding merit, character, and reputation in his civilian and Air Force communities. So it went without saying that we felt George would be an excellent witness for the defense. We had found him to be truthful and cooperative in everything we tried to do to prepare for the trial, even though our efforts were completely disjointed due to time and distance from our client and from one another on the defense team. We bet his life on his credibility, as did he. We had our two best defense witnesses to call, Colonel Lucio E. Gatto and Lieutenant George C. Schreiber.

CHAPTER 23

Colonel Lucio Gatto

DR. LUCIO E. Gatto graduated from Harvard Medical School in 1938. He went through a residency in psychiatry at Temple University Medical School while in the U.S. Army Medical Corps. He was certified by the American Board of Psychiatry in June of 1950 and received a master's degree in psychiatry from Temple University Medical School in June of 1951. He was a clinical associate professor at the Philadelphia Institute of Psychiatry and served as the chief of professional services for the U.S. Air Force, as well as the Far East Air Materiel Command. He was the chief Air Force psychiatrist for the Far East Air Force, as well. In short, he was the top psychiatrist in the Air Force at that time. I took George to Japan to meet with him in June of 1953 as a part of our trial preparation. He immediately took a liking to George and to me. He was a fatherly figure and was of a mind to help George and me in George's defense.

Colonel Gatto was somewhat short in stature and long on qualifications. He chaired a board of psychiatrists to meet and speak with George. I advised George to tell his entire story to the board, even though most defense lawyers would have criticized me in those days for not keeping the client's rights protected under Article 31 of the code. That was the privilege against self-incrimination. There was no privilege in those days between a psychiatrist and a patient, such as exists today. The privilege today is as sacred as the attorney-client privilege, under which anything that a client says to his attorney and vice versa is privileged. One may not compel the repeating of anything that is said between them without the client's knowing waiver of the privilege.

After qualifying the doctor, Mike Braun offered into evidence as a defense exhibit the psychiatric board's report dated June 18, 1953. To qualify one as an expert, counsel proffering the opinions of the expert witness must review with the witness, under oath, the education, training, and experience of the witness in a particular field or science to show that the witness possesses knowledge of the field that the average person of average intelligence does not possess. Dr. Gatto was obviously a well-trained and well-educated psychiatrist. The effort to introduce the report of the board he had chaired was objected to by the prosecution on the grounds that it contained "incompetent evidence," and the prosecution cited the Manual for Courts-Martial, 1951, page 204, second paragraph. This paragraph was an anomaly in the law, as it precluded opinions as to the mental status of an accused being introduced into evidence and said that such opinions as contained in reports were hearsay and not admissible. It went on to say that the report could be received into evidence as past recollection recorded or by a stipulation. The prosecution was not about to stipulate to the report, since it was helpful to the defense. The manual went on to say that the court could examine the document if any member of the court objected to its exclusion and that the law officer should examine it to see if further examination into the mental status of the accused should be conducted. This was all totally inapposite and confusing. This rule was modified to eliminate the ability of a court member to object, so as to permit the members to read the report. In this case, no court member said anything.

Major Farnell then excused the court and conducted a hearing outside of the earshot of the court members. Mike asked Billy Holland to stipulate as to the board's conclusions, and Billy refused to do so. The inquiry began in closed session as to how the board conducted its examination of George. Dr. Gatto was asked if he had formed an "independent opinion as to Lieutenant Schreiber." Colonel Gatto asked Mike, "Independent of what?" Mike said he was referring to Gatto's opinion as opposed to all of the other members of the board. What Mike was attempting to do was to qualify Dr. Gatto as an expert so that his expert opinion, rather than the collective opinion of all of the members of the board detailed in the written report, would be allowed to be expressed and received as evidence. Under the Hearsay Rule of Evidence, the report was to be excluded from being introduced into evidence and read by the court members. Holland's objection was a good one. Mike then asked Dr. Gatto if he needed his memory refreshed, and Dr. Gatto referred to the report to testify as to his "independent opinion." The testimony was allowed as past recollection refreshed by the contents of the report, and the court was allowed to receive Colonel Gatto's opinions.

Gatto said that George was not suffering from any mental defect, disease, or derangement when he was examined and that he was capable of recognizing "the difference between right and wrong and adhering to the right." This was the classic test used in criminal cases to determine if an accused was suffering from a mental disease or defect, which is needed to raise an insanity defense to a crime. Dr. Gatto went on to say that George was capable of understanding the charges against him and in cooperating in his defense. He then went on to say that, "for the period of time surrounding approximately September 27, 1952, this officer's mental status and behavior revealed evidence of an underlying severe anxiety state, manifested by evidence of excessive worry, constant internal tension, startled reactions, and irritability related to his duty assignment in Korea. This anxiety state could have served within his given combat security assignment to produce a greater than average difficulty in adhering to the right so as to avoid certain offenses against the military code. The anxiety reaction is considered severe enough to have prevented him from recognizing the difference between right and wrong."

This testimony would normally have been "a home run" for the accused in any normal court, as it was sufficient to give the court the basis for an acquittal or, if not that, at least for a finding of manslaughter if they wanted to acquit Schreiber or find him guilty of a much lesser offense than premeditated murder. It got even better for us as Dr. Gatto's testimony continued.

He said that he had reviewed the information as to the facts surrounding the incident as given to another medical officer prior to the board convening, and that he had listened to George's account of events. He said that he had then reviewed George's actions at the time of the alleged offense. He then reviewed George's behavior as related by George. He said, "We evaluated him – not just the content of what is being brought forth, but the emotional operations and acts that are revealed by his behavior." He said that he also reviewed statements of others who were present at the "alleged time." Mike again asked Gatto to recount the facts, and Gatto said he needed his memory refreshed. So he read from his report, which contained extensive facts. (The report is set forth in the book)

Among the important facts was the emphasis made by higher authority to Schreiber on the seriousness of his pending position in Korea, on the presence of extreme dangers, including regular attacks from guerrilla forces and nightly intruders into the ammunition supply depot that he was to be charged with protecting, and that he would be the officer responsible for safeguarding the depot. His position as the sole Air Police officer would require extreme vigilance on his part. He was advised that the depot was subjected to enemy snipers who shot to kill. He was told to become very proficient in the use of his weapons for his own protection. He was placed into a combat situation. Doctor Gatto testified that Schreiber was "quite shaken up by his original briefing concerning the dangers of his new assignment and the fact that he found the security situation quite disorganized and his men poorly trained and inexperienced in covering the area involved. He felt a sense that a low ebb of morale was present. He was constantly bombarded by a sense of frustration and futility in which he could not gain any real control of the situation, no matter how hard he tried or how long he worked. His fears and anxieties over the situation were further increased by his knowledge that approximately one month earlier a nearby Army bomb dump had blown up."

Colonel Gatto went on in detail, telling the court that Schreiber suffered from a lack of sleep and that he would be up all night most nights to look after his men, as the attacks were primarily at night under cover of darkness. He told of George working "incessantly with a sense of futility and frustration." He told of Schreiber's men being pinned down by snipers and said that George would have to lead his remaining guards to relieve the men being attacked. He told that George was "in one damn nightmare." He told of how, when the infiltrators were apprehended, they were turned over to the Korean national police and, more often than not, they were then released by the police and allowed to attack again. In those days, the national police were a corrupted lot who dealt in the black market and were often complicit in provoking the depot attacks so as to allow weapons and munitions to be stolen and turned over to them for sale to bandit gangs and guerrilla forces. These police were employed by the Japanese during World War II and often served as guards of Allied prisoners of war. They were among the cruelest of guards. My own experience at K-10 was that they instructed the thieves in their own forces as to what vehicles should be stolen. Pusan was busy with stolen Jeeps and trucks painted in bright colors. The national police guards were totally corrupted, in my experience. They hated the Americans and used us as their source of loot to be sold in the black markets, which they controlled. As thieves escaped with items into the neighboring village, the Air Police were prohibited from entering the village to apprehend the thieves and bandits who had just tried to kill them.

Dr. Gatto told of how George was on medication to prevent the swelling of his hands, feet, and face from the hives following treatment with penicillin as a result of dental abscesses over his upper front teeth. He said that the use of Benadryl and Ephedrine "would have impaired his physical stamina and also played a part in increasing his emotional reactions to his entire situation." He then said, "It would be possible that, in a drowsy state, an individual's attention to details happening could be inaccurate." Dr. Gatto testified as to George's high sense of moral and ethical values and of his work as the Air Police commander of his guard unit. He told that Schreiber had a close personal friend killed in Korea in 1946 while on guard duty, and that George was now in a highly dangerous combat condition that heightened his anxieties. He said that these anxieties "under certain situations of stress might cause impairment of this officer's ability to adhere fully to the right as is indicated in Air Force Manual160-42, entitled 'Psychiatry in Military Law,' dated September 1950, Page 19, Paragraph 16b (2) (b)." The Manual, while not providing a complete defense, speaks of a situation where an accused suffering from severe anxiety reactions, such as described by Colonel Gatto, could find it difficult to avoid committing offenses against the code, and that such a reaction can be reported as rendering an accused's "adherence to the right more than normally difficult. This may then be taken into account by the court in extenuation of the offense. However, individuals with the reactions falling into this category are criminally accountable."

It was self-evident that Colonel Gatto was trying his best to assist in George's defense. After our meeting in June in Japan, he told me that he felt he would be helpful to George's defense. George was facing the death penalty, and such evidence from the Colonel could help us to avoid such a verdict, let alone a conviction for premeditated murder. On cross-examination by Major Holland, Colonel Gatto was asked to repeat what Schreiber told him. At first, Mike objected, but then said, "The defense doesn't want to keep anything out. We withdraw the objection." In an abundance of caution, Major Farnell then asked if George had been advised of his right to remain silent under Article 31 of the military code. Colonel Gatto replied that he didn't know, but said that, "Lieutenant Shaines of the defense was there and listening to what we said to him. But so far as reading the Article 31, I don't know." He did say that, as senior member of the board, he had cautioned George that anything he said could be used against him. He then went on to tell the facts as George iterated them to him.

Major Farnell then questioned the witness further about George's ability to adhere to the right.

Q. "I see. and what you are speaking of is an impairment of that ability, but the impairment didn't actually take away the ability, is that correct?"

A. "If I may be allowed to qualify my answer, I may be able to answer. It is true that in all of this there are impulses to do certain things, strong impulses. We learn in our American way of life to develop certain controls, certain inhibitions, which we feel is the culture we live in. Now, if individuals are moved into a slightly different culture that may be associated with warfare – it may not necessarily have to be the combat type – in an area where there will be underlying tensions, such individuals can develop anxieties, certain frustrations, certain feelings that have an effect or influence on these normal controls, controls established by individuals and society in which we live. If you can picture a governor on an automobile moving along at a certain speed, and not beyond that limit, it would be almost as though the spring controlling the governor would be under greater tension, so that under certain circumstances, the limit would be overreached. Similarly, under certain circumstances, either in warfare or in situations that are associated with warfare – and I say advisedly not necessarily at the front but in areas again where tensions are present – the control of an individual's conduct or inhibitions he would normally have over these impulses to aggression, they can be affected and be decreased."

Q. "Now was this intent in your opinion the result of a mental defect, disease, or derangement?"

A. "Repeat that please."

Q. "Was this intent in your opinion the result of a mental defect, disease, or derangement?"

A. "Insofar as I call an anxiety state an emotional disturbance, which can imply simple impairment, I would answer yes."

Q. "Did this impairment completely deprive the accused of his ability to adhere to the right?"

A. "Not completely, but rather [made it] more difficult to do so."

The president then asked some questions, namely when was Gatto's report written. Dr. Gatto said that his examination was held on June 18th and the report was dated June 30th. He said that he had reviewed some additional information, such as statements of witnesses. He told of an initial report, and said that this was the more detailed report. With the following question, the president obviously tried to demean Doctor Gatto's testimony.

Q. "And the information obtained is, in essence, the statements of the patient plus your observation of his emotional condition during this one-and-a-half-hour to one-hour period?"

A. "That is correct, except you must conclude also the experience and understanding that we had evaluating the material that is being offered or brought out by the individual."

The president by his question was signaling to the members of the court to disregard Colonel Gatto's testimony. It is a well-known ploy among trial lawyers to try and minimize expert testimony adverse to their client's cause to bring out the very limited time spent with the patient before arriving at an opinion. Colonel Gatto countered by reference to the combined experience of the members of the board and their understanding of human frailties. The question was not lost on me, even though I was a neophyte as a trial lawyer.

Major Farnell then gave the court the following instructions.

"Let me complete my instruction. You have heard the testimony of Colonel Gatto on the matter of the psychiatric examination. He is known in the law as an expert witness, because he is more qualified in the field of psychiatry than the ordinary man. You are advised that there is no rule of law requiring you to attach controlling significance to his testimony merely because of his position as an expert witness. You should, however, consider with due regard for his qualifications the testimony of this witness and attach such weight thereto as, in your fair judgment, it reasonably deserves in light of all of the circumstances, including your own common knowledge and observations. Further, the opinion of Colonel Gatto as to the mental responsibility of the accused has been received in evidence as the opinion of an expert witness. In specifying the data upon which his opinion is based, Colonel Gatto testified that it is based in part on facts presented to him, which for the most part was hearsay evidence. The court is instructed that this reference to such facts may be considered by the court only with regards to the weight to be given to Colonel Gatto's opinion and not as independent evidence bearing on the guilt or innocence of the accused."

We were all asleep at the switch, perhaps because the trial had been going on all day. The instruction was the worst piece of judicial gobbledygook and obfuscation ever recited in a court of law. It required our attention as soon as he mouthed the instruction, but we were too slow. We failed to object and did nothing to correct him. What he intended to say was that experts often rely on facts given to them to arrive at their opinions, and that the facts used in reaching those opinions are not necessarily proof of the facts as referred to and relied upon by the expert. The facts used in giving the opinion should not be used to judge the weight of the opinion, as the court was instructed. The opinion, rather, should be judged upon the expert's qualifications and alternative validation by competent evidence of any of the facts relied upon by the expert. If any fact relied on by Colonel Gatto was incorrect, you can bet that the prosecution would have been all over that as a basis to cross-examine him and to make him vacillate about his opinions. It is common for the cross-examining lawyer to change a few facts in the cross-examination of an opposing expert witness and then to ask if his opinion would be the same assuming a change in the facts relied upon by the witness. But such was not the case here. Major Holland had no basis to dispute the facts relied upon by the colonel as he iterated them to form the basis for his testimony.

Between the president's question demeaning Gatto's opinion and the instruction of Major Farnell, we lost the momentum from our very best witness, Colonel Gatto. Remember that he sent his report to us at the 5th Air Force JAG office, but it was never delivered to the defense until the eve of trial. We received the report only after I had phoned the Colonel to ask him of its whereabouts and after we searched for it with some help from Jake Hurley, the executive officer of 5th Air Force JAG. I remembered what Colonel Gatto had said to me while I was in Japan with George and, fortunately, somewhat late in the day thought of it. But, nevertheless, we sought it out because of his statements to me that he would be helpful to George's defense. He certainly tried to be. He was the chief psychiatrist in the Air Force at that time, but his opinions were for the most part disregarded by the court. Colonel Charles Loewenberg at 5th Air Force was highly motivated to hide this report, given that it was his office that had recommended the charge of premeditated murder. Colonel Gatto effectively and forcefully took away that claim and that of premeditation on the part of Schreiber by sharing his expert opinions that Schreiber in his actions was governed by uncontrollable anxiety and fear.

CHAPTER 24

Schreiber Tells His Story

JUST BEFORE GEORGE testified, we put Colonel Lee V. Wiseman on the witness stand as a precursor with the intent of reinforcing Schreiber's testimony. Colonel Wiseman was one of the youngest full colonels on active duty in the newly formed Air Force. He was barely 30 years old at the time and commanded the 75th Supply Group. This was the operations group that supplied the entire war effort of the 5th Air Force in Korea during the war. George had been assigned to the 543rd Ammunition Supply Depot, which became a part of the group on February 1, 1953. Colonel Wiseman had visited that depot shortly after arriving in Korea on January 1. He met Schreiber and said that Schreiber's commander had told him of exemplary performance as an Air Police officer and as the adjutant for the 543rd. It was common for junior officers to be given a primary assignment and to also to hold several other assignments within an organization at that time. The Air Force suffered from not only a paucity of logistics, but of trained officers.

After being notified that he was to be charged with murder, Schreiber was transferred to K-10, where he was placed under quarters arrest and in my custody. He was given the job of chief of training in the Management Procedures Analysis Division of the Supply Directorate K-10 on April 2, 1953. In his testimony, Colonel Wiseman rated his performance as "excellent." He said that Schreiber was an excellent officer and commented that, "I don't believe Lieutenant Schreiber would tell a lie."

The court then recessed until 1230 hours the next day.

The day started with a stipulation that a canvass was attempted by the OSI, including the publication in three newspapers circulated in the Pusan area of a notice seeking the identity of Bang Soon Kil. There had still been no identification of the deceased. The stipulation was to reinforce our theory that the deceased was not a Korean.

After a statement that George Schreiber was aware of his rights not to testify in his trial, he was sworn in and began to tell his story as to what happened on the night when Airman Thomas Kinder killed Bang Soon Kil. George said that he was 25 years old and that he was a second lieutenant in the U.S. Air Force stationed at K-10, Korea. He told that he "engaged in eight years of interscholastic competition in basketball during high school and college, two years of intercollegiate baseball, George was chosen a member of the 1950 All-Star basketball team." That was the equivalent of being on the All-America team in football. He could have been a pro basketball player, and his prowess was the subject of numerous newspaper articles in both Indiana and Illinois during his college career. Indiana was the heart of basketball country in the United States in those days. He told how he studied education at Valparaiso and, upon graduation in June of 1950, sought employment as a teacher in his hometown. He was employed as a grammar school and junior high school teacher in his hometown of Brookfield, Illinois. He taught the fifth and sixth grades, as well as handled the athletic program in junior high school. He told of how he organized a teenage recreational center in Brookfield "in which we took care of their athletic and social outlets." He remained a teacher for one academic year. He told of how he missed the draft in 1946 by one day, as the draft for World War II which ended on October 15, 1946, his birthday – when he turned 19 and would have been eligible. The Korean War draft made him tops on the list to be drafted, so in the spring of 1951 he enlisted in the Air Force Officer Candidate Program. He was accepted and reported to Lackland Air Force Base in June of 1951. He attended officer candidate training for six months and, in December of 1951, he was assigned to the Air Police. He told of how he was selected to be an Air Police officer, "When we were asked our choices for fields in the career field of the Air Force, only a very minimum number asked for Air Police – people who had prior experience," he said. "At this time, there was a critical need and a shortage, and as a result a quota was sent to the OCS [Officer Candidate School] informing them they needed a goodly number. In the end, it was an alphabetical choice in my being selected in the field. I disliked the assignment intensely. I had no experience. I was sent TDY [temporary duty assignment] to Tyndall Air Force Base, Florida, for a period of three months and then to Spokane, Washington. At that base, I learned more about Air Police fields, and I lost the ill feeling I had towards the field." He then returned to Spokane and volunteered for an overseas assignment. He was designated to go to FEAMCOM in Japan.

He was then asked about his medical issues. He told of a blow to his mouth in 1948 that led to abscesses developing over his front teeth. He previously had no reaction to penicillin, but told of how he had experienced a strong reaction of hives just before leaving for Japan. He was then taking ephedrine and Benadryl every three to four hours. He told of how the pills made him sleep a lot, how he had traveled to Japan by ship, the *General Breckenridge*, and that he slept a good deal of the voyage. He arrived in Japan in late July 1952.

The idea behind all of the preliminaries was to put Schreiber at ease on the witness stand by having him testify as to his history, which he could readily recall, and to set up certain facts to support Colonel Gatto's helpful opinions. Schreiber told us that he reported to Lieutenant Colonel Percy R. Follis at Far East Air Logistical Forces. Colonel Follis interviewed him and told him that he would be assigned to an Air Police job at a Far East Air Materiel Command Air Base. He was asked if he was single, and he replied that he was. He was thereafter told that he would be assigned to a base in Korea. That was the Air Force policy at the time, to send the single officers to the combat areas whenever feasible. The same system was applicable to the JAG officers assigned there. He told of the things that Colonel Follis told him about his prospective assignment to Korea, namely that the Air Force was losing a great deal of equipment in Korea and that the service was experimenting with the use of sentry dogs to guard the supply depots. Schreiber said:"He informed me the unit to which I was being sent, the 543rd Ammo Supply Depot, was the first unit in Korea to receive these dogs, inasmuch as that unit was the one having the most trouble, losing the most materiel and, just plain speaking, in the lousiest possible condition,"

George continued to explain that the command had four or five units in Korea spread out from K-14 to K-9. Colonel Follis personally accompanied George on a tour of these units, briefing him on the condition of each and advising him on what to expect at the 543rd. George arrived at the 543rd around August 15, 1952, and immediately started to work. He told us of the poor shape of the unit and how its poor performance had exceeded his expectations. "Everyone was boss; everyone was sergeant of the guard; everyone was Non Commissioned Officer in charge, – whether he was an airman third class or sergeant or tech sergeant," Schreiber said. "The group had many bosses and no one on the hill. I refer to our bomb-dump area." He told of how there was no record keeping or any administrative records of any kind. "There was nothing, so it was easy to start from the bottom and work up," he said.

He said that the Air Police section had virtually no equipment – personal or Air Police equipment. There was one "broken-down Jeep" and tentative use of a 6x6 truck. Assigned to the unit , about seven qualified Air Policemen, and a group of about twenty-five airmen who had been relieved of duty in other sections and reassigned to the guard unit. "The men were completely without any discipline, without any working schedule," he said. "I could not distinguish between an airman third class and an airman basic and the NCOIC (non-commissioned officer in charge) – no rank, no authority rendered, no respect rendered to the men who were in charge. The men came and went to duty as they saw fit. There had been an occasion prior to my arrival, which I feel certain is the truth, where guards would report for duty with a case of beer under their arm to take with them to the hills. If a man wanted to go to work, he went. If he didn't, he went to the sergeant and told him he wasn't going to work. At that time, they had indigenous guards, although we referred to them as guides, inasmuch as it turned out they were in this group who were stealing from the dumps and received their share of the profits."

George continued to tell of the organizational structure he implemented, how he set up work schedules and started to build a functioning unit. He built new fences around the dumps and began regular training classes, which included a ten-week Air Police training program. "These people were completely uninhibited," he said. "A field-grade officer would arrive on the base and would be shown no respect by any member of the squadron, and more so not by the Air Policemen's unit. I remember the first time Colonel Follis and I arrived and went through the main gate. They had on fatigue uniforms, fatigue caps, an old .45 of some kind of Jap design. They were in a slumping position, gave us a wave as a sign to come on through. That was the status of the discipline. But I could not blame these airmen. There was no one there who took any interest." He told of four officers who had been there before he arrived and were removed because of fighting among themselves. He said he blamed the conditions there on the lack of leadership and not on the airmen.

We had George tell about his constant education of his airmen in formal classes, so as to prepare them for their duties. He told of his primary duties as AP squadron commander and as adjutant to the group. He told of having been assigned to ten additional secondary duties. He told of how he got to know each of his airmen and how he worked at least seventeen hours each day. He explained that he felt it was important to be with his guards during the night and that he would sleep for some of the morning hours. He told of how men would have previously been under fire and that the officers didn't care and would contradict one another. He organized teams to relieve the attacks on his men when shots were heard. He said that he continued taking his capsules until the end of October, as his feet would swell.

We then got to the night of September 26th. Schreiber said that he was in bed at 2300 hours and was awakened by a phone call on the base phone system. He got out of bed and walked to the phone, which was located a distance away. He talked to Sergeant Toth, who told him that a Korean had been picked up in the bomb dump and that a struggle ensued. Toth said that he had to subdue the Korean by force and had brought him to Air Police operations. He told Toth that he would be right down. He returned to his room and dressed. He said Lieutenant Penabaker was the duty officer, and he told him what Toth had said. Schreiber continued that he and Penabaker went to the operations office. He didn't know what time he arrived but, as the guard was changing, he assumed it was midnight. The first thing he noticed was the Korean on the floor with four of five APs standing around.

He was then asked who was there at the time. "Here is my point," he responded. "Since the entire incident has been brought about, I have heard many witnesses testify they were in the office and so on." He said that he didn't remember such folks being there. He did remember that Toth was there when he arrived. He asked Toth what had happened. Toth told him that he apprehended the man in the bomb dump and that he had tried to escape. Toth said that he had caught him and brought him in. Toth explained that, while he was bringing the Korean in to the operations office, the man had tried to grab his .45 pistol, whereupon Toth stopped the vehicle and struck the man with his pistol. He bent down to look at the man and noticed a bruise on his face and blood on his hair. He asked if the man had any identification and was informed that there was none. He could not say how the man was dressed, other than to say he had on dark clothing.

Schreiber was then asked what he did. He said that, since the man had no identification, "I had no recourse but to release this man." He felt it was useless to turn him over to the national police, as they were working with the thieves at that K site. "I told Toth to take this man out, get him out of here, which Toth proceeded to do," Schreiber said. He said that Ed Penabaker was in the room, as well as Sergeant Addleman and a few airmen. He said that Kinder was not in his sight at the time. As Toth was removing the man, Kinder came in and walked to the gun room. "I told Kinder to take his carbine and his clips and go and assist Toth," Schreiber said. He had no memory of Kinder being in the room before that, and he didn't say anything else to Kinder except, "as Kinder was walking out, he turned around and said, in what I thought to be in a joking way – to be funny – 'Is that an order, sir?' And I said, 'Yes, that is an order.'" He then said that he asked for some coffee and sat down with Addleman. Penabaker then left. He said some people may have passed in and out of the room, but he only remembered being there with Sergeant Addleman. He was working with Addleman and heard shots fired in the bomb dump. He then saw Sergeant Rumpf sitting at a desk and told him to go to the bomb dump and find out what the shots were. After five or ten minutes, Rumpf returned and reported "that the Korean had been shot."

Upon learning of this, Schreiber called the K-9 dispensary and asked that they meet him at the squadron area to proceed to the bomb dump in the mountains. He then got a Jeep and drove to the main gate to await the arrival of the ambulance. Upon its arrival, he led the ambulance to the bomb dump. He saw a guard signaling to him, so he pulled up about five hundred yards from the ammunition dump. He saw a group standing and a figure on the ground on the side of the road. The ambulance stopped beside him, and the medics got out. He noticed Airman Renteria with his dog and, because he recognized the dog as vicious, he told Renteria to keep away. He said it was dark and that here were no lights and no moon, but he saw the man placed on a stretcher, put into the ambulance, and driven away. "I asked someone at that time what happened, and someone said Kinder shot a gook," he said. Schreiber then got in the Jeep, followed the ambulance out, and drove to operations. He then drove to the K-9 dispensary. The entire place was in darkness. He went into the office and saw several medics – men running in and out and walking in a hurried fashion. He inquired about the man and, after about ten minutes, he was told that the man was either drunk or drugged, that he had a gunshot wound, but that he would be all right. He returned, asked for Kinder, and was told that he had gone to chow and then to bed. He instructed the man on duty to phone the hospital in a few hours so as to inquire as to the man's condition so that he would know it in the morning. He returned to the BOQ and went to bed.

In the morning, he got up between 7:30 and 8:30, had breakfast, and went to AP operations. He inquired about the condition of the man and was told that the Korean had died during the night. Someone had put the information in the logbook and typed up an incident report for him to sign. That was sent to the commanding officer, as was the case each morning.

After submitting the report, Schreiber received a phone call from the 17th Air Police investigator. He was told that they wanted to see Kinder regarding the incident on the previous night. He accompanied Kinder to the investigation. As they were driving, Kinder asked him what to say. "I turned to him and said tell them what happened," Schreiber said. He said Kinder had told him that the Korean had charged at him and that he shot him.

In his answers to the next few questions, Schreiber exhibited his nervousness and talked too much. He was asked if he went with Kinder to the investigator's office. He said that he did. He was then asked what he was doing and where he was while Kinder was being interviewed. He said that part of the time he was in the Provost Marshal's office. He then continued to ramble and started discussing Sergeant Addleman and Kinder. He rambled on about how many of his men told of being shot at and knocked down by intruders, and bragged of their exploits while on guard in the hills, where the bombs were being stored. He continued on, telling the court that he cautioned his men not to make too much of the incident, as "it seemed to be putting coal on the fire or something, and everyone was telling great stories of battle threats, that they were going to get the Koreans. They were going into the hills even then, and to be perfectly frank, I was becoming more afraid of their action in the hills." He told that, as a result, he had prepared a lesson plan designed to calm his men down. He said their fear was obvious and was being covered by excessive tales of bravado. In the class, he cautioned the men not to let their imaginations run away with them. "We had a couple of storytellers down there for some time. And they had great stories to tell – which, in my opinion, were dreamed up only to try and impress other people with their ability," he said. "I cautioned these people not to talk about this incident, not to make something out of it that it isn't, exciting their own fear."

He continued to ramble from one subject to the next. He was not impressing the court and was talking far too much in response to a simple question. I figured that Mike and Jesse knew what they were doing in letting Schreiber ramble. I now know that this was a classic error in such a trial. It is far better to hold the witness close in his testimony and to elicit what it is that you as the attorney want the court or the jury to hear. By rambling on as he did, Schreiber opened up a large area of questioning by the prosecution, since the scope of cross-examination in military courts was limited to areas covered on direct testimony only. Allowing George to continue got into areas that hurt him, in my opinion. He told of how two of his airmen had been fired upon from a distance of forty yards and that they were "so shaken and afraid that they were throwing up, purely nervousness on the spot." He told of his men threatening to get long knives and kill Koreans with them. "They were getting in more fear and more jumpy, if they continued."

All of this rambling, in my judgment, was designed by Schreiber to show how he was suffering from an anxiety reaction, etc. George's bravado on the stand seemed to me to contradict Doctor Gatto. I think that, in reality, for all of his calm demeanor, Schreiber was a nervous wreck and too proud to admit it. He would have done better with this court had he done so. Some of the court members had flown in combat. From my experience at the 8th Fighter Bomber Wing, where I shared quarters with at least ten pilots, these guys were nervous wrecks and didn't try to hide it. Their usual routine after coming in from combat missions was to spend fifteen to forty-five minutes in the latrine puking their guts out. What they couldn't puke, came out as diarrhea. They were never embarrassed, since flying in all-weather night fighters through the Korean mountains, often at low levels and at supersonic speeds while wearing G-suits, was enough to terrify the most aggressive warriors. In making light of the fear and upset attitudes of his men, Schreiber did himself a big disservice. I blame Mike and Jesse for that. George should have been curtailed when his answer was not responsive. You will notice that neither of the prosecutors made any effort to object to his answers as non-responsive. In fact, they probably relished it.

We continued on to show what an exemplary officer the accused was. We introduced a photograph of George with the Commanding General of FEALOGFOR. He told of how the General gave him a promotion to first lieutenant just ten months after receiving his commission. He then was asked about his transfers, which left him at K-10. He had been sent there after the investigation was reopened, and he was placed on quarters arrest. It was now mid-afternoon, and Billy Holland asked for a short recess, which was granted.

Major Billy Holland began his cross-examination by asking about Lieutenant Penabaker and what time he left the office on the night of the killing. Schreiber said he couldn't remember. Holland then asked if Schreiber remembered a phone call that he made to Penabaker after he had been transferred to K-2 at Taegu. Schreiber, instead of answering the question, asked Holland for the approximate time of the call. Schreiber finally admitted making a call "concerning this incident."

Holland then continued with his questioning.

Q: "At Air Police operations that night, why did you warn Lieutenant Penabaker of his rights under Article 31 over the telephone?"

A. "Lieutenant Penabaker was the duty officer of the day on the night of the incident."

Again, Schreiber was not answering the question and seemed to me to be evasive. Billy Holland pressed him.

Q. "'Why did you?' is the question I am asking."

A. "May I finish explaining, sir? When I was informed in February that there was an incident in September being investigated by the OSI, I felt it was my duty to him as a personal friend to inform that the investigation was going on. And he asked me if anything was wrong with this incident, and I felt it was the only thing to do as a friend to let this man know."

Holland then asked Schreiber when in February he had been informed of the investigation. He suggested that Schreiber's recollection of events was faulty and that he was being evasive in responding to questions. Holland then reminded Schreiber that he was informed of the investigation on January 27, 1953. This was all designed to show that George's memory of events was faulty.

Holland pressed on with his questioning.

Q. "You called a meeting of all people in your squadron and warned them of their rights also?"

A. "May I have permission to answer the question? I did not warn anyone, Major. I informed them that they had certain rights under Article 31. I did not call a special meeting. I had just returned shortly from a provost marshall's conference in Japan. I had not seen my men, not any of them, for nine days. I had my normal classes, normal get-together with the troops in my command. At that time, I had been informed that there was an investigation. At that meeting, as a part of the instruction, I told the men who were present at that time, I saw no need to worry them about possible trouble in the bomb dump. So, as a result, I released the new men early and told these people and asked them what was going on. I wanted to be informed, informed of any OSI investigation going on. I proceeded to ask them who had already been interviewed, what the nature of it was."

He was asked if Toth and Kinder were present. He replied, "no," but asked if he could go on. The Law Officer, Farnell, cautioned him to wait for the next question. I think Farnell was also seeing the hole that Schreiber was digging for himself by talking too much and by not remembering details. He didn't remember if he said anything to Airman Mullins. He was vague on what, if anything, he had said to Sergeant Borchardt. He was asked if he cleared the 6x6 truck out of the gate and answered by saying, "If I did clear it out of the gate, it was normal procedure, sir."

George found it difficult to answer a direct question, which put him more in the category of being an unreliable rather than a credible witness. He professed that Holland was confusing him when he was asked if Mullins and Borchardt were at the scene of the shooting after Schreiber drove there. He didn't know, he said. He didn't recall if Kinder was there. He said he remembered seeing Renteria. He didn't remember seeing the man's face at the bomb dump. It got worse.

Q. "When did you first find out that Kinder shot a Korean?"

A. "I think I stated previously. I am not sure it was that night out there in the process of coming in or if it was the next morning when

I got to Air Police Operations, I was informed that Kinder had shot a Korean."

This testimony flew in the face of every other witness' testimony and, frankly, was not credible. I guess that when one is subject to an investigation and then charged with premeditated murder, a lot of different scenarios go through one's mind. After a while, you convince yourself as to the facts that seem most helpful to you, and you forget the facts that could tend to incriminate you. I really never thought that George was lying, but I think he developed a selective memory to conceive of and to construct his own legal and moral defense. He was doing himself much harm in doing this. Holland was getting a lot of good answers for the prosecution, so he pushed on.

Q. "When you found out Kinder shot the Korean, you put him on the truck to take him out the gate to release him and not out to the bomb dump to shoot him? Is that true?"

Mike Braun, the IDC 9 individual defense counsel said: "We object. There are three questions in one."

Law officer: "I believe it is a proper question. Objection overruled."

A. "Major Holland, when a vehicle leaves the area, there are several men on for the purpose of posting. To take the Korean out to release him is not the only purpose of it leaving. A truck with people in it has more to do than just go out and . . . "

IDC "Has the witness completed his answer?"

Law Officer: "Do you wish to continue with your answer?"

A. "As to Major Holland's question, this shooting is going on nightly. I knew they had left the area. I knew the man was in the truck with them because they finally end up in a bomb dump. I knew they had the Korean with them. I told them to take him."

Q. "Wasn't Kinder due to be relieved?"

A. "Kinder had been relieved from the post, but not necessarily from duty. We have several men. Because they are taken off of the post, they are not off duty completely, if other things come up. A man doesn't work six hours and then go to bed, Major."

Q. "Let me ask you this. Since Kinder shot the Korean and you knew it the next day, as you previously testified, didn't it seem odd to you that he shot a Korean on the post while you already told him on the night before to take the Korean out and let him loose?"

A. "Not at all."

Q. "When did you first realize any irregularity in the incident?"

A. "When the OSI started to interrogate me."

He was asked if that was around February 15, and Schreiber said that it could have been. He then added, "I have had many interrogations by the OSI personnel."

Schreiber was getting testy and tired. He didn't like the way it was going and the fact that his version of events was being questioned. To me, he sounded arrogant. So Holland asked him if he was being impertinent. Schreiber replied that he didn't mean to be, but he was. Schreiber refused to recognize any irregularity other than that he should have had the Korean taken out for medical treatment in the first instance.

Q. "Other than that, the only time you realized anything was wrong was when the OSI started investigating you, or interrogating you?"

A. "Irregularities?"

So Schreiber said that they didn't know anything was wrong until February 15, 1953, then Holland dropped the hammer on him.

Q. "Did you or did you not on February 7, 1953, cause a letter to be prepared in which you signed your name on it and sent it to Toth containing the words to this effect: 'Remember I am the responsible officer. You are reminded of your rights under Article 31. It would be better for all concerned if no one would make a statement.' Did you or did you not send that letter to Kinder?"

A. "Yes, sir. I did."

He then advised that he so informed Sergeant Borchardt about it. He couldn't remember if he had sent a letter to Mullins. Holland had

Schreiber in a death grip, and he was not about to let it go. Schreiber insisted that he was only trying to protect his men. On the one hand, he said that he counseled them to tell the truth if interrogated. And, on the other hand, he told them that it would be better for all to say nothing and invoke the right of silence under Article 31. His positions were inconsistent – he knew it; we knew it; the court knew it; and the prosecution knew it. His story was unraveling, so he retreated. "Sir, the only reason that I made that statement was because of the fact that I was not present with these boys." he said. "I know the methods the OSI use. I had seen the methods the OSI uses on airmen."

It got even worse as Schreiber went on.

A. "So, advising them of their rights under Article 31 to an eighteen year old is far from being a regulation. I further knew these people would be shaken up if they had anything to be shaken about."

Q. "Do you mean to tell this court that Kinder never told you about the incident when Kinder was first involved with the shooting of the Korean?"

A. "I did not hear him say anything."

Q. "Kinder never explained to you what happened about this incident when he was the very person who shot the Korean?"

A. "He shot who? I have testified before that someone said there was a person in the Air Police Operations' that night who was injured.

A. "He did not."

Schreiber was then asked if he made a prior inconsistent statement to a James J. Donahue, an OSI investigator. He said he didn't recall such a statement. In my experience, that is not the same thing as saying I did not say that. It leaves the impression that maybe he did. Mike tried to object that Donahue had not testified and that the cross-examination was improper. He was rebuffed in his effort by the law officer.

He was asked how long he saw Kinder that night, and he said, "Twenty seconds." He was asked if he told Penabaker the following morning that he "had the Korean shot." He denied making such a statement. He was asked if he ordered the logbook changed, which he denied. He was asked if he told Kinder that they would coordinate their stories he denied that. He was asked if he changed the roster to read that Kinder was changed to Post 12 instead of Post 13. He responded, "No, sir."

The court was then permitted to examine Schreiber. First came Major Simpson, who asked him if he knew that everybody is made aware of their rights to remain silent when being interrogated. The answer was obvious. He was then asked why he called Penabaker to remind him of his right to remain silent. Good question, poor answer.

Lieutenant Colonel Eslick came next. He asked about why the men passed their clips in through the window that night. Schreiber said it was normal procedure, as there were usually twenty-five men passing in clips. The operations and gun room were small, and Schreiber explained that it would be too crowded for everyone to come inside. Eslick continued to question Schreiber about his saying he didn't recognize who was on the hill after the shooting. He said he heard Borchardt say in court that he was on the truck. He said that he knew Toth was on the truck because he had told him to take the Korean out. He continued asking about how the guard was mounted and how the guards retrieved the dogs to go on post. Schreiber explained that some posts were one and a half miles apart, and that posting often took two hours. He said that trucks are constantly going back and forth in the transition carrying guards and dogs each way. He said that the corporal of the guard, sergeant of the guard, and the NCOIC would then be checking the guard once posted to see that everything is all right. Lieutenant Colonel Eslick then continued with his questions.

Q. "If this Korean was being taken to the gate to be released, and this truck has guards on it to be posted, would it have been necessary to put additional people on that truck to escort that man to the gate?"

A. "First of all, sir, when you take a man out, you just don't take the man to the gate. We will send an interpreter on with them, and they continue on their way. However, when we pick people up at night, you just direct them to take this person out in the village away from our area. Airman Kinder said he apprehended the person, or someone told me that he apprehended him. Kinder came in, and I said, 'Take him out of here.'"

Q. "What I am trying to find out is the answer you gave to a question by the trial counsel, and you answered his question that it wasn't unusual to put a Korean on the truck going out the gate to post the guard?"

A. "Yes, sir. It doesn't necessarily mean this particular unit."

Q. "But if the truck was posting the guard, would you leave it to go to the village before posting the guard? Was that the usual procedure?"

A. "That went through the village, sir."

Q. "On the way to the dump?"

A. "Yes, sir."

It was now Colonel Perry's turn to question Schreiber. He asked about Schreiber observing the condition of the man on the floor of the operations office. Schreiber said that he thought the man was unconscious and that he was thrashing around. He knew the man was injured in "resisting arrest." Perry then continued with his questioning.

Q. "Is that a customary incident so far as operations are concerned? Usual incident? Normal incident?"

A. "With regard to what, sir?"

Q. "In respect to having an individual in a beaten-up condition on the floor of the operations shack?"

A. "I cannot say it is usual."

When asked if he investigated the circumstance s reported by Toth in beating the man, Schreiber said that he made no investigation. Perry went on cross-examining Schreiber, whose answers were not direct and not candid.

Q. "Didn't you say it is a responsibility of a responsible officer to look into unusual instances?"

A. "Colonel, when one of my men is assaulted in the bomb dump, there is no investigation I can make. When one of the Orientals who is in the bomb dump and apprehended there attacks one of my men, I have no desire or reason to believe other than what the Sergeant told me. He told me this man resisted apprehension and had gone for his weapon. It was apparent to me a struggle had ensued."

He was then quizzed as to what he said to whom about taking the man out. He said he told Toth to take the man out. He thought that his order had been to release the man in the village. He said that when he went to the dump after the shooting, he didn't realize it was the same man that was shot. Perry pressed him as to his responsibility to investigate the matter. Schreiber disagreed, saying that such an investigation was the responsibility of the 17th Air Police investigation section. "I have nothing to say, nothing to do. I took the men over to them for investigation," Schreiber said.

Q. "Going back to the Air Police operations shack again – you have heard numerous witnesses testify that they concluded from the activities in the operations shack that the apprehended individual was to be taken out and shot."

Mike moved to strike that question on the grounds "that it is contrary to the evidence. Many witnesses have not so testified. It shows misconstruction of the evidence, sir."

Law Officer: "Objection sustained." Perry was tipping his hand. He was ready to convict Schreiber. In fact, there were not "many witnesses" who said any such thing. Mike asked for a recess so we could consider challenging Colonel Perry remaining as a court member. The president denied the request. It was not his prerogative to do so, and Farnell granted it.

We met outside and discussed challenging Colonel Perry. We decided to do so. The law officer ordered us to continue with Schreiber's testimony. We wanted Colonel Perry to be sworn right then, and that we be allowed to be question him about his obvious prejudice against Schreiber as was apparent to us by his question. Farnell said that he would permit us to examine Perry, but only after Schreiber completed his testimony. Perry began again, pressing further with his questions.

It is permissible to challenge a court member for cause during a trial if that member shows that he has determined guilt or innocence of an accused before all of the evidence is heard, arguments completed and instructions given as to the law by the judge. In such a case the challenging party has a right to examine the challenged member under oath and the rest of the board votes to either uphold or reject the challenge.

Q. "It has been testified during this trial, in your presence, the impression was received by at least one individual who was present in the operations shack on the night of 26 September, that it was concluded to take the Korean out and shoot him. Recalling that evening, Lieutenant Schreiber, can you think of anything that transpired in that group that you observed or took part in that could possibly have given the impression to anyone person present?"

A. "Yes, sir, if I may allowed to explain. I had previously told the guards that in the performance of their duty, if it was going to be a pitched battle, going to be you or him, make damn sure it is you that is not attacked and shot. Now, when this incident occurred, I can't say truthfully – right now I can't recall it, but it is possible that I asked when this man resisted apprehension – why didn't you use your weapon, use your dog. I may have made a comment that if these people don't stop coming in, they will fight on sight and we should shoot them. But so far as telling anyone anything specific to do to this Korean, no, sir."

That was the first time in all of the months that I had been associated with Schreiber that he ever told me anything remotely close to his response to Colonel Perry. Did it do anything for him to say that? I doubt it, as it showed a lack of compassion in one sense. But it was designed to show that Schreiber was loyal to his people to a fault.

An article appeared in *The New Yorker* entitled "The Kill Company," dated July 6 and 12, 2009, and written by Raffi Khatchadourian. It was remarkably like what Schreiber said, as it sent a message to the soldiers in that company with the ultimate result that four of the young GIs in Iraq were charged with murder. The Army initially sought the death penalty, but then settled on going for life imprisonment. It bears out the fact that the only thing we don't really know about the future is the history that we haven't read. Take a group of teenagers and kids in their early twenties. Train them to use weapons. Scare the hell out of them. Tell them to shoot to kill if they feel they are facing an enemy. Then we are no different than any other group of trained killers who shoot first and determine the reality of the situation later. If that is to be our nation's strategy and what we teach our kids who fight our wars, then we should accept it and not prosecute them for doing what we know they might do under the strained circumstances when they are in fear for their lives and their safety. They have the absolute right to be afraid and in fear. When this fear is masked with bravado then it is encouraged by the rush of adrenalin and testosterone, killing will happen.

Captain McClain then took his turn. He asked George about the morale of his troops in September. George said that it was improving and, with some people, it was very high. He told of how he taught the eighteen- and nineteen-year old kids that he commanded, played football with them, and showed an interest in them. He told of how he helped them to get high school diplomas and of how they responded to him and the jobs they had to do. He told of how his entire squadron held a special formation on Christmas to honor him and present gifts to him. "I didn't know what to say, he said. "It was the first time in my life I ever had anything like that. So, from that, I believe the men respected me. They had given me a pen, a cigarette lighter, cigarettes, and so on. I just never had anything like that."

McClain then asked if anyone in his organization held any animosity toward him. George responded that he knew of only one person. It was Rumpf. Schreiber described him as a man of low moral character, being married and living in Korea with an Oriental to whom he was not married. He said he was angry because he was demoted in the organization because of his inefficiency. Schreiber said that he didn't recognize the animosity at the time. Then McClain continued with another question.

Q. "One last question – the night of the incident in September, do you remember discussing anything with Penabaker prior to his departure, to the effect that Penabaker may have said, 'Shall I make a report on this?' And did you reply you would take care of a report, referring to the OD report?"

A. "I don't recall saying anything about that incident at the time. My thoughts were that it was a normal incident. I may have said I don't believe there is any need to make a report. It is just another Korean. I can't truthfully recall saying that to Penabaker."

Did that last answer reveal the true Schreiber? The thought that it was "just another Korean" upset me greatly. Did George have some Germanic coding in his DNA that left the rest of the human race as something less than him? I still don't know. I do know that his background was one of prejudice and thinking that Koreans were to be regarded as lesser humans. His answers bothered me then, and they bother me now. This gentle grammar-school teacher, beloved by his students and pupils, held hidden prejudices. Could it be that there was also violence in his makeup? The court members were perceptive in digging out such remarks. Perhaps we did not fully understand our client, nor did we comprehend what he was saying at the time. He did himself no good in his testimony.

Major McCann then asked about Schreiber having completed FBI School at Tyndall Air Force Base and of his briefing before coming to Korea. He then asked an interesting question.

Q. "In your training and briefing, I assume – well, I will say – do you understand the term 'shoot to kill'?"

A. "Do I understand it?"

Q. "The meaning of the term?"

A. "Yes, sir. I believe I do."

Q. "What were the instructions issued to you by your superiors concerning such accused in the performance of their assigned duties?"

A. "Sir, I never instructed anyone to shoot to kill. I never instructed them to do anything like that. The boys asked when this man got after us, 'What do we do when they shoot at us?' I said, if you are being shot at, return the fire. If you see an individual, if he has materiel, .50-caliber machine guns or flares, or anything like that, blow your whistle or holler. If there is no action on that, fire around and over the man's head. If there is no action on that, send the sentry dog after the man. They are trained to grab hold of the person and will resist any shaking off by the individual. If the dog is loose, don't fire. We don't want the dog killed. After that, if the man is getting away, shoot to cripple the man. If the man has a weapon and you see his weapon, shoot to stop him firing. If, after that, shoot to kill. And if that man over there has a gun pointing at me to kill me, I told those men to shoot him."

Schreiber said those were the instructions that he issued. He was then questioned about Toth. He said that he respected Toth in the performance of his duties and regarded him as a good airman. McCann then asked Schreiber where he thought Toth would discharge the individual. Schreiber said he thought Toth would drop him at the crossroads of the highway surrounding a small village outside of the gate, "where the other people were." He asked about Schreiber's and Toth's conversation as to what had occurred between Toth and the man. He asked about Schreiber's orders that night.

Q. "Did you give any other orders?"

A. "The one I stated in my previous testimony. The man on his way out the door – I took it as a snide remark to be ignored – I heard him say, 'Is this an order?' And I said 'yes.'"

The president asked Schreiber why the Korean was lying on the floor and not sitting or standing.

Q. "He was injured and he had no identification? Is that correct?"

A. "Yes, sir."

Q. "And you instructed someone to take an injured man with no identification out into the bomb dump and turn him loose in town?"

A. "May I preface my remark?"

Law Officer. "Sure you can."

A. "Yes, sir, would be my answer. Colonel, the injuries to these Korean people in and out of our bomb dump were numerous. They would get caught on barbed wire, erected to hold anyone out, and the hole wasn't big enough to let them through. They would carry out too much ammunition and stumble and fall. We had our own four indigenous guards who let them in, and those people were injured. American medics do not accept Koreans. They did not at that time. They would be taken to a Korean hospital located at K-9 Air Base. However, many Koreans refused any medical treatment. It was an irregularity, I agree. Now, this individual had the most antagonism in my mind. But no matter what my feelings were, I should have taken that man to a hospital no matter what my feelings. But he had been in the bomb dump and had tried to get a man's weapon. He did not appear to be the kind of man looking for assistance, and I wasn't about to give assistance at that time."

Colonel Eslick then had more questions about the Korean on the floor. Schreiber now said, "He was in a moving condition." He then asked why, after the man had been shot, Schreiber took such an interest in him and inquired after him at the dispensary. He asked if Schreiber ever had any other Koreans shot in the dump. Schreiber replied that he had, and that he always called for an ambulance. Eslick then asked if there was a procedure in place to calculate the number of carbine rounds fired from a weapon. Schreiber said that there was not. The prosecution again weighed in with questions as to procedure when Koreans have no identification and are caught in the bomb dump.

After a recess, Mike said, "The defense, as said, some time ago challenged Colonel Perry for cause. In his general demeanor, he was hostile to the accused." That is something appellate records don't show, namely demeanor, sneering, harsh voices, hand and head gestures, and the like. So it was good for Mike to indicate on the record not just Perry's questions, but his behavior and demeanor in asking them. Colonel Arthur C. Perry was put under oath and took the witness stand. Mike questioned him.

Q. "Isn't it true that a while ago, while questioning this witness, you raised up on your elbows and, with a scowl on your face, put this question to the witness: 'Numerous witnesses have testified that their conclusion was the Korean was to be taken out and shot?"

A. "As to the first part, I was not conscious of such actions, if I did do that. I noticed several nervous tendencies on the part of the defense counsel in a similar way. So far, as the question is concerned, it must be read."

The reporter then read the question. Mike proceeded to ask him, "In your own mind, in your own heart, do you still believe numerous witnesses have testified to that, Colonel?" Perry then asked him to clarify "numerous" and said that he rephrased his question after the objection was raised to it.

He also said, "There has been an abundance of testimony concerning the impression received in the Air Police operations shack. My one and only effort was to tie down any possibility as to what happened in the shack. As far as a number of witnesses who testified to that extent, I will not state the number, and I certainly have kept an open mind so as to listen to the closing arguments of both sides and also to discuss the matter with the members of the court."

Mike then asked him how many witnesses testified to that, and he replied Penabaker used the word "impression."

Farnell then asked us if the challenge was withdrawn, and we said no, we stand on it.

The court closed to deliberate on the challenge. After five minutes we reconvened, and the president announced that a majority of the court had voted not to sustain the challenge of the defense. We then called Lieutenant Colonel Percy R. Follis to the stand. Schreiber's turn was over.

CHAPTER 25

End of the Evidence

LIEUTENANT COLONEL PERCY R. Follis was the top cop in the Far East Air Logistic Force, based in Tachikawa, Japan. His title was Staff Provost Marshal. His area of responsibility for FEALOGFOR encompassed Japan, Okinawa, the Philippines, Bataan, Guam, Korea, and Iwo Jima. The 75th Air Depot Wing was the paymaster for FEALOGFOR forces.

Captain Jimmie Kinnis, our club officer, would regularly pilot the C-47, "Goonie Bird", with the payrolls to these far-flung bases. The ride to Baggio in the Philippines was always fun, as we bought our Alhambra cigars there. Also, seeing some other fabled Oriental spots was a blast, as Jimmie usually found that there was bad weather requiring him to land in Hong Kong or sometimes Bangkok for at least a day. Since the Air Force paid in cash in those days, it was required that another officer or two accompany the boxes of money as guards. I was always happy to do this.

Percy Follis said he first met Schreiber in the middle of August 1952. He told of how he had Schreiber stay with him for a few weeks for orientation. He said that FEALOGFOR furnished about seventy-five percent of all logistical personnel for all Air Force units in the Far East. He advised the court of the location of all of the bomb dumps in the Far East. He said that out of the eight bomb dumps in the

Far East, the most troublesome were the two in Korea. The theft and pilfery were very high. He selected Schreiber for the AP job at Pusan because, "...it was the most important of all Air Police assignments in the Far East Air Forces due to the enormous amount of thefts, pilferage, plus sabotage, plus the fact that Pusan was the center of much of our guerrilla activity."

He accompanied Schreiber to Korea to acquaint him with the problems firsthand. He told Schreiber that his job would be "one of the toughest jobs" in the Far East. In his briefing to Schreiber, he noted that there were several hundred guerrillas in the area, that some of our people had been killed by guerrillas, that a radar site within a few miles of the bomb dump was wiped out by guerrillas, that five Marine guards had been killed, and that several of our personnel had been shot at by guerrillas while traveling on the road. He told of the Army bomb dump next to ours having been blown up on June 16, and our dump being blown up on June 30. When the Army dump blew up, forty to fifty Koreans were killed. He got to the 543rd with Schreiber around September 1, 1952.

When he introduced Schreiber to the fifteen Air Policemen at the 543rd, he couldn't tell if they were Korean workers or Americans because there was no uniformity of dress or insignia of any sort and the men had disheveled appearances and long hair. He told how Schreiber started with this rag-tag group and built an organization that was sharp, military-like, and efficient. He had fifteen more APs and ten sentry dogs assigned to Schreiber. Schreiber developed the sentry-dog policy for the entire Far East. Then, as George requested, he assigned additional dogs and men to Schreiber. He told of how Schreiber developed a protocol as to how many hours a day the dogs could work, their ration needs, and their training. His report was disseminated throughout all of the military services. As a result, they all began to use dogs. George also prepared articles at Colonel Follis' request on military discipline, on the job training, and other subjects. In all, at least twelve were published in *The Far East Air Force Bulletin*. He estimated that Schreiber was working eighteen to twenty hours a day. As a result, he was worried that Schreiber would burn out, so he instructed Major Vanderhoven to relieve George of the added duty as adjutant. He told of how his men liked him, how he fought for and got them radio-equipped Jeeps and all-weather uniforms, how he arranged for coffee to be delivered to the men on duty, and how he fought for promotions for his men.

He was asked how he rated Schreiber. He said, "I consider Lieutenant Schreiber to be a superior officer, far ahead of any police officer or provost marshal assigned to me, including one lieutenant colonel I had for two years. I have as many as six positions I would like to put Lieutenant Schreiber into." He said that he was about to be transferred to the United States and that he wanted to bring Schreiber along as his first assistant. He said that he would certainly believe Schreiber under oath.

The purpose of Percy Follis testifying was to give the court confidence that Schreiber was a man of much integrity and that they could well believe his testimony as opposed to that of Rumpf and Kinder. It still bothers me, because I believe that Kinder, being young and stupid, concocted a story to cover himself and shift the blame for his killing of the Korean from himself to Schreiber. Anyone with any common sense knew and should have known that the cold-blooded murder of another unarmed human being was a crime. Nothing in Schreiber's makeup – including his devout Catholicism, his chosen profession as a teacher, his volunteering to serve his country, his sense of devotion to his men, and his obvious love of his duty in the Air Force – would lead any thinking person to believe that he ordered the man murdered.

Schreiber's testimony in the trial left much to be desired, but that was as much the fault of the defense counsel and the Air Force. We had almost no time to work together as a defense team and no time to prepare Schreiber for the trial and for his testifying at his trial. He never would have given the rambling, non-responsive answers that he gave on direct examination or cross-examination if he had been properly prepared. I feared then and I fear now that George's rambling testimony, not just the command influence, was his undoing. Although the influence of the General and his press release was difficult for the court members to disregard. Their commanding general had pronounced Schreiber guilty of premeditated murder before they ever heard any testimony. That is very compelling when you are subject to his whims and desires as a career officer. Remember, Mike Braun and Jesse Bryan and I, had never met as a team with George Schreiber to prepare him for the ordeal of the trial, until the afternoon before the trial was to begin. I was totally unprepared to handle Schreiber. Even though I had tried numerous cases by that time, I had never tried a premeditated murder charge. I was doing okay as a trial lawyer in JAG, but this was, as Jesse said, the "most important trial of my career" – his and mine.

At that time, the defense rested its case. Farnell asked if the court wanted any witnesses recalled, and the president said no. With that, the evidence was closed. The prosecution had the right to give both an opening statement and a closing statement at the close of the trial, giving it an advantage, since the first argument and also the last would come from the trial counsel.

Major Billy Holland said that he had a brief opening statement. It turned out not to be so brief. He recapped all of the testimony in the case. The best of his arguments was that witnesses said that Schreiber said, "that the Korean would be taken to the bomb dump and shot or shot at. That was the point made by the defense. In order to kill someone, you had to shoot at him." This was a very good argument, in my opinion. At the close of his opening argument, Major Holland said, "The only thing left in this entire matter is premeditation. Exactly what is premeditation? Where was the premeditation? Right back in Air Police operations – Kinder said he had the intention to kill when he left Air Police operations before he took the man out there because the man was beaten up so badly it could not be explained."

At that time, Holland requested a five-minute recess. It was now 1525 hours (3:25 pm) on August 16, 1953. Upon the resumption of the trial, the president said that the court wanted to adjourn for the day, whereupon Farnell adjourned until 8:15 a.m. the next day, as requested by the president of the court.

We worked together to formulate a closing argument, which Jesse O. Bryan IV was to make the following morning. Promptly at 8:15 a.m. on August 17, the court reconvened. Jesse rose and, in clear words and with an Alabama drawl, said, "Sir, the defense will not make a lengthy argument. The case has been, itself, quite lengthy and quite exhaustive." That statement said a lot. Unless you have held the life of a client in your care and thoughts, involving your skill, your words, your concentration of thought, and your ability to persuade coupled with a sense of determination to protect a client and friend you believe to be innocent of a heinous crime, you have not felt the type of exhaustion that Jesse was referencing. It was first an exhaustion of thought, of ideas, and a physical demand beyond belief. I have tried cases in my entire career, and no case has ever come close to surpassing the Schreiber case in exhausting me in all ways. Yet our professionalism demands that we appear in the courtroom in a composed and unaffected way, lest we err to our client's doom. In this case, we were climbing a legal Mount Everest. We all knew Schreiber was factually innocent, yet we couldn't climb over the mountain called command influence which pervaded the trial.

Jesse argued the case for Schreiber. He continued by saying that he would concentrate his argument on the "primary issue of the case. . . . And that issue is purely and simply whether Lieutenant Schreiber (1) gave an order to kill a human being, and (2) the second specification of Charge II, whether Schreiber, together with other persons, entered into an agreement to do away with, to kill a human being." He went on to say that if we could not "analyze the evidence and submit the facts in a manner which will be helpful to the court in arriving at its decision, final argument itself has no value. Therefore, in considering the evidence, we will at times take it from the viewpoint as though there was no defense evidence at all, so that the court can analyze it from that point."

He then continued to say that a conspiracy involved a "meeting of the minds." He posited the question, "Did those three persons or any part of them voluntarily come together and make an illegal decision?" He went on to explain to the court, "Either there has been a meeting of the minds, or there has been an order." His point was that Schreiber was tried for two charges – entering into a conspiracy with Toth and Kinder to commit murder or, alternatively, ordering Kinder and Toth to commit murder. Our point was that it could not have been both. However, Jesse then said, "tis possible, under certain circumstances, there could be both. Certainly there is no proof of that in this case. And the court well knows that where there is no direct evidence to prove a fact. And where the dependence is placed upon circumstances, every reasonable hypothesis must be excluded. And has that been done in this case?"

He then went through the evidence used by the prosecution to show that Schreiber ordered the killing. He said that Rumpf never heard such an order. Addleman was the only one to say that he heard such an order, but after a lengthy cross-examination and having his previous statements brought to his attention, Addleman said that hearing such an order was not his best recollection. I tried to put a hypnotic trance on him, if you will, so that he forgot every interrogation and everything that happened to him. I tried to put him back in that office, in that room, and when he came out, he said what they heard was "Take him out and get rid of him." He did not say anything such as, "Take him out and kill him" or "Take him out and shoot him." So, ultimately, the testimony of Addleman was that there was no order to shoot or kill this person.

Jesse then addressed the testimony of Penabaker, who testified that he reached a "conclusion." "Based on what?" Jesse asked. Penabaker had testified that he heard Schreiber say, "Take him out." He based his conclusion on what he heard after the Korean was killed. "Gentlemen, then and there that if he knew at that time, he would not have been interested in trying to find out what happened," Jesse said. "He was asked by the law officer, 'When did you reach that conclusion?' And he gave an answer in which he said, 'I have been told so many things, been interrogated so many times, so many reports were read, so many OSI investigations made – I don't know when I reached that conclusion.' And again, in logic, gentlemen, Penabaker was the duty officer. Do you think any duty officer would stand by if such a decision had been reached? Of course not. Penabaker has become so confused, and he admits it frankly. He doesn't know whether he is coming or going anymore. So, what stands, gentlemen, is the only piece of evidence he heard, 'Take him out.'" What Jesse was alluding to was something that every officer and court member knew – that Penabaker, in his capacity as the duty officer, was the ranking officer on duty that night. The duty officer acts in the stead of the commanding officer of the organization on the spot and has the responsibility and the right to keep law and order in the organization. And that includes the right to countermand an illegal order of another officer and to place persons under military arrest if need be to maintain good order and discipline. In short, if he had heard Schreiber order his men to commit a killing, under the circumstances, he had the right and the duty to countermand that order and to place Schreiber under arrest. A failure to do so could involve him as an accomplice to murder. I believe that Penabaker well knew this, as he previously sought military counsel to protect him under the circumstances.

Jesse continued on to discuss Kinder and his testimony. He repeated Kinder's testimony as to what he said he was ordered to do. "Take your carbine and clip and go with Toth. Is that an order, sir? Yes, that is an order." Jesse continued, "Were you ordered to shoot him? No."

Jesse added, "There is no testimony from Kinder that he ever received an order to shoot or kill any person. It was put in the record when Kinder was testifying on his previous case. He testified he presumed. It was presumption on his part. He went on to point out that the first time Kinder talked it was a presumption on his part as to what Schreiber meant. The second time he considered it his opinion that is what Schreiber meant. And, at a third time, it was his opinion as that, that is what Schreiber meant."

"Which, gentlemen, raises a very serious question," Jesse continued. "It shows definitely there was no order to shoot. That seems to be beyond dispute. It does raise a serious question because Kinder has said he did have that presumption or consideration or opinion, whether Schreiber was in agreement in giving that order that night. That raises a serious question. If Schreiber was in agreement in the way he gave that order that night, was Schreiber guilty of negligence? Naturally, when the defense went into the facts of this case, that question arose. Here was an officer, considered superior by anyone who had contact with him. A remarkable instance – not too remarkable – the respect for a superior officer. How could men like that be negligent and give an unclear order or something that some people say they could not understand, or drew certain opinions and presumptions. It was for that reason we had to delve deeper into the situation that existed at that time." Jesse then alluded to the fact that Schreiber had been pushing himself with too much work and taking the medications. "In driving himself, he could overcome these medicines. Viewing it in the best light of the prosecution, we don't contend he was negligent under those circumstances, even if the order was unclear."

He pointed out that Schreiber was on the stand for three and a half hours, and that he testified consistently. "There has been testimony of the character witnesses, solicited and unsolicited. And, gentlemen, you heard one captain come here to say no one asked him to come as a character witness. But knowing George Schreiber, he wanted to come and testify. Men of the caliber of Colonel Wiseman, Colonel Follis, Major Westland, and other persons who appeared, persons who had the sincere and devoted interest of the Air Force of the United States in their hearts. They don't want eight balls. They want good men who are patriots. They left their duties to come here and testify to the character of Lieutenant Schreiber, to his honesty, to his truthfulness, to his veracity, and to the manner in which he conducts himself and his duties. Nothing I could say about Lieutenant Schreiber in the short period I have had contact with him could outdo what these men, with their responsibilities, came here especially to tell you gentlemen, to assist you in making your decision." This was a powerful argument to acquit, since they could acquit on the evidence of Schreiber's character alone, if they were so inclined. It also gave a reason for them to believe George's testimony.

Jesse, being from the Bible Belt, then quoted the Bible. "To get your minds in the proper frame for what I am about to say, and to show you the reasoning that I want you to pursue for a few moments, I want you to follow me for about five or six lines of the words that David, in the 58th Psalm, said. 'Do ye indeed decree what is right to your God? Do ye judge uprightly ye sons of man? Yea, in your hearts you devise wrongs; your hands thereon use violence. The wicked go astray from the womb. They err from their birth speaking lies. They have venom-like stings, like the deaf adder that stoppeth her ear.' Listen to the words of wise old David. 'The wicked go astray from the womb and they err from birth.'" He pointed out that we read into the record eight stipulations of testimony from people who had known George from the age of four years to twenty-five years. All of these people and those who testified for him said, "I believe him in a court of law. His general reputation for truth and veracity is good." Jesse repeated Colonel Wiseman, "Lieutenant Schreiber does not lie."

Jesse continued on. "Gentlemen, the reason I am getting into this character evidence is this – because the law officer will charge you, before you go out to consider this case, that character evidence in and of itself is sufficient to put the reasonable doubt in your mind that will allow you to bring back an acquittal. That is why it is so important. One time, gentlemen, there was a man in the Pennsylvania Station trying to make a telephone call. He was a country boy from down around the Bible Belt, like I am. And he put a nickel in the slot, dialed the number, and got his number. And the person said at the other end, 'I can't hear you. I can't hear you. There is so much noise from the outside coming in. Close the door.' And so the country boy closed the door. And then what he said went audibly and plainly to the person he was talking to. That brings to mind this, gentlemen. I know in our everyday living we can't help but overhear what people's opinions are on this case. I believe Major McCann said someone talked to him about the case before trial. And he got up and left, and he said I don't want to hear this. I want to hear the facts of this case as presented to me before a court of justice. So that is what I am asking you to do. I know that this is a small compound. I know you can't – nobody can help hearing a little drift of things here and little drifts there. I want you to do one thing. Like the man in the phone booth, don't form your opinion on what other people think before you consider the evidence before you today."

Jesse then pointed out errors in Holland's statement summing up, such as his quoting witnesses as saying Schreiber said, "Take him to the bomb dump." No one so testified, and it was not in the record.

We had the benefit of getting a daily copy of the transcript of the trial. We found no such testimony from anyone. Holland objected and was shut down by a ruling that the argument was perfectly proper.

Jesse pointed out some areas where he and Major Holland disagreed in their recollections, such as quoting Addleman's testimony and the medic, Gillette, saying he was not qualified to render an opinion as to the cause of death. Jesse said, "Major Holland has no doubt been hearing things in different ways from the way I hear them. And I am sure he is not being unintellectual or dishonest when he says that. And neither do I want him to think I am unintellectually dishonest when I wrote down Addleman's words." He then cited Kinder saying that, "I was worried about the morals of the thing." He then shifted to Renteria's testimony that he was fifteen feet away when Kinder said, "Die you son-of-a-bitch gook, die." Jesse asked, "Wasn't he worried about the morals? Wasn't he indeed?" He then discussed Major Simpson asking Schreiber why he considered it necessary to warn Lieutenant Penabaker of his rights under Article 31. He said there were numerous cases in the Board of Review and the Court of Military Appeals where persons were not advised of their rights. Jesse said "So, gentlemen, there are a lot of procedures the boy might have had in mind. But I think it is incumbent upon myself to shed light on such things as this." This was a very weak part of Jesse's argument and, in retrospect, he should have done better or left it out of his closing remarks. Jesse then started to argue the law that was applicable to the case, and Holland objected. Jesse then said,: "I will say this then. Here is what I believe. I believe that seven years of college, four years of practice in law will back me up – that if you got a person that could help your testimony and you don't call him, then the law presumes he would be adverse to you. On cross-examination, he asked the question, 'Schreiber, did you spread the word around, and this and so.' They called me up and told me he was going home. I believe that is a very good presumption. If Donahue were here to testify, he would do so."

Jesse's arguments were lagging, and his words started not being reflective of his thoughts. He was obviously agitated by Holland's interruption and his objection, and he burst out at Holland in a loud and demanding tone with, "Sit down and quit walking around."

Law Officer: "What was that please?"

Defense Counsel: "I am just saying for him to sit down so he would not distract the court or myself."

Law Officer: "I believe if you stay at the table, either way, doesn't make any difference."

Here, Farnell's lack of trial experience came through. Of course it was a distraction, and it accomplished exactly what Holland had intended – it got Jesse flustered and saying things that made little sense. With any trial judge worthy of the name, Holland would have been cautioned to cut it out and to sit down. Our client's life and freedom were at issue, and the cheap tactics should never have been tolerated. But we had a military judge who obviously was fearful of allowing an acquittal of Schreiber.

Jesse regained his composure and argued, "You are all going out to decide a very important case. You are reasonably seated in your chairs. You look down at your hands now and you, in your power and in your wisdom, have the life or the death of a human being in your hands. Is not life so precious that you could send a man to prison for the rest of his life or sentence him to be hanged until he is dead on mere supposition and 'I suppose,' that 'I presumed,' that because that is the way morals go. The man with the morals, I presume, or I suppose, he said it on his own trial. I presume and I suppose. Is not life so dear that all suppositions and opinions such as that can send a man to his death or away for life?"

Jesse ended by telling them that if they found Schreiber guilty, they had only two choices – death or life in prison. He again pointed out Schreiber's character and deeds previously in his life as being completely contradictory to his having been guilty. He finished by saying, "Gentlemen, and I want to state to you again that the law officer will tell you that character evidence in itself is sufficient to bring about the reasonable doubt. And then, gentlemen, after considering all of this evidence, if in your mind there is reasonable doubt – there is nothing in my mind and I know nothing in my heart and nothing in my mind, gentlemen – you will come back and you will have me and this lieutenant stand up before you and you will tell him he is not guilty."

Major Holland, also having the right to close, then stood up and went through all of the things that Schreiber testified that he remembered about the events of the night of the shooting. He remembered what everyone said, what he did, and what he said. Holland then said, "I would like to say that Schreiber's testimony differs not one bit from Weeks, Rumpf, Penabaker, Addleman, Mullins, and Kinder." He continued with Weeks' testimony that he was in the operations office about 1:30 to 2:00 and saw Kinder come in. He noted Weeks' testimony on how "Kinder looked like he had seen a ghost," and how Schreiber put his arm around Kinder, patted him on the back in a joking manner, and told him to get a cup of coffee. Holland said, "Weeks, the witness called by the defense, not only did Weeks contradict Schreiber, but it seems the scene he discloses fits into the theory that an order was given. Schreiber had said he never saw Kinder until the next morning." He then recalled Borchardt's testimony. Schreiber said he didn't leave the AP office, yet Borchardt said that Schreiber was standing by the 6x6 truck and told him to get in. Schreiber said Kinder was in the operations office only half a minute. Mullins said he was in operations and had gone in and come out for over a ten minute period of time. He went on to say that Mullins "observed Lieutenant Schreiber in conversation with Kinder and Toth while in the office. Mullins said he heard Toth say, 'Shall we take the Korean out to the bomb dump like we used to?' Schreiber denies this. Mullins says he was coming back to the APO and Schreiber told him to go along. Schreiber denies he was outside at the time." He then argued that Rumpf said that he saw Schreiber talking with Toth and Kinder for a number of moments. He recalled Rumpf saying that he had asked Schreiber where the Korean was taken to, and that Schreiber had answered that he was taken to the bomb dump to be shot or shot at. Schreiber denies this. Holland dealt with our effort to discredit Rumpf, and said in argument, "If Rumpf wanted to lie to get Schreiber, he could have really stuck him by saying he heard the conversation between Schreiber, Toth, and Kinder."

Holland then discussed Sergeant Addleman's testimony, saying that Addleman had placed Kinder in the office for ten to fifteen minutes, not half a minute as Schreiber had said. He recalled Addleman saying that Schreiber told Kinder two things. "Addleman says he heard Schreiber tell Kinder two things – I know the defense can argue about this. He said the first testimony in here was 'Take him out to the bomb dump and shoot him.'" Where did he get that in his mind? There was an objection from Jesse that Holland was misquoting the evidence. It was overruled, as it should have been, as counsel are permitted to state what their recollection of the evidence was or what it tended to prove.

Holland went on. "Then, through an admission by the defense counsel that he put the man in a hypnotic trance – whether he is a hypnotist or not I do not know – in a hypnotic trance and he got him to say, 'Take him out to the bomb dump and get rid of him.' Addleman said the first thing that came to his mind was, 'Take him out and get rid of him.' The second thing, 'Take him out to the bomb dump and shoot him.' Schreiber denies making that statement. And, furthermore, Schreiber admitted that the Korean would never have been released in the bomb dump."

As Billy Holland continued his argument for the prosecution, he got stronger. Jesse, sensing that we were losing the battle, started objecting on the grounds that Billy Holland was misquoting the evidence. This annoyed the members of the court, as such objections were overruled since the arguments were proper. Jesse got on Holland's nerves, and Holland started arguing with Jesse. I think Jesse thought he could disrupt the argument to our advantage, but it had just the opposite effect. It was damned annoying and won nothing for us. The Law Officer, Farnell, kept telling Jesse that it was okay for counsel to argue his recollection of the evidence.

Holland continued with his strong points. He argued that Penabaker testified that he heard Schreiber say that the Korean was beaten so badly it was decided to kill him. He went on to say that this was more than a conclusion, it was the gist of what Penabaker overheard. He then dealt with Penabaker concealing information from the OSI, saying that "the reason he concealed it was because he didn't want the boy prosecuted." He said that Schreiber was his roommate, and that every motive of Penabaker was to help Schreiber. "The defense states Penabaker could not have known on the night the Korean was to be shot because he asked Schreiber the next day what happened. Penabaker himself said he knew that night that the plan was to kill the Korean, and the next day he asked to find out if the plan had been carried into execution."

Jesse, now more alarmed than ever with that argument, asked Farnell if the defense could reply. Holland shot back, "No." Jesse retorted, "We didn't ask you. We asked the law officer." Again, Holland started to address Jesse. In a very annoyed tone of voice, Jesse said, "Please don't talk to me." Jesse then said to Farnell, "Sir, will the defense be permitted to rebut?" Farnell responded, "The objection will be overruled. I will consider that later." Of course, we were not permitted to rebut the argument of the prosecution. They had the opening and closing remarks as a matter of established law. It would be like the umpire in a baseball game allowing an extra inning at bat for the underdog.

Holland continued, obviously concerned by Jesse's interruption. "If I misled the court, that is not what I mean. I say the reason Penabaker asked the next day is not because he wanted to know what happened, but what the final decision was. He wanted to know if they carried the plan into execution, as was concocted the night before. That is what I mean by what he said."

Holland would have been better off leaving it alone. In my opinion, Penabaker changed his story to the OSI to save himself from prosecution. Considering my discussion with him, there is no doubt in my mind that he was threatened that he would be charged with being a conspirator if he didn't change his testimony and implicate Schreiber. Such were the tactics of the OSI. As a prosecutor in several court-martial cases, I became very much aware of the high-handed and low-minded tactics of the OSI investigators, generally. Like the Royal Mounted Police, they always got their man. The Royal Mounted Police had a reputation for fair play. The OSI had a reputation for dirty tricks. We had a lot of NCOs in the OSI in Korea. They loved to flex their authority, particularly against accused members of the Air Force who outranked them, such as Lieutenant Penabaker and Lieutenant Schreiber.

Holland argued that Schreiber called Kinder over to him and said, "Hey, Red, do you think you can shoot this Korean?" – or words to that effect. It got worse for us. He then said that Kinder said to Schreiber, "I don't think I can. I would rather not."

Holland quoted the rest of the conversation as follows.

Schreiber: "You will do it if I order you to, won't you?"

Kinder: "Yes, I suppose I would," or words to that effect.

Schreiber: "Get your carbine and clip and go with Toth."

Kinder: "Is that an order? Will you take the responsibility if this thing goes to higher authority, if anything comes out of it?"

Schreiber: "Yes, I will take the responsibility."

Holland concluded, "That is entirely different from what Schreiber says."

Holland continued on to say that Kinder's story was backed up "by all of the other witnesses." His argument drove these points home, but they were totally and unremittingly not true. The evidence was quite the opposite.

Holland said the defense tried to show that Kinder testified differently at his trial and that we were unable to do so. That is quite true – not because it wasn't so, but because Farnell made a ruling that we could not use Kinder's prior testimony to impeach him, and if there were inconsistencies, we couldn't use the prior testimony as affirmative evidence as to what happened that night.

Kinder eventually pled guilty in his trial as part of a deal to incriminate Schreiber. Holland went on. "The facts also show that the decision to kill the Korean must have been formulated in Air Police operations by Schreiber. The truck left there and headed directly to B-14. Toth and Kinder did not have a chance to speak in the truck. Toth was in the back, and Kinder drove, and Mullins was in the back. The truck stopped at the bomb dump and left Kinder and the Korean off and left in a short time. What cause could there have been, other than Schreiber himself. It doesn't sound natural that a Korean who was without an identification card, who could hardly walk, and who Schreiber thought attacked these guards would be released without questioning, just like that."

He raised the issues of why Kinder was in the bomb dump after his shift ended, why Schreiber told Rumpf that he would take care of reporting the matter, and why Schreiber told Addleman that he would take care of all reports and not to enter the Korean's name in the logbook. Of course, no one knew the Korean's name, or even if he was a Korean. Billy Holland asked twice, "Does it sound natural?" He then told that Schreiber called everyone together and told them of their rights under Article 31. He said Schreiber called Addleman and told him there would be no sweat if his poor memory continued.

There was no such evidence in the record to support a great part of Billy's persuasive arguments. A lot of it was not even remotely connected to any evidence in the case before the court. In reality, it didn't matter that most of his argument was his imagination. He had a job to do, and, by God, he was doing it with the concurrence of the law officer, and I believe to the delight of Colonel Perry and the president of the court.

After his very well presented diatribe and interpretation of the evidence, actual and imaginary, Holland took up Schreiber's character. He said Schreiber's character was not on trial. "He is on trial for a specific act – premeditated murder and conspiracy to commit premeditated murder. A person of good character has no more right to go and commit premeditated murder than a person of bad character.

The law must be upheld no matter who commits the crime."

He continued. "I got one further thing to say, which I forgot." I held my breath. What now, Billy? Holland then quoted Kinder as telling how Schreiber said it would help the morale of the troops and keep the natives out of the bomb dump if Kinder killed the Korean. Of course, that wasn't the evidence, but it really didn't matter. Billy had nailed his case tight with his version of events and statements that never appeared in the record of trial or in any investigator's statement.. He finished by saying that, with all of his education and experience, Schreiber had the worst memory of any witness. "He, with all of his education, remembers less than all of these other fellows."

This was the most egregious argument based on solely the lawyer's imagination as to what was testified at trial I ever have witnessed in my very long career as a trial lawyer.

Jesse made one more effort to correct the many arguments made by Billy and his quoting other non-existent evidence and statements so well contrived and argued. Farnell rebuffed him by saying, "I believe, and it is the Law Officer's understanding under the law, the trial counsel has an opportunity to make rebuttal on what the defense counsel has said. I can see a situation developing where that can go on and on. I believe you are interested in correcting the misquotations of the trial counsel?"

Jesse acknowledged Billy's new arguments and that we had no chance to rebut them. Farnell ended it by stating the law. "I am going to deny that request, and I will instruct the court that the quotations of witnesses on the part of both counsel are of course, the counsel's recollection of the witness' testimony and does not necessarily reflect the actual testimony of the witness." Jesse then said, with a look of disbelief on his face, "The defense will never be given an opportunity to answer statements made by trial counsel?"

Farnell said, "I believe the ruling of the law officer is clear." Mike then said he didn't think that Farnell quite understood what we were saying and why we were asking. Without saying it, both Mike and

Jesse were in shock at what Billy Holland was allowed to get away with in his summation. He intentionally lied, misquoted witnesses, and made up evidence, all under the umbrella of his recall of the evidence. I thought to myself, "Billy, you have just committed murder in plain sight of us all, and you are about to get away with it." Where the hell did conscience and ethics come into this picture? The law is clear, but it is not a license to kill in a courtroom. But it sure was this day. It was now 9:30 in the morning on August 17, 1953, and we asked for a short recess. At precisely 9:35 a.m., the court was back in order.

Farnell then gave the stock set of instructions to the court. "It is your duty as members of the court to determine the facts of the case, apply the law to those facts, and determine the guilt or innocence of the accused. I will now instruct the court as required by Article 51c of the Uniform Code of Military Justice." He made sure that the members had a copy of the Manual for Courts-Martial, 1951. He then read to the members the parts of the Code that dealt with the charges against the accused.

Premeditated murder is murder committed after the conscious decision is made to kill another. Farnell went on. "A murder is not premeditated unless the thought of taking a life was consciously conceived and the act or omission by which it was taken was intended." He told them that once the intent was formed to kill, it is immaterial how soon afterward it is put into execution. He instructed on the lesser included offenses of unpremeditated murder, involuntary manslaughter, and negligent homicide.

Farnell reviewed the elements of each of the lesser included offenses and referred to the provisions of the Code. He read from the Manual and told the court members where to look for explanations of such offenses. Of course, not a soul present had any belief that the court would acquit Schreiber of the more serious crimes and find him guilty of a lesser charge, but it covered the law. Following the letter of the law from a procedural point was all-important if the convictions were to be upheld on review and appeal. Farnell instructed that Schreiber was a principal offender if he aided, abetted, or counseled the crime and clarified that he need not have been present at the scene of the shooting. His charge to the court was repetitious, repeating over and over how and why Schreiber could be found guilty. He then went into a convoluted instruction of conspiracy, saying, "The agreement in a conspiracy need not be in any particular form, nor manifested in any formal words. It is sufficient if the minds of the parties arrive at a common understanding to accomplish the object of the conspiracy, and this may be shown by the conduct of the parties. The agreement need not state the means by which the conspiracy is to be accomplished or what part each conspirator is to play."

My friends in the press corps had good time with this, suggesting that mental telepathy worked as well as anything.

Farnell talked about the fact that, even if one is mortally wounded by another means other than the means charged in the case, it doesn't mean the accused is not guilty because, if the act complained of accelerated the death, it is sufficient. "The law declares that one who inflicts an injury on another and thereby accelerates his death shall be held criminally responsible. Therefore, . . . "... In this connection, if any life at all is left in a human body, even the least spark, the extinguishment of it is as much homicide as the killing of the most vital being."

He then instructed on mental responsibility, the old "knowing right from wrong" test, and the ability or inability of the accused to adhere to the right. He missed the point of Gatto's testimony and the finding of the psychiatric board as to why Schreiber had a lack of detailed memory of events on the night in question. We never raised a psychiatric defense other than as a very valid explanation from the top psychiatrist in the Air Force to explain Schreiber's lack of recall of some of the events and people that night.

Farnell ended his soliloquy by instructing the court members that they could acquit Schreiber based on the evidence of his good character, coupled with the presumption of innocence. "This evidence of the accused's good character may be sufficient to cause a reasonable doubt to remain as to his guilt, thereby warranting an acquittal. On the other hand, the inference of innocence to be drawn from such evidence may be more than offset by the other evidence in the case tending to establish the accused's guilt. As members of the court, the final determination as to the weight to be accorded to this and all other evidence in the case rests solely with you."

Farnell then told them that if they had a question of law he was available to them to answer it and that he would reopen the court for such questions. He then told them about reasonable doubt, but never defined it for the members. This would have been a reversible error in a civilian criminal case.

With this, the court was closed at 1020 hours (10:20 am). Precisely forty minutes later, all had been determined, and the court was reconvened. The president asked, "In announcing the findings of the court, if it finds the accused is guilty, is it necessary that the finding be stated in terms of two-thirds, or all, in this particular instance?" Farnell told the court members that they only needed to announce, "two-thirds of the members present concurred in the findings." Fifteen minutes later, at 11:15 a.m., the court reconvened and found Schreiber guilty of the charges and specifications. This practically represented a world record for such a case, particularly for one in which an ambulance driver testified as to the cause of death and a fellow who would not have been called an intern, who had never conducted an autopsy let alone examined the body, gave his opinion. I don't mean to be picky or to make excuses, but the entire case was a farce., and the members of the American press corps in attendance said so to me and to others. Command Influence was alive and well in Korea in August of 1953.

Upon hearing about the trial, Governor William Stratton of Illinois referred to the trial and conviction of Schreiber as being a miscarriage of justice and a sham. It was.

CHAPTER 26
The War Raged On

AS THE EVENTS concerning Schreiber, Toth and Kinder were unfolding, the war around them continued. During the winter of 1952-1953, the war on the ground seemed to be stalemated into a kind of trench war, with casualties on both sides mounting. The F-86 Sabre jets would patrol along the Yalu river dividing Korea and China. MIG pilots flying a superior aircraft would catch the UN planes as they were low on fuel and heading south to return to base. During these engagements, a lot of UN pilots would run out of fuel and have to bail out of their aircraft. They would try to head to Cho-do Island, about sixty miles southwest of Pyongyang, the capital of North Korea. The United Nations Forces maintained an air-rescue detachment on the island in order to rescue such pilots. The UN pilots, at a disadvantage in numbers of aircraft, had to rely on their skills in aerial combat to achieve victories, even though they were flying aircraft that did not measure up to the capabilities of the MIG-15s. In one memorable air battle on February 18, 1953, near the Sui-ho Reservoir on the Yalu River, 110 miles north of Pyongyang, four Sabre jets attacked forty-eight MIGs. The Sabres shot down two MIGs and caused the crash of two others taking defensive action. All four Sabres returned safely to base. This, however, was not the norm, since the Russian pilots and their aircraft and armaments were usually superior to the UN pilots, armament, and flight capabilities of the aircraft being flown by the UN. With speeds approaching Mach 1, faster climb rates, and flight ceilings of fifty-five thousand feet or more, the MIGs could and did strike at their discretion, especially on the P-51s left over from World War II, the newly minted F-80s, and the early versions of the F-86 and F-94.

The Far East Air Forces flew nighttime missions over North Korea from Japan and Okinawa. They ran afoul of superior night fighter-interceptors, and losses mounted on the aging B-29 bombers and crews. The B-29s had to rely on darkness and electronic jamming for protection, but this proved no match for the interceptors and the anti-aircraft ground fire. As B-29 losses mounted in late 1952, the Bomber Command compressed bomber formations to shorten the time they spent over their targets, which increased the effectiveness of their jamming devices. The 5th Air Force joined with the Navy and Marine Air Arms to provide fighter escorts for the bombers. The losses of the bombers were greatly reduced after January 1953 as a result. The 5th Air Force fighter bombers and light bombers joined by the Navy and Marine aircraft kept up attacks on supply routes, equipment, and troops near the front lines. They often flew these missions within three thousand meters of the American front lines so as to target areas threatening the American positions. B-26 light bombers of the 5th Air Force took out bridges and railroads and attacked the stalled trains and vehicles.

In March of 1953, the Red Chinese government was agreeable to exchanging injured and sick prisoners of war. The exchange commenced on April 20, and on April 26, sessions to discuss an armistice recommenced at Panmunjom. The South Korean government of Syngman Rhee was dead set against the armistice talks and threatened to boycott them and to continue the battle with the north and China alone if need be.

While most analysts called these last months of the war a stalemate, General Otto P. Weyland, the Far East Air Forces Commander, disagreed. "To accept the theory of stalemate is to completely ignore the innumerable advantages of air power as a predominant weapon for destroying the enemy fighting machine and to acquiesce to the dangerous rule of thumb whereby military success, regardless of cost, is measured in terms of geographical gain," Weyland said.

Ultimately, the later version of the F-86 was superior to the earlier aircraft. It could fly at Mach 1.05 speeds and exceed fifty-thousand feet in ceiling. As a result, the UN gained air superiority. By the end of the hostilities, the Air Force claimed destruction of 184,808 enemy soldiers, shot down 976 aircraft, and destroyed 1,327 tanks, 82,920 vehicles, 10,407 rail cars, 1,153 bridges, and 65 tunnels. It also claimed 593 barges and vessels. We lost 1,041 aircraft. It was the beginning of the end for the manned heavy bombers.

There was never a declaration of war by the United States, as President Harry S. Truman took the issue to the United Nations Security Council and not to the United States Congress. Truman argued that if the administration did not use the term "war," a president could send troops anywhere in the world for any purpose. Thus, Korea would become a "police action," the first of many such presidential decisions to wage undeclared wars and to alter the constitutional system of government in the United States forever. After the initial victories in Korea in the early days, Truman made two serious miscalculations. He ordered the 7th Fleet to defend Taiwan and insisted that the Chinese Nationalist forces on Taiwan cease any operations against the Chinese mainland. With no fear that Chaing Kai-shek would make incursions from Formosa (now Taiwan), the Red Chinese moved their armies away from the southeast coast of China, as they no longer feared a Nationalist Chinese invasion. Without this concern, they were urged by Joseph Stalin, the Russian Communist dictator, to engage their forces with Russian assistance into North Korea, and the tides of war were shifted.

Truman and his Secretary of State, General George Marshall, were more concerned that if the United States escalated the war in Korea, it would have to weaken its forces in Europe. Truman and Marshall were reluctant to shift forces from Germany to Asia, thus leaving Europe open to incursion by Stalin. When the Chinese started to cross the Yalu on bridges spanning the river, General Douglas MacArthur ordered the air forces to destroy them, but he was countermanded by General George C. Marshall, Secretary of Defense. This gave the Chinese free reign over the outnumbered and outgunned American armies and Marine battalions, who had to retreat fighting for their lives.

There was a clash of wills. Asia had been largely ignored by the administration in Washington following the Japanese surrender, and MacArthur was the U.S. policy maker in the Far East. He wanted a war and a victory and was willing to take on Red China. Truman wanted a stalemate so as not to weaken the U.S. position in Europe, where the Soviet Union was creating a bloc referred to as the Iron Curtain countries. Truman's war strategy created untenable situations for the thousands of men who fought and died in the Korean "police action." While Harry S. Truman remains, in my view, one of our most heroic national leaders, he gravely miscalculated Stalin, who was a master at world geopolitics. Truman came to power as a compromise vice president on the death of Franklin Delano Roosevelt during World War II because too many politicians didn't like Henry Wallace's left-leaning politics as vice president under Roosevelt. Truman was a country boy from Missouri who gained favor with a political machine in St. Louis and later gained a seat in the Senate. From there, he went to the then-nondescript position of vice president, which a former vice president, the late Alben Barkley, once said wasn't worth "a warm bucket of spit."

With a minimal commitment of manpower and equipment, Stalin pressed on in Europe and Asia and took control of county after country, including Poland, Germany, Latvia, Estonia, Lithuania, Hungary, Czechoslovakia, Yugoslavia, and Albania. He also gained considerable power and influence over Red China and Korea. Declaring the Sakhalin Islands to be Soviet territory, he also took a part of Japan as a Soviet prize for coming into the war in Asia just before it ended. Russia still occupies the islands today, as the Soviet Union and Japan never entered into a peace treaty following World War II.

Armistice talks began in July of 1951. By October 28, there was an agreement on a line of demarcation between North Korea and South Korea. On November 12, General Mathew Ridgeway, the new commander in Asia, ordered General James Van Fleet, commander of the 8th Army, to halt offensive operations and commence active defense of the front. We were officially in stalemates both at the front lines and at the negotiating table at Panmunjom. All of the United Nations Forces had been ordered to establish a holding position along the agreed-upon line of truce. There were still many bloody battles fought over useless territory close to the front. There were nightly firefights and patrols reconnoitering one another's positions. Those of us who were there continually asked one another, "Why are we here?" There was then no purpose to the static war, other than kill or be killed.

The treaty talks dragged on until newly elected President Dwight D. Eisenhower, who took office in January of 1953, ordered the 7th Fleet to cease its defensive blockade of Formosa, gave notice to the Chinese government that the United States was going to henceforth attack bases in China, and readied the fleet for the use of the atomic bomb with little secrecy. Two weeks later, on July 27, 1953, the treaty of armistice was signed, even though the South Korean government had to be coerced into agreeing with it.

Truman's style of micro-management of the battlefields during an armed conflict has since prevailed in every war, declared and undeclared, since Korea. Henceforth, presidents would send our military forces anywhere in the world, such as Lebanon, Panama, Granada, Cuba, the Persian Gulf, Somalia, Bosnia, Iraq, Afghanistan, and elsewhere, as the geo-political strategies changed. Korea foreshadowed the future strategy and tragedy of undeclared wars where our young men are sent to die and, worse, to be maimed.

In this undeclared war, the United States incurred the following casualties: 33,568Americans killed in action and 3,275 dead from non-combat injuries. There were 103,284 Americans wounded in action in firefights with enemy forces. A total of 1,789,000 Americans served in the Korean theater during the war from June 1950 to July 27, 1953. There are still 8,176 Americans missing in action and never accounted for. South Korea sustained 1,312,836 military casualties, including 415,000-plus dead. Other casualties included 3,094 killed and a total killed and wounded of 16,552. Estimated communist casualties were two million. The Korean populace loss exceeded one million people killed and missing.. In August of 1999, the Congress of the United States approved the wearing of the Republic of Korea War Service medal, although there were not then and there are not now any active service folks serving on active duty eligible to wear the medal. At last, the battle in Korea was recognized as an official war.

Of the thousands of MIAs, many were placed in labor camps in China and died of malnutrition, excessive work, or disease. The Chinese government has never cooperated in finding or documenting the thousands who were transported to China as POWs.

In the July 1983 edition of *Airman* magazine, the following quotation appears:

"To this day, the potential for renewed fighting exists. Sabres and MIGs armed with guns have since been replaced with supersonic aircraft bearing missiles. The North Koreans still threaten the South Koreans, and the UN command still maintains their defenses. The armistice was not a peace treaty, thus, technically, the war has not ended."

Tragically, that piece could have been written in 2009. The war still has not ended, and threats of its resumption are heard around the world as North Korea again threatens to invade the South. Meanwhile, the United States seeks sanctions, answers, and diplomacy as North

Korea, with its stagnant economy but large army, has a nuclear weapon and is developing the missiles to deliver it. Is another war the answer? With more millions waiting to kill and be killed, I hope that the world has learned something from the awful conflicts it has endured since the Korean armistice. But it doesn't seem so. Conflicts rage in Africa, the Middle East, the former states of Yugoslavia, and in our own wars in Iraq and Afghanistan. Conflicts threaten to break out in Iran as well. Is eternal vigilance the real price we must pay for peace?

CHAPTER 27

The Appeals

AFTER THE CONVICTION and the certifying of the record of trial came the appeals. The first appeal went to the Air Force Board for Review, which was at the time the intermediate appellate court. After that was the highest appellate court, the Court of Military Appeals.

Appearing as appellate counsel for Schreiber were Latham Castle, the attorney general of Illinois; Granville Beardsley, the first assistant attorney general of Illinois; Major Jesse O. Bryan IV, associate special appellate defense counsel; Colonel A.W. Tolen; and Major Norman F. Carroll. Despite the formidable talent appearing on behalf of Schreiber, the Board of Review, in a rather lengthy opinion, bought none of the many arguments advanced on behalf of the accused and upheld the conviction of Schreiber. The board adopted Penabaker and Addleman as the key witnesses verifying that Schreiber gave an order to kill the Korean. The board also grouped the eleven points raised on appeal into four categories – impropriety of trial by 5th Air Force, insufficiency of the evidence, instructional errors, and trial errors.

As to the first group, the board found that the defense had raised nine contentions.

The court dealt with the argument that Schreiber could not obtain a fair trial due to the hostility of the staff judge advocate of the 5th Air Force and its commander. The issue was raised in our motion for appropriate relief. The board found that the granting of the motion seeking a change of venue is discretionary with the law officer and at the discretion of the SJA and then at the discretion of the convening authority. The board members said that there had to be a showing of a clear abuse of discretion. They went on to say that the press release issued before the trial indicating the guilt of Schreiber was not an issue, as we didn't show that any member of the court had seen it. Additionally, they said, the release was really about Toth and not the accused, as his name was only "incidentally mentioned." They further found, "The press release does not indicate that the convening authority had any personal interest in the outcome of the proceedings or had prejudged the guilt of the accused." This statement is incredulous, since the convening authority in the press release says that Schreiber ordered the killing. The board then continued on with the farce. "What we have said concerning the innocuous nature of the press release in connection with the convening authority is of equal application to contention that the staff judge advocate was similarly disqualified by reason of his participation in the preparation of the press release. The latter individual has been particularly singled out for criticism by the defense, since the majority of the defense's complaints are laid directly at his door. . . . The contentions advanced by the defense are extremely serious in their implication that the staff judge advocate was personally so hostile, prejudiced and, vindictive toward the accused as to deprive him of a fair trial."

They went on to say that they examined the affidavit appended to the Assignment of Errors by Major Holland. "We find no basis in fact for any imputation that the staff judge advocate displayed such bias, animosity, and hostility toward accused as to deny him his right to properly prepare for trial and present his defense." In fact, except for consistently interfering with the preparation of Schreiber's defense by secreting potentially favorable evidence in his desk drawer, not allowing the defense counsel the opportunity to meet and prepare the defense except for the afternoon before trial, failing to allow the depositions desired by the defense to be transmitted and conducted, refusal to provide a place for the defense team to meet with the accused and one another, throwing Jesse and me out of his office, chewing out Farnell for agreeing to give us a one-day continuance, and generally being an unpleasant bastard, the SJA was okay, so far as the Board of Review was concerned. It has always surprised me at how clairvoyant certain appellate judges think they are in discerning the real facts needed to properly decide an appeal. Bear in mind, most of the appeals court judges are either elected politically or appointed based on political connections. Once installed, many seem to take on a magisterial air of self-importance and superior knowledge of human affairs. This seemed to me to be the case with the three-officer Board of Review in this case. The boards of review in the Air Force were comprised at that time of three officers of field-grade rank, selected essentially by the Air Force staff judge advocate or his staff. It became painfully obvious to me that none of them forgot that the Air Force chief of staff initiated this case.

The board also made predictable decisions on the third, fourth, fifth, and sixth contentions of the defense, which, "laid at the door of the staff judge advocate, were shown to have involved the prosecution staff and the investigating officer." The board made short shrift of our arguments, saying that we eventually got to see all of the documents which had been withheld and that we were content that the depositions had not been sent forward, as we relied upon stipulations. "When the defense made a request therefore, copies were made available, insofar as possible," the board said. "In connection with the requested depositions, the accused apparently was content to substitute the stipulated testimony of the witnesses."

The words "insofar as possible" and "apparently" are critical to an analysis of this decision. We knew from interviewing witnesses, such as Toth, Penabaker, Addleman, Mullins, and others, that the OSI agents questioned them repeatedly and scared the hell out of them. This was followed up by Major Holland and Lieutenant Roth outright threatening them with being charged either as accomplices or co-conspirators in premeditated murder, thereupon getting these fellows to "cooperate" with the prosecution. They made no secret of what happened in talking with us. Hence their many written statements given to the investigators and the prosecutors were and should have been of great significance to us in planning the cross-examination of these many witnesses. We were told that they were simply not available. So much for "insofar as possible." As to "apparently," why the hell did we bother to raise the issue if we were satisfied? Again, the board in its superior knowledge of what "apparently satisfied" the defense was dead wrong. Otherwise, we would not have raised it at trial and on appeal.

As to our claim of repeated questioning of witnesses before the trial by the prosecution team, which we claimed amounted to the "brainwashing" of certain witnesses, the board issued the following response. "The use of the term 'brainwashing' by appellate defense counsel is an unfortunate one, since there is not the slightest indication that so abhorrent a practice was indulged in by the prosecution. We can attribute the use of such language by counsel only to the zeal of advocacy. Any intimation that the testimony of the government witnesses was fabricated or colored by the efforts of the members of the prosecution is utterly unsupported by any evidence adduced by the defense." It later wrote, "Although there were discrepancies and inconsistencies in the testimony of many of the prosecution's witnesses, there is no basis for the contention that the prosecution staff, by its pre-trial interviews, so conditioned the minds of the witnesses that they testified untruthfully against the accused." What about the fearful performance of Penabaker on the stand? He had to impale Schreiber or else he was going to be an accused in the case. He made no bones about it when I spoke to him before trial. He was a frightened specimen. What about Addleman on the stand, saying that he had been questioned so many times that he didn't know where the truth was? And his best memory was in favor of Schreiber, in spite of all of the "brainwashing." Don't forget, the appellate lawyers raising these issues were two of the top law enforcement officers in the country – those of the attorney general and first assistant attorney general of the state of Illinois, appointed by Illinois Governor William Stratton to help right an injustice to one of Illinois' citizens, George C. Schreiber. The national press covered this trial and to a man felt that Schreiber was railroaded into a conviction. Any fair-minded person in attendance related the same sentiment to me. It was an exhibition of command influence at its worst, or maybe at its best.

The next issue dealt with was the allegedly "impartial Article 32 investigation." The board held that the investigator's "function is merely to make the required investigation and report the results to the military commander – to provide the latter with a fair, factual basis to guide him in the exercise of his discretion." The board went on, "Even conceding arguendo that error was present in the appointment of the same investigating officer for both the companion case (Kinder's) and the instant case, there is no showing of prejudice to the substantial rights of the accused. Absent prejudice to the accused, a failure to comply substantially with the requirements of Article 32 is not such an omission as requires disapproval of otherwise valid findings."

The board, in dealing with our Motion for Appropriate Relief, satisfied itself by saying, "We have considered the defense's contentions, both in their individual and collective effects, and we are unable to find sufficient substance therein to impel the conclusion that the law officer arbitrarily abused his discretion in denying the defense the relief requested." That relief was to move the trial out of 5th Air Force headquarters, since it became apparent to us, the defense team, that our client was not going to receive fair treatment in the pre-trial preparation of his case or at the trial itself. The Board of Review in its omnipotence was satisfied. We were not, and I am not to this day, satisfied that justice was not perverted for some reason that only the chief of staff can tell us, but he did not tell us anything.

To allay the public's suspicions, the board took the unusual step of stating the following as a part of its decision. "We have endeavored to lay at rest any questions in this regard primarily to allay the suspicions of those unfamiliar with the contents of the record and the proceedings had herein. The board has received and has considered the numerous petitions, resolutions, letters, and telegrams from friends, neighbors, acquaintances, and civil and fraternal organizations on behalf of the accused. Throughout these communications, there appears an undertone of dissatisfaction with the impartiality of the court-martial, which sat in judgment on the accused. In our view, any claim that accused was deprived of a fair and impartial trial by reason of any of the circumstances adverted to by the defense is wholly without merit. Each of the members of the court was subjected to voir dire examination by defense counsel. The defense was satisfied with the impartiality of members of the court since it did not exercise any challenge for cause against any member of the court. The trial itself was conducted in an orderly and judicial manner. Accused was ably and forcefully represented by capable counsel, both appointed and of his own choice. Accordingly, we do not hesitate to state unequivocally and emphatically that in our considered opinion the accused was afforded a just and fair trial on the merits."

What about the sneering and misguided questioning by Colonel Perry, the most outspoken and opinionated member of the court, and our challenge for cause? What about the hostility shown throughout the trial by Major Holland and Lieutenant Roth? A trial can be conducted in a fair and orderly fashion without the belligerent tones and arguments initiated by Holland and Roth during the trial. I was there. Jesse was there and had consulted with the appellate team, even providing an affidavit to append to the record as to the shabby treatment of us by Colonel Loewenberg. When I read the opinion, it was with astonishment as to how such serious cases were to be reviewed by the

Board of Review. Could every member of the press who sat through the trial have been so wrong? Fairness is perceived, as is unfairness. The press corps to a person felt that the trial was a sham. I spoke with all of them, as I tried to discern their reactions throughout the trial to see how we were doing. I repeatedly got answers that Schreiber was being screwed and that the prosecution witnesses had been so coerced and coached in their testimony that we were doomed. These men had far more courtroom time than I had, as they covered many noted trials for the press at home.

I was disheartened by all of it, so much so that after the trial I turned down a position working for the commander, Far East Forces in Tokyo. The offer contained a prompt promotion to captain and involved working with the military government in force in Japan. The senior lawyer for General MacArthur and his successor was Stephen Simes, a lawyer from Portsmouth, New Hampshire. His father was a municipal judge and active practicing lawyer in Portsmouth. He indicated his pleasure at having a hometown boy working on his staff. He was a top civilian employee, enjoying the equivalent grade in the civil service as a major general in the Army. Likewise, Mike Braun, who was the chief counsel for Mitsubishi, offered me a job to stay in Japan and work with him. I was so disheartened by what went on that I opted to accept neither position and returned to the 8th Fighter Bomber Wing as acting SJA. When I was offered the chance to return to the United States, I took it and was assigned to Otis Air Force Base on Cape Cod. From there, I was given the opportunity to be the second officer assigned to Portsmouth Air Force Station, in my hometown. The Air Force was building a large SAC (Strategic Air Command) base in Portsmouth, and there was a lot of apprehension as to what the base would mean to the local community. I had a staff sergeant assigned to me, and we would go to speak at Rotary Clubs, Kiwanis Clubs, Exchange Clubs, and the like, including church groups, civic organizations, and in towns and cities in southeastern New Hampshire. We were in uniform, and I would introduce myself as being from Portsmouth. After a ten-minute speech, we showed a film called *The Mount Clemens Story*, which was about the establishment of a SAC Base in Mount Clemens, Michigan, and its beneficial impact on the surrounding communities. When my service on active duty was up, I left the Air Force and became the staff judge advocate of a reserve wing at Hanscom Air Force Base in Bedford, Massachusetts, where I served until transferring as a weekend warrior to the 817th Bomb Group at Pease Air Force Base in Portsmouth, New Hampshire, serving in the JAG office. Over time, I perceived that military justice was in a constant state of improvement over what I experienced in Korea. While the Schreiber case was a once-in-a-lifetime experience for me, it deprived the Air Force JAG of a potential career officer. I truly loved being on active duty in the Air Force and could have had a rewarding and mutually beneficial career, but for my upset at what I witnessed in Korea at 5th Air Force headquarters. As they say, it was another time in history.

Suffice it to say, the board went through every other argument raised at trial and by the appeal, such as any proof as to the cause of death. No autopsy was performed, and no competent witness testified as to the cause of death. These arguments were rejected. "It is significant to note that there is no evidence that the injuries inflicted on the victim by Toth were so serious as to as to lead eventually to the victim's death. On the other hand, there is substantial evidence that the gunshot wound caused the death of the victim or at least materially contributed to or hastened such result." They relied on Dr. Robbins' testimony that the gunshot wound in the chest would cause shock, and the shock would be a contributing factor to death."

Here is what the doctor testified:

Q. "Which would be the most likely to be the main cause of death in the event a victim dies? Blows on the head or the bullet?"

A. "I can't answer that because I don't know the exact pathway of that bullet."

Q. "Assuming it went in where I told you?"

A. "I could not answer that."

Q. "Do you know how hard the blows were?"

A. "No, that is why I cannot answer the question."

Q. "You don't know what caused the death. Is that true?"

A. "No, I don't know what caused the death."

There was no such testimony as relied upon by the Board of Review – it simply never was said at the trial by Dr. Robbins. Colonel Mathews asked the doctor if a gunshot wound would cause hemorrhage. The doctor said it could or could not, depending upon its pathway.

Q. "Is it possible for a bullet to go through a man's body without causing a hemorrhage?"

A. "Yes."

Q. "In your official opinion, did this bullet going through this individual accelerate his death?"

A. "I have no way of telling unless I knew the exact pathway of the bullet . . . "

Q. "Would shock be a contributing factor towards his death?"

A. "A contributing factor? Yes."

The court went on with Major McCann asking the questions.

Q. "Concerning your answer to Colonel Mathews' question concerning shock from a shot through the chest, would the same condition result from severe blows inflicting injury on the head?"

A. "You mean would it cause shock?"

Q. "Yes."

A. "Yes."

Note, the record consistently mixes up Colonel Perry and Colonel Mathews and attributes remarks and questions to each that really came from the other. Both exhibited similar hostility to the defense and the accused throughout the trial, in my opinion.

Suffice it to say, Dr. Robbins never testified that the gunshot wound would be a contributing factor to death "in this case." The most he said was it could be under certain circumstances, but he didn't know. This gaffe on the part of the board was enough to overturn the decision, but they were not likely to do so, given the attitude previously expressed. They also erroneously stated, "It is significant to note that there is no evidence that the injuries inflicted on the victim by Toth were so serious as to lead eventually to the victim's death." Again a material misstatement of the evidence, as the doctor said those injuries could be a cause of death, but again offered no opinion absent an autopsy. The board conjured up its view of the evidence to mistakenly support its conclusions. It concluded that Kinder's shot was a contributing cause of death or at least accelerated death, contrary to the only credible testimony in the case to the contrary.

The board also ruled, "Although accused stoutly denied giving any order that the Korean be killed, the facts and circumstances surrounding the commission of the offense as described by the prosecution's witnesses, together with the accused activities subsequent to the incident, compel the conclusion that the accused did in fact knowingly participate in a plan to extinguish the life of the victim."

At the appeal, appellate counsel argued that the testimony of the prosecution's witnesses should be given little or no credence because of patent ambiguities, demonstrated inconsistencies, obvious contradictions, inherent bias, and apparent self-interest. The board said, "Kinder's version of the conversation with the accused which led to the shooting was substantially corroborated by the testimony of others present." This was simply not true and was the basis for our challenge to Colonel Perry for cause. Namely, this was a corrupted interpretation of the evidence based upon supposition and authority and not upon the record of trial. The board had a statutory duty and authority "to weigh the evidence, judge the credibility of witnesses, and determine controverted questions of fact." Having done so, they said, "We arrive at the same conclusions as to the accused's guilt as did the trial forum."

As to the conspiracy charge, we had alleged and argued that if Kinder was to be believed in saying that he was ordered to shoot the victim, that it wasn't a conspiracy. In this instance, the board made the determination "that Kinder did not shoot the victim under the compulsion of any military order allegedly given him by the accused." Now they had retreated from the position previously found that Schreiber ordered the shooting. They went on to say that, upon being assured that the accused would take full responsibility, "Kinder agreed to shoot the victim and thereafter proceeded to his part in the offense. By such agreement and conduct, Kinder entered into a conspiracy with the accused to commit an unlawful act."

Coming from a Board of Review, this was, at its best, inconsistent and flawed thinking, since earlier the board stated that there was substantial evidence from several witnesses that Schreiber ordered the shooting, So, when convenient, they believed Kinder, who said he followed an order to shoot. And to establish a conspiracy, they do not believe Kinder, but said he was a participant in a plan to shoot the victim. Either he was part of an agreement among co-conspirators or he was following an order. It could not be both, unless you were an appellate judge on that board. Then it could be both. That is what I mean when I say a lot of appellate judges believe somehow that, since they were elected or appointed, they became possessed of omnipotent powers to say and do as they wish so that the decision will end up as they want it to be, regardless of the justice involved or, for that matter, the jurisprudence involved in the matter at hand. These folks operate under the theory that "it is what it is, because I say that is what it is." They also gave as an added reason that Kinder was held to have been a co-conspirator with the accused. They ignored the fact that Charlie Weir had cut a deal with the convening authority that, if Kinder testified against Schreiber and pled guilty to the charges and specifications, he would be freed and returned at once to active duty, which is precisely what occurred. So much for "Kinder was held to have been a co-conspirator with the accused."

The next issue was whether Farnell gave an adequate instruction on premeditation, lesser included offenses, circumstantial evidence, and the weight to be given to accomplice testimony and to testimony of witnesses who were substantially impeached. The board totally dismissed Colonel Gatto's testimony and the findings of the psychiatric board. It said, "Upon this state of the record, we cannot conceive that any real issue was presented as to the accused's mental ability to deliberate and to consciously participate in the events of the fateful night. Hence, we hold that there was no necessity for the law officer to instruct, sua sponte, that the court members might consider evidence of accused's drowsiness in determining his capacity to premeditate." In fact, the board was correct, because after Farnell gave his instruction on the meaning of premeditation, no objection was raised by the defense. In such a case, if you snooze, you lose. Here, Farnell said, "As the terms indicate, premeditated murder and unpremeditated murder are identical except that the former requires proof of premeditation while the latter requires no proof of this element." So what did the board say? "Although the language used by the law officer as set forth above is susceptible to misinterpretation and its further use ill-advised, we do not feel that the court-martial was in fact misled thereby." How the hell do they know, clairvoyance again?

The board gave two reasons for determining Farnell's instruction adequate. The first was that Farnell said the offense required "at the time of the killing, the accused had a premeditated design to kill." Second, the board said, "He thereafter elaborated on the definition and concept of premeditated murder so as to make it abundantly clear that the intent involved in that offense was the specific intent to kill." Therefore, the board ruled, there had to be intent to kill in unpremeditated murder, as well otherwise it would be negligent homicide. In any event, we blew it at trial by not contemporaneously objecting to the mishmash of definitions given to the court on the offense by the law officer, Major Farnell.

As to the failure to instruct on circumstantial evidence, the board said that they didn't know what we had in mind in requesting such an instruction at trial. They then said that appellate defense counsel said it should have been given because the conspiracy charge was based upon circumstantial evidence and not direct evidence. The board said, "Initially, it must be observed that in the military, it is not essential that the proposed instruction correctly state the principle of law involved, the law officer being under a duty to properly instruct the court where the giving of an instruction on the subject matter is required by law upon request." While conceding that there was circumstantial evidence of a conspiracy, they concluded that, "if believed," there was adequate direct evidence of a conspiracy in the case, such an instruction was not needed. They conceded that all courts did not agree with this, including several federal courts of appeal, citing language that said, "The requirement seems to us a refinement which only serves to confuse laymen into supposing that they should use circumstantial evidence otherwise than testimonial. All conclusions have implicit major premises drawn from common knowledge; the truth of testimony depends as much on these, as do inferences from events."

In short, they decided that the instruction, which we and the appellate defenders knew was critical, was as likely to confuse the jury. "To elaborate this into an inexorable ritual, or to articulate it for different situations, is more likely to impede than to promote their inquiry," the board said. The conclusion was that no prejudicial error was committed.

Next was the request that the court instruct on the weight to be given to accomplice testimony. The board said no request was made at trial, and the law officer did not have to sua sponte so instruct.

The next item involved trial errors. At trial, there was an appropriate objection to trial counsel asking about a statement alleged to have made by Schreiber to one James Donahue. We objected, since no one by that name was listed as witness by the prosecution and, no matter how it was answered, it would have been prejudicial. The board said in the first instance that it was proper cross-examination. It then hedged its bet by saying, "Finally, even assuming the impropriety of the question and error in failing to give admonitory instructions, we are unable to discern a reasonable possibility that the error influenced the court or substantially prejudiced the members of the court in view of the accused's denial of the statement attributed to him and the abundance of otherwise competent evidence of guilt contained in the record."

As to the law officer permitting Colonel Perry to continue questioning Schreiber after an objection to his highly prejudicial statement of the evidence was sustained by the law officer, and not allowing a contemporaneous vote on the challenge for cause of Colonel Perry, the board ruled the defense arguments "lacking in substance."

Last was the law officer's refusal to allow the defense to make further rebuttal of Major Holland's introduction of new arguments in his closing argument and, also in closing arguments, his misstating the evidence by misquoting testimony of a witness. "We find no error in the law officer's disposition of the request," the board said. "The trial counsel has the right to final closing argument, but the defense should be afforded an opportunity to reply where trial counsel has introduced new matter in his final argument." They found that Major Holland argued no new matter, and that any misquotation of testimony was for the members of the court to recall their own version. Of course, the idea of argument is to persuade a particular point of view based on competent evidence and not to mislead the jury or court in its recollection of what was said, as did Major Holland in his final argument. In short, the Board of Review concluded, "It is our opinion that the record of trial is free from substantial error, the accused was afforded a fair and proper trial, and the findings and sentence are correct in law and fact."

The next appeal was to the Court of Military Appeals, the Supreme Court for the military. However, before dealing with that matter, it is instructive to point out that in my request for all of the records, I was given two documents that were attached to the Board of Review's decision. The first questioned how they could reconcile Kinder having testified that he acted under an order from Schreiber and the finding of an agreement to sustain the conspiracy charge. The other memorandum says the writer prepared a footnote to assist the board in dealing with the obvious inconsistency. It went on to express concern about Colonel Charles Loewenberg chewing out Major Farnell and the obvious issue of General Anderson's press release. The author of the memorandum went on to state that the Association of the Bar of the City of New York had recommended that there be adopted in the Canons of Ethics a proscription forbidding counsel from either side discussing a pretrial statement or confession made by the accused or suggesting conclusions with respect to the ultimate facts or the evidence to be adduced in a case or discussing the guilt or innocence of the accused. The writer went on to say that, had such a press release been issued in England, it would probably result in the finding that the accused had been deprived of a fair trial.

The Court of Military Appeals, in a rather brief decision considering the issues, made the following conclusion. "Without reviewing in detail the testimony of these witnesses, we note that the court-martial accepted the essentials of their testimony and arrived at the conclusion that the accused was guilty. The Board of Review after examining the evidence in detail, and specifically 'evaluating the varying motives underlying the testimony of each witness,' arrived at a like conclusion. Its opinion is set out in full in 16 CMR 639. Since credibility is a matter to be determined by the triers of fact, and no clear abuse of discretion is shown, we shall not disturb these findings."

And thus, Schreiber's fate was determined. But the resulting uproar and pressure upon the Air Force – from both the U.S. senators and several congressmen concerned with the case as well as the Governor of Illinois – was so great and intense that, after two years in confinement, Schreiber's confinement was terminated by the Secretary of the Air

Force and his dishonorable discharge from the service was reduced to a dismissal from the service. It is also noted that he was allowed to collect his full pay and allowances for several months after his sentence, something that I noticed in writing this book. As the acrimony against his conviction increased, from such organizations as the American Federation of Labor and the American Legion, George told me that he received a pardon from President Eisenhower. However, I have not been able to validate this statement. Although it would surprise me if he did not receive such a pardon, never in the annals of the military have so many newspapers, citizens, and organizations protested so loudly and righteously about an injustice to one of its heroes perpetrated by his own government.

CHAPTER 28

Sentencing and Beyond

BEFORE THE SENTENCING phase, Major Holland read for the record Schreiber's date of enlistment, his rank and rate of pay, his date of birth, the fact that he had no prior record of convictions, and the fact that he was not now in restraint. The court then recessed for lunch until 1300 hours.

One interesting thing about military courts is that they started when the presiding officer said they would, not minutes later. In my experience, this has been rare in civilian courts, where the rule is hurry up and wait, sometimes for hours or even days of delay. Precisely at 1300 hours, the court reconvened.

The law officer now told Schreiber that he could present evidence in extenuation or mitigation of the offenses of which he stood convicted. He had a choice of making a sworn or unsworn statement as he wished, or he could say nothing. If he made an unsworn statement, he could not be cross-examined on it, but the prosecution could rebut anything contained in the statement. He was also told that he could speak directly or through his counsel. He could also provide a written statement in mitigation or extenuation. What he could not do is now claim his innocence, as he had been convicted.

Mike then said, "The defense and the defendant have nothing further to add to what has already been stated as a matter of record."

Farnell referred the court to the manual for approved forms of sentencing and then closed the court for ten minutes to reconvene at 1320 hours. At precisely 1320 hours, the court reconvened. The president then stated, "Second Lieutenant George C. Schreiber, it is my duty as president of the court to inform you that the court in closed session and upon secret written ballot, two-thirds of the members present at the time the vote was taken, concurring sentences you to be dishonorably discharged from the service, to forfeit all pay and allowances, and to be confined at hard labor for the term of your natural life."

The court adjourned at 1325 hours on August 17, 1953.

The sentencing phase was very swift. In view of its findings of guilt, the court members had two choices – death or life in prison. No one felt death would be an option, as it would call too much attention to an already corrupt proceeding. The press went wild, calling the trial a sham and a show trial, and impugning the new military justice system as being like the old "drumhead justice" system.

I was once again Schreiber's keeper. He was delivered to me with orders for me to deliver him to the Army Stockade at Tokyo, Japan. Naturally, we felt glum and disassociated from reality for a while. No one knew quite what to do with Schreiber. He was now a convicted murderer and, certainly anywhere else, would have been a flight risk. He was now in confinement at K-2. On the appointed date of our departure, we flew to Tachikawa and were then driven to the Army Stockade in Tokyo. In my recollection, it was a fortress-like building. It seemed ominous, dark, and dank to me. A captain came to greet us. He told me not to be concerned, that George would be well treated. From all accounts I received from George, he was well treated, everything considered. I was emotional, had lumps in my throat, and fought back tears. I perceived that George had the same sentiments. We embraced, said nothing, shook hands, and I departed. That was the last time that I ever saw him.

The record of trial was corrected on October 23, 1953, to show that Colonel Mathews, the president, really said that the sentence was with the concurrence of three-fourths of the voting members, not the two-thirds indicated in the record.

On November 2, 1953, Lieutenant General Samuel E. Anderson entered the following order.

"In the foregoing case of SECOND LIEUTENANT GEORGE C. SCHREIBER, AO 2219359, United States Air Force, 75th Supply Group, 75th Air Depot Wing, APO 709, only so much of the sentence is approved as provides for dismissal, confinement at hard labor for five years, and forfeiture of all pay and allowances. The forfeiture shall apply to pay and allowances becoming due on and after the date of this action. The record of trial is forwarded to the Judge Advocate General of the United States Air Force for review by a Board of Review. Pending completion of appellate review, the accused will be confined in the United States Army Stockade, 8044th Army Unit, APO 500, or elsewhere as competent authority may direct."

I did hear from George again. On Sunday, November 8, 1953, he wrote to me. He said that even though he had promised to drop me a line, until this week he really had nothing to tell me. He asked me how things went for me after he last saw me and asked if I was married yet, which I was not.

He went on, "Probably be best for me to go back and start at the time I last saw you. Jesse got fouled up on his scheduled departure and, as a result, didn't leave until the latter part of September. He met with my relatives on the coast and went from there to Texas to get married. However, he didn't get married, reason unknown, and proceeded to his ol' Alabama home, where he promptly broke his ankle, reason unknown. Then, last week, he drove his new Buick up to Chicago, where the boys had a little get-together. The boys I refer to are Jesse, Granville Beardsley, who is assistant attorney general of Illinois and who is taking the case to higher courts, and Clayton Kirkpatrick, who is a reporter at the *Chicago Tribune* and who is really crusading to get the attention of the president when the appellate proceedings start. Bob, the response at home has been terrific. Over seven thousand signatures have already reached the desk of Ike, the senators and reps of Illinois, Indiana, and Michigan, and the secretary of the AF. The AF of L is solidly behind, and the American Legion has started a defense fund in Chicago, which at the latest report I got had over one thousand dollars at the end of the first week. The teachers and kids and people of the hometown have really organized and have some kind of 'day' planned, which is to come off the 14th of November, and their goal is to sell 5,400 tickets at a buck a flip. Everyone has been going all out to help, so I think it will be a success. Did you know that Mom had been on TV twice and had spoken to several large organizations at their meetings? She has been wonderful the way she has withstood all this pressure. Almost every day there is some sort of article in the paper, and they consider this amazing since this sort of thing usually wears off after the first few weeks. Keyes Beech, dean of the foreign correspondents, was out to see me a few weeks ago and said he will be back. He reports for the *Chicago Daily News* and some other papers, the names of which escape me. Braun has really been swell about coming out to see me during the past two and a half months. Of course, I see dollar signs in his eyes, but nevertheless it helps to see and talk to someone."

"Whew, that was a long paragraph. I stayed in that room, under the same circumstances as the one in Korea, for two weeks here, and then had the very lucky break of running into this captain who is in charge of the dispensary here. As a result, I have been working over here helping out with the administrative work and just shuffling papers around. He sees to it that I get all the breaks and just makes life very enjoyable considering the circumstances. Certainly a far cry from that place of initial confinement, Bob."

He then wrote that he had received a letter from Colonel Wiseman, and shared some news from his letter:

"Had a chat with Major Holland a week or so ago and, believe me, that man has things on his mind. I feel sure that he will go to the Pentagon upon his return and get some of these matters off his mind. I don't believe he is sleeping well at night. To me, it's a good indication."

"Thought you might get a kick out of that, since you know the inside details on the whole thing. He is now stationed up north somewhere. The review by the 5th, which cut the sentence to five years, was a very fast one, Bob."

George then recounted the numerous errors contained in the trial transcript. There were hundreds, if not thousands, of errors as to what was said at trial. "As it turned out, Braun never did get an opportunity to authenticate or sign," George wrote. "In fact, he didn't get a chance to even see the finished product after they spent over two months correcting it. Major Farnell said there were over 100 pages of corrections, but I found a hell of a lot of them when I read it on Thursday and Friday of this week. We sure drew a lemon in the court reporter . . . "

"Jesse signed a blank authentication paper which also had Braun's signature block on it. And I can't blame him for doing that, since they undoubtedly would have held him over. However, the AF never let Braun see it or sign it, so today his signature block is still empty. Their excuse? Not enough time! What a load of shit! After two months they say that. The AF ordered Farnell to personally bring the copy over to 5th and not let Braun see it. He said that the newspapers made it happen. Farnell was in the middle, so he could do nothing but play like the errand boy. Isn't that a blast in the old phistaris?"

George said that Mike Braun was reviewing the record of trial and that he was going to send a memorandum with the record to Assistant Attorney General Granville Beardsley via the *Chicago Tribune* facilities in Tokyo to Chicago. After that, he said Beardsley will fly to Washington to compare his transcript with the one provided to Mike, and that he would confer with Jesse before preparing his appellate brief. "I don't know exactly what else they have in mind, but if the senators go through with their demands for a complete investigation of this whole thing, I believe we will be needing you again, Bob," George wrote. "I won't go into what this may include, but I think you know. Rep. Hoffman, who lives in the next village to mine, is really up in the air over this thing, so there is no telling where it will end up."

George wrote that he understood he would be leaving Japan soon and wanted to be sure that I wrote to him, which I did. He told me how they held up his mail for seventeen days, but it was not done at the stockade. The implication was that it was the OSI at the behest of 5th Air Force commander. He said that the newspapers "made quite a big stink about it, so now they are extra careful."

At the very bottom of his typed letter, he penned the following. "I'm still the captain, don't believe the Greek; been playing any v-ball lately?" That last part told me that George was still in good spirits and had not lost hope that he would be exonerated. "The Greek" was Captain Jimmie Kinnis, a former cab driver from Detroit and the club officer. We played a lot of volleyball to pass the spare time at K-10, and George was captain of our team, being an excellent and tall athlete. Strangely enough, we both felt that justice would ultimately prevail for George, and neither he nor I as his captor, friend, and lawyer let it worry us. We were young, patriotic, spiritual, ambitious, and felt the service that we loved so well would soon come around. We believed that the fact we had run into some corrupt individuals along the way was an abnormality. Sadly, we were wrong on almost all counts.

In Illinois, Indiana, and Michigan, the press was in an uproar over what the reporters who had witnessed the trial called a "farce" and "a complete miscarriage of justice." The senators and congressmen took note and were demanding answers, but none were being offered. The trial had been a fiasco. Jesse had written to the appellate defense counsel assigned to be the military lawyer for the appeal to the Board of Review. "My own feelings in the matter are that I most certainly want to see this case all the way through the finish," Jesse wrote.

It is quite impossible for the record of trial to come anywhere near reflecting the hostility and animosity that attended the entire proceedings, from the Article 32 investigation down through the sentence. Of course, I realize that those are, for the most part, matters for collateral attack. I have attached copies of Jesse's letter to Major Norman F. Carroll and his response. Senator Everett Dirksen from Illinois, was demanding answers from the Secretary of the Air Force and from General Nathan Twining, the AF chief of staff. If one had not experienced it, the aura of hostility and the desire to treat Schreiber and his defense counsel as persona non grata permeated the atmosphere at 5th Air Force (Rear) in Taegu before, after, and during the trial. These matters were not lost on the members of the press. Hence the very stupid press release by Lieutenant General Samuel Anderson issued before the start of Schreiber's trial on August 11, in which he argued the case for the prosecution. The hostility was seen in the little things – like preventing Schreiber from entering the Officer' Club at 5th AF headquarters, not giving the defense counsel any place in which to work and interview witnesses, withholding Gatto's reports, giving us no typist or typewriter to use, forcing the matter to trial before we could fully prepare, failing to grant Mike a travel order when he wanted it, which denied us at least another day and a half to work together, the hostility of the staff judge advocate and the president of the court, Colonel Mathews, and Colonel Perry, a court member. In short, there was no collegiality. Colonel Loewenberg, the SJA, could not address Jesse, Mike, or me in a civil tone of voice. This permeated down through his ass-kissing staff. In spite of everything, we all believed Schreiber to have been innocent, and we resented the way in which he and we were treated. We all remained loyal allies in what we felt was a need for justice in the newly organized Air Force.

My next letter from George was dated December 8, 1953. It was newsy, upbeat, and friendly, but did not express the same degree of assurance as to his vindication as before. I am publishing his letter with this chapter as well.

17 November 1953

AFCJA-32

Major Jesse O. Bryan, IV,
Office of the Staff Judge Advocate,
Headquarters Eastern Air Defense Force,
Stewart Air Force Base, N.Y.

Dea Major Bryan:-

The record of trial in the case of Second Lieutenant George
C. Schreiber, wherein you acted as defense counsel, has been
received at this office. I have been assigned to represent
Lieutenant Schreiber as appellate defense counsel. It is
noted that XXXX. Lt. Schreiver's request for appellate defense
counsel, dated 29 August 1953, requests that you represent him
before the Board of Review. Since that time General Harmon has
received a letter from the Attorney General of the State of
Illinois, dated November 6, 1953, wherein it is stated that the
Attorney General has assigned Mr. Grenville Beardsley to
prepare a brief on behalf of Lt. Schreiver and to make an
oral argument before the Board of Review in his case. This
letter also disclosed that Lt. Schreiber has requested his
counsel in Tokyo to forward his copy of the record of trial
to Mr. Beardsley.

You are no doubt familiar with the fact that as a matter of
practicality and to prevent an unnecessary expenditure of
public funds, there is a general policy that defense counsel
in the field will not represent an accused before the various
Boards of Review and that such accused will be represented by
Judge Advocates assigned to the Appellate Defense Section in
the Office of The Judge Advocate General. In view of the lapse
of time since Lt. Schreiber's request for your services and
his evident acceptance of representation by Mr. Beardsley, it
is requested that you make known your opinion and desires in
this matter.

Sincerely yours,

NORMAN F. CARROLL
Major, USAF
Appellate Defense Counsel

11-17-1953 letter N.Carroll to J.Bryan

HEADQUARTERS 4707TH DEFENSE WING
Office of the Staff Judge Advocate
Otis Air Force Base, Falmouth, Mass

20 November 1953

Major Norman F. Carroll
Office of the Judge Advocate General
Headquarters USAF
Washington 25, D.C.

Dear Major Carroll:

I am in receipt of your letter of 17 November 1953

Mr. Beardsley was appointed to represent Lieutenant Schreiber by the Governor of Illinois after pressure was brought by The ~~Tribune~~ Chicago Tribune and the people of Illinois.

Information from Tokyo leads me to believe that the record of trial does not truly reflect the ~~proceedings~~. Before leaving Tokyo I read a rough draft of the trial and noted thereon the errors that I thought the reporter had made. Major Farnell, the legal officer, and I were in agreement as to many of the errors. It was my understanding that Mr. Braun, the civilian counsel, would have an opportunity to review the record of trial and at General Johnson's request, I turned a rough draft over to Mr. Braun with my recommendations noted, and departed Tokyo the next day for the Zone of Interior. Further, assuming that the trial counsel would note the corrections I had made in accordance with paragraph 82e, MCM, 1951, I signed the authentication sheet . I have been led to believe that Mr. Braun was not allowed to examine the corrected record of trial. As a result, the authentication sheet that I signed has been attached to the "new" record of trial and naturally I do not know if any of the errors noted by me and the law officer have been made.

You will have to contact Lieut. Schreiber in regard to his desires in this matter. However, I feel quite certain that he is desirous of my services in an appellate capacity and he certainly has amply reason if, in fact, the record is "fouled up."

My own feelings in the matter are that I most certainly want to see this case all the way through to the finish. It is quite impossible for the record of trial to anywhere near reflect the hostility and animosity that attended the entire proceedings, from the Article 32 investigation down through the sentence. Of course, I realize that those are for the most part matters for collateral attack.

My experience on appellate matters is void and, as a result, I would not attempt to proceed nor would I desire to be without your services, preferably as your assistant or your associate.

Trusting that this answers any questions that you may have in regard to my feelings in the matter, I remain

Sincerely

Jesse O. Bryan IV
Major, USAF
Staff Judge Advocate

11-20-1953 letter J.Bryan to N.Carroll

8 December 1953
Tuesday Evening

Dear Bob,

Received yours of the 26th and was sure glad to hear
from you. Got a real boost out of that new address of yours;
One State Street. Number one place of business, now what
about the man in the business? Heh, Heh, Just kidding Bob,
I know you will be successful. It may take a little time
to get all the needed experience and it may also take time
to get up in the higher earning brackets, but think of the
freedom kid, and smile. How I do envy you.

From what mom told me, Jesse broke his ankle while out
playing football or something with his sisters kids in the
back yard. My aunt said he created quite a sensation, while
in Chicago and strolling around the Palmer House with his
uniform, ribbons wings etc., and sporting a cane. I can see
it all now. Don't think his oil well deal is off, just post-
poned. She is still in school, just 21 and still a spring
chicken. Jesse picked up a new Buick while enroute to his
new assignment. The inclosure will explain the mixup about
the record of trial and may enlighten you even farther. I
get a kick out of the AF giving me an appellate defense counsel
even tho I had specifically requested Jesse. I intend to
continue to ask for him. It would be the best if as Jesse
puts it in his reply to Major Carroll, he could act as an
associate in the case. I definitely want Jesse to be there
and if it boils down to a question of one or the other I
will choose the boy from Alabama. I haven't heard from anyone at home on the subject yet and will be interested in hearing
what Mr. Beardsley has to say on the subject. Jesse is now
stationed at Otis AFB, Falmouth Mass which should put you
two fairly close together. Hope you can give him a ring or
at least drop him a line. I know he would like to see you
and imagine you can be bought up to date on the happening
much better by him than I can.

You would never guess who was in to see me today. None
other than the Greek himself. I refer to one C. J. Kinnes,
Capt, USAF, complete with wings, brag rage, and looking
mighty sharp. We had a nice chat for an hour or so and then
he had to take off for K-10. He had the "goony bird" over for
repairs or something. Tells me he has a wide eyed moose over
here now and is enjoying her company. What a guy to tell
that to-- me who is in the worst condition of his life along
those lines. He is due to go home in January. Mike is still
trying to make out with everyone elses moose up at the club.
Kinnes is now the club officer and says they lost money last
month. I had a nice letter from "The Captain" a few weeks

12-08-1953 letter George to Bob-pg1

ago and he is now working for the Celotex Corp in Detroit.
His address: 319 West Hayes
             Hazel Park, Michigan
I'm sure he would enjoy hearing from you, so break down.
The Greek was telling me today that Danny Egan took a spill
while playing volly-ball not too long again ago and made
a most beautiful swan dive into the moat. It must have been
hilarious to see.

I am on orders to leave for the states this coming Sat-
urday but the boy I work for here is doing his best to get
me a delay until after the holidays. We both think it would
be best to hold off so the family could relax and have a
more pleasent holiday. However, the AF is not holding still
so I will probably be on the ship as scheduled. Ironic part
of the whole thing is that I am going back on the Breckenridge, the same one I came over on. What a blast in the butt.
If I do leave I won't be able to write to any more than four
people and not more than two letters a week. Another kick
since I do like to get postage and write.

Your new type of life sounds excellent Bob. I bet you
are really giving those women the rush act, mitt apartment
and all. From what I saw of Boston the few times
I was there, it looked like good stamping grounds.

Best I sign off for now kid. Hope you can contact
Jesse out at Otis. If anything happens on your end that
you would like me to know write to my mother and she will
forward the info to me in her letters. I'll be writing
again the next chance I get, don't know when but I will
keep you up on the events if at all possible. Have a few
for the ol' Hawk on New Years Bob. Someone has to drink
my share. Good Luck Buddy, see you

                        Your Buddy
                        George
                        George

12-08-1953 letter George to Bob-pg2

CHAPTER 29

Post Trial Press Reports

AFTER SCHREIBER'S CONVICTION, the reaction in Schreiber's hometown was instantaneous. In a report in the Logansport, Indiana-based *Pharos-Tribune* on August 19, 1953, Schreiber's mother, Mrs. Anne Schreiber, said, "It wasn't in George's character to do what they say he has done." The article describes his mother as grief stricken. His father, Clifford G. Schreiber, said, "He hated everything communism stood for – he just went out and enlisted. . . . He was fighting against dictatorship. . . . We feel that the trial was an example of dictatorship."

An article in the October 11, 1953, edition of the Cedar Rapids, Iowa, *Gazette* indicated that Schreiber insisted he was innocent. "His commanding officer and returning dischargees from his outfit all swear by him," the article said. It went on to quote Chapell H. Donfell, a Chicago attorney and state adjutant of the Military Order of World Wars. "Unquestionably, there were extenuating and mitigating circumstances not presented," Donfell said. "Such a decision in a civil court would be unanimously denounced as a flagrant miscarriage of justice."

The article went on to quote Anne Schreiber, George's mother, as saying, "I simply don't know how it is going to turn out, but everybody's been so wonderful. You never know who your friends are until you need help."

The same article also indicated that Illinois' congressmen as well as U.S. Senators Everett Dirksen (R) and Paul Douglas (D) declared they wanted to see transcripts of Schreiber's case. There was such an outcry of thousands of ordinary and important folks. Individuals such as Governor Stratton of Illinois and the two U.S. senators, Dirksen and Douglas, and organizations such as the American Legion, the Chicago Labor Council, the Pipefitters Union, and many others began writing, protesting, and speaking out against Schreiber's conviction. The discrimination against Schreiber and his defense counsel as evidenced during the trial was so obvious and outrageous, I believe that if people were informed nationally, through a program like *60 Minutes*, it would have been seen as a national shame and would have caused an outpouring of criticism like what happened in Illinois and Indiana. There was no such program back then, and the Korean War was not in the daily headlines like the Vietnam War. Thankfully, the press covered the trial in some force, and what was obvious to me throughout the proceedings – namely that Schreiber was being framed – became obvious to the astute members of the American press who witnessed the trial.

The Waterloo Daily Courier (Iowa) of October 11, 1953, carried an article indicating that "hope is eternal in a mother's heart, and Mrs. Anne Schreiber, who worried out the war service of two sons, is anxiously awaiting today's news of a third son who was convicted of murder in Korea." It goes on to say how George had begun a life term in a Tokyo stockade and describes him as a former Valparaiso University basketball star. The article went on to say,

"Back in his elm-shaded hometown of Brookfield, near Chicago, a mass protest swelled. Petitions were launched by the school board and Schreiber's former boss, Superintendent M.W. Hummel. Some 5,000 signatures urged President Eisenhower to study the case."

Anne Schreiber indicated that she received letters every two weeks from George and stated that he wrote mostly about home. Even when he went on trial, he wrote simply that he'd "had a little trouble in the line of duty." "No details," she added with a sigh.

On May 19, 1955, *The Logansport Press* (Indiana) carried a story from Lompoc, California, indicating that an Air Force officer had been released from prison after serving 20 months of a five-year sentence for the murder of a South Korean. He said he would continue fighting to clear his name.

"First Lieutenant George Schreiber was ordered released from prison by Air Force Secretary Harold Talbott, but the Secretary also ordered him dismissed from the service," the article stated. "The dismissal is equivalent to a dishonorable discharge for an enlisted man, and Schreiber, 27, will lose his veteran's benefits and rights to military pensions and services."

"'I am not screaming for mercy or crying sour grapes,' said Schreiber as he left the U.S. disciplinary barracks at Camp Cooke. 'All I want is a cold appraisal of the whole thing.' The former Brookfield, Illinois, schoolteacher, a 240-pounder standing 6–foot-6-inches tall, added that he felt he was 'morally correct' and was innocent. He blamed what he termed a misinterpretation of an order for his conviction." The article went on to say that the school board in Brookfield, a Chicago suburb, voted "complete confidence" in Schreiber and said that he is welcome to return to his old teaching job.

The Vidette Messenger of Valparaiso, Indiana, on September 2, 1953, carried an article entitled "Schreiber Petition is Planned Here." The article told how plans were being formulated to draw up a petition in the interest of Lieutenant George Schreiber, a former Valparaiso University basketball player who was convicted on August 17 by court-martial of ordering the killing of a South Korean. It indicated the petition would be similar to the one that thousands of George's friends in Brookfield, Illinois, and neighboring communities were sending to President Eisenhower requesting a review of the case, according to Mel Doering, a spokesman for Omega Chi Beta fraternity of which

Schreiber is a member.

"Our fraternity for three months has been conducting a campaign among our members to demonstrate our firm conviction that George has been innocently [sic] accused by the Air Force in connection with the shooting of a Korean civilian at Pusan Air Base last September," Doering said. "It was not and still is not the intention of our fraternity to solicit contributions from persons outside our organization. However, we have already accepted unsolicited contributions from a number of generous people in the community, and we would like to take this means of announcing that we stand ready to receive any donations that others in the community would care to make."

Doering went on to state that many people had indicated they wanted to make financial contributions to help George but did not know where to send contributions. The article ended with the information that checks should be made payable to Clifford G. Schreiber, with the contributor's name and complete address accompanying the donation.

In the Dickson, Illinois, *Evening Telegraph* of April 13, 1954, an article entitled "Castle Argues Sentence of GI," with a dateline of Washington, D.C., indicated that Attorney General Latham Castle of Illinois had submitted arguments to an Air Force Board of Review in an attempt to get the five-year prison sentence of 2nd Lieutenant George Schreiber of Hollywood, Illinois, reduced. The article went on to say that Castle and Illinois Assistant Attorney General Granville Beardsley had submitted arguments that the five-year sentence was not justified to the board reviewing the sentence. "The Illinois officials contended that evidence that Schreiber ordered an enlisted man to slay the Korean was unsubstantiated," the article said.

An article entitled "Governor Directs Castle to Aid Officer Held for Slaying" ran in *The Dickson Evening Telegraph* on September 10, 1953, with a Chicago dateline. "The State of Illinois acted Wednesday to assist an Illinois Army Officer under life sentence in Tokyo for the fatal shooting of a Korean.," the article said. The article indicated that Governor William Stratton conferred with Illinois Attorney General Latham Castle about the case of Lieutenant George Schreiber and directed Castle to do whatever was possible to help Schreiber in his fight against the court-martial conviction. It then went on to state that Castle assigned his first assistant in his Chicago office, Granville Beardsley, a member of the Judge Advocate General's staff in World War I, to handle the case. Beardsley said that his first move would be to get a copy of the court-martial record to study it for possible errors. Beardsley also said that he would review the record and would seek permission to appear before the Air Force Board of Review in Washington and to file briefs as would be done in a civilian case. Beardsley said that if he failed before the Board of Review, his next move would be to file briefs before the Court of Military Appeals and make oral argument. He said that the Court of Military Appeals is comparable in the military to the United States Supreme Court.

The Cedar Rapids Tribune (Iowa) on September 10, 1953, carried an article entitled "Chicago Union Leads Fight for Convicted GI" with a Chicago dateline. The article explained that leaders of one of the largest labor unions in the Chicago area had been enlisted in the fight to win justice for Lieutenant George Schreiber. Martin J. Ward, business manager for the AFL Pipefitters Local 597, said that a resolution urging a fair trial was scheduled to be adopted by the then-thousand-member local union. Schreiber's father, Clifford, had been a member of the union for 35 years. Ward added that he was confident the resolution would be approved by the Chicago Building Trades Council and the Chicago Federation of Labor. He said it would also be presented to the Illinois State Federation of Labor at its annual convention in Springfield in October.

Arthur J. Meany, a business agent for the union, said he had known Clifford Schreiber and his family for years. He asserted that such a crime would be completely out of character for the elder Schreiber and for his three sons, of which George was the youngest. Mr. Meany went on to say, "There are a lot of questions that went unanswered after that court-martial. . . . For one thing, why did the Air Force make an investigation and clear everybody, and then reopen it a year later when one of the witnesses had been discharged."

In *The Kingsport News* (Tennessee) of August 7, 1953, an article entitled "Convicted GI Says Training Insufficient" appeared with a Cleveland, Tennessee, dateline and indicated that a 20-year-old Cleveland airman convicted of murder by a military court-martial had written his mother that he was assigned to military police duty without training.

The article reported that, "Airman 1st Class Thomas L. Kinder, sentenced to life imprisonment in the death of a South Korean civilian, said in a letter, 'If I had attended [police] school, I would have known better than to obey the order that was given me.' Kinder said he was ordered by superiors to shoot the Korean. The two other Air Force men, Lieutenant George Schreiber of Hollywood, Illinois, and former Airman Robert W. Toth of Pittsburgh, Pennsylvania, are also charged in the case. Kinder was the first of the three to be tried. The conviction has received widespread publicity in Tennessee, and many groups have requested a review of the case or a new trial for the young servicemen."

The article continued, "In Nashville, Governor Frank Clement's office announced that it has received a letter from a White House official saying that Kinder's case will be fully reviewed by proper authorities. The letter was from Special Presidential Counsel Bernard Shanley, who also said Clement's offer to provide special counsel for Kinder's defense would be allowed if Kinder so desires."

The article went on to say that Air Force Secretary Harold Talbott had also notified Senator Estes Kefauver (D-Tennessee) that the "question of clemency should be considered carefully during a review of the case." The article added that Bradley County Republican Chairman

D.J. Marler had said he had received a letter from State GOP Chairman Giles Smith of Knoxville and Republican Representatives Harold Reese and Howard Baker concerning the Kinder case. The letter said, "We want to do everything in our power in his behalf. We think that he has been mistreated as a result of circumstances over which he had no control."

The Kingsport News(Tennessee) on August 27, 1953, carried an article entitled "Change of Plea Complicated Case for Tennessee Airmen." The article stated that Attorney Edward T. Cole, who was appointed to seek an appeal of Kinder's conviction, said the trial record showed Kinder's military attorney recommended that the Cleveland, Tennessee, airman change his plea from not guilty of murder to guilty of involuntary manslaughter. Cole said the defense lawyer, Major Charlie Y. Weir, told the court-martial Kinder's change of plea denotes fault but not guilt in the killing of the South Korean. Kinder at first was given a life sentence for his part in the slaying, but an Air Force general reduced the sentence to two years. Kinder said he killed the Korean, whom he shot on orders of a superior officer, Lieutenant George Schreiber. Cole said that Kinder's change of plea indicated his attorney felt there was no maliciousness in Kinder's action. Cole added that there must be an element of negligence in a plea of guilty to manslaughter, and Kinder showed no negligence since he followed an order.

The real fact is that Charlie Weir had orchestrated a deal for Kinder with the Commander of the 5th Air Force through Colonel Loewenberg. The deal stipulated that if Kinder would testify against Schreiber at Schreiber's court-martial, he would be immediately released from confinement, restored to active duty, and his sentence would be remitted, which is exactly what happened. Within a few days of his testimony against Schreiber, Kinder was back in the United States on active duty as if nothing untoward had ever happened to him. His story was either totally or mostly false and was concocted to serve his own interests. To make a deal, he had to help to convict

George Schreiber and protect himself. He heard what he wanted to say he heard that night in September of 1952. Kinder knew exactly what he was doing when he shot the man. Schreiber's major mistake was in trying to cover up the stupidity of both Toth and Kinder in killing the Korean. Schreiber was trying to protect his men. That, too, was stupid, but it was in Schreiber's mentality that the protection of his men from all harm came first. In his mind, he was somehow both a leader and a big brother to his men. This may have been admirable in other settings, but in war-torn Korea, it was a dumb move. It is out of such good intentions that, when the rules are bent, people fall into difficulties that they never envisioned. Such was the situation for George Schreiber. He did not give any order to kill anyone, but once the killing happened, he remained loyal to his men at his own peril. While Toth was overtly supportive of Schreiber, he, too, was self serving in his recollections at trial, as was Kinder to a fault. Their own self-preservation was paramount to them. That was apparent to me as I listened to their testimony at trial.

In an article published in the *Charleroi Mail* (Pennsylvania) on August 19, 1953, Airman Kinder is quoted as saying that the killing of the Korean was to cover up the fact that he had been pistol-whipped as a suspected thief.

The Modesto Bee (California) on June 6, 1953, carried an article in which Colonel Charles L. Loewenberg, 5th Air Force Judge Advocate, said Schreiber, age 25, was arrested at an air base near Pusan and charged with premeditated murder and with conspiracy to commit murder. Loewenberg said Schreiber allegedly ordered the shooting of Bang Soon Kil on September 27th after Bang was apprehended by Kinder in a restricted area on an air base near Pusan, pistol-whipped by Toth, and taken to Schreiber. After the alleged order from Schreiber, Loewenberg said, Toth allegedly selected an empty revetment on the base for the shooting, and Kinder allegedly did the actual shooting. Quoting from an article published in the *Oneonta Star* (New York) on May 28, 1953, the article purports to quote Robert W. Toth, who was honorably discharged from the Air Force in December of 1952, as having been arrested on May 13,1953, while at work and five days later was back in Korea for trial by court-martial. Toth said he was told by arresting Air Police that he had the right to get a civilian lawyer, "but I told him I didn't want an attorney – that was because I could not afford one." It goes on, "And, of course, I was shook by the arrest and the speed with which I was taken from Pittsburgh, that I wasn't sure just what to do."

The same sensation of shock at being returned to Korea was expressed in a separate interview by Toth's co-defendant, Airman 1st Class Thomas L. Kinder of Cleveland, Tennessee. Still in the service, Kinder was picked up at Osceola, Wisconsin, where he was on duty as an Air Policeman.

Another article in the Modesto Bee reported that President Syngman Rhee of South Korea had been advised of a proposed truce only an hour before it was presented to the communists the previous week. The Korean general who represented the Republic of Korea had boycotted that meeting at Panmunjon. Rhee repeatedly vowed to fight on alone if an armistice that did not provide for unification of all Korea was signed. In Washington, U.S. State Department officials said the idea of a unified Korea would be pressed at a peace conference to follow any truce agreement. The Allies presented their plan in secrecy at the request of the Allied Nations. The negotiations were then recessed until the following Monday. Members of the South Korean National Assembly blasted the Allied proposal, as it did not provide for a reunified Korea.

An article appeared on August 17, 1953, in the *Corpus Christi Times* (Texas) indicating that Schreiber had been convicted and sentenced to life imprisonment. It went on to say that both Toth and Kinder were arrested in the United States and returned to Korea for trial. Kinder was still in the Air Force at the time, but Toth had been honorably discharged some months before. Toth was the first discharged serviceman to be returned to a foreign theater to stand trial under the 1951 Code of Military Justice. Toth was arrested and returned to Korea within five days, and this kicked up a storm of controversy in the United States. This case was to become a test of the constitutionality of the Uniform Code of Military Justice provision that said a discharged serviceman might be returned to a foreign theater to stand trial on charges of a serious crime if he cannot be tried in the courts of the United States.

In September 1953, *The Daily Times-News* of Wilmington, North Carolina, featured a significant article by Don Whitehead emanating from Washington, D.C. In that article, Whitehead said, "One bullet among the millions fired in the Korean War has kicked up a legal storm over how much power the armed forces should have in seizing honorably discharged veterans for trial by court-martial. The echoes of that one shot, in theory at least, may affect Army, Navy, and Air Force veterans discharged from service in the past two years and in years to come. Involved in the argument – which may yet reach the Supreme Court – are these questions, among others: 1. Does the military have the right to arrest a veteran, a civilian, and transport him without a preliminary hearing nor advice of counsel to a distant country to stand trial for a crime allegedly committed before he left the service? 2. Can a veteran using his honorable discharge as a shield dodge trial for a crime he might have committed before his discharge?"

The article continued, "The shot that started this controversy was fired in September 1952 at an Air Force Base near Pusan, Korea. The bullet snuffed out the life of Bong [sic] Soon Kil Kong [sic], a South Korean who had been caught in a restricted area at the air base. The Air Force, after investigating, didn't classify Bong's death as something that was justified in protecting U.S. property. This chain of events followed Air Force Sergeant Robert Toth, 21, of Pittsburgh, Pennsylvania. He came home to pick up the threads of civilian life again and got a job in a Pittsburgh steel mill."

"Last May," the article continued, "Toth was at work as usual when

Air Force military policemen suddenly appeared at the plant. The MPs permitted Toth to make one telephone call before they put him aboard a plane. Toth called his mother. He asked that someone pick up his work clothes at the airport because military police were taking him back to Korea. They had given him GI clothing for the journey."

"And then the story began to unfold. In Korea, the Air Force said Toth was being returned to stand trial of the murder of Bong Soon Kil," the article read. "Soon there were announcements that two other airmen still on active duty had been arrested in the same case, Airman 1st Class Thomas L. Kinder, 21, of Cleveland, Tennessee, and Lieutenant George C. Schreiber, 21, of Hollywood, Illinois."

"The official story was that Kinder was on guard duty when he caught Bong in the restricted area, and Toth, the sergeant of the guard, pistol-whipped the Korean. Then, the story continues, Schreiber, the officer on duty, said something about 'getting rid' of Bong, which Kinder later testified he understood as an order to have the man shot. Schreiber denies issuing such an order. Then the official story concludes that Toth and Kinder drove Bong away in a Jeep, and Kinder took him aside and shot him to death."

"A court-martial sentenced Schreiber to life imprisonment and gave Kinder a similar sentence that later was reduced to two years. Both cases are now under review. But Toth never went on trial. A few days after his arrest, an attorney for Toth charged the Air Force had denied Toth his constitutional rights to a preliminary hearing and benefit of counsel. A federal court was asked to free Toth from Air Force custody," the article continued.

"On the other side, the Air Force contended it acted merely in accordance with the laws approved by Congress and that Toth was given every legal consideration under the Uniform Code of Military Justice. He was not arrested, the Air Force said, until the action was approved by the Secretary of the Air Force after a careful review of the facts."

"The Air Force cited articles of the Code as authority for Toth's arrest and his transportation to Korea to stand trial. The articles cited were part of the Uniform Code of Military Justice that became effective in July of 1951 and provided:

'Any veteran is subject to arrest and trial by military court – even after an honorable discharge – if he is charged with having committed while in uniform a crime punishable by five years or more in prison. However, this action is authorized only in cases where the accused cannot be tried in a U.S. civil court.'

"Ever since 1863, the Armed Forces have had authority to arrest and try ex-servicemen for any frauds committed against the government while they are in uniform," the article continued. "Four years ago, Congress began considering ways to close loopholes through which ex-servicemen have escaped trial for major crimes because neither military nor civilian courts had jurisdiction in their cases. There have been several celebrated cases in recent years pointing up these loopholes. One case that is often cited is the case of Major William V. Holohan. Major Holohan was an agent of the U.S. Wartime Office of Strategic Services, the OSS, which was the forerunner to the CIA. He had parachuted into Nazi-held Italy to work with partisans in the underground resistance. The Army said Holohan was shot to death by an American sergeant who plotted the murder with an American lieutenant (both OSS agents) after they disagreed with Holohan over the distribution of arms to communist partisans. Both denied the allegations."

"But neither of the accused men had been brought to trial," the article continued. "The Army could not try them because they had been discharged to civilian life. A federal judge ruled they could not be extradited to Italy for trial because the Germans, and not Italy, had controlled the place where the crime was committed."

"Holohan was killed before the new Uniform Code of Military Justice was enacted. But the Toth case shows there is still doubt as to the full authority of the Armed Forces in the arrest of a civilian."

The article continued, "U.S. District Court Judge Alexander Holtzoff, after listening to arguments on both sides, said, 'It seems appalling to the court for the Air Force to seize a civilian in Pittsburgh and immediately transport him to Korea for trial without a hearing of any kind.' He termed the action 'very drastic and somewhat arbitrary' and said it 'shows the danger of arbitrary policies.' Holtzoff freed Toth under $1,000 bond, pending an appeal to higher courts by the Air Force. Holtzoff's ruling, in granting Toth a Writ of Habeas Corpus, was limited to the question of whether the Air Force had authority to take Toth to such a distant point as Korea for trial. The judge said the law did not specifically authorize such an action. The Air Force contended that if it has authority to move a man one inch then it has authority to move him ten-thousand miles. In the Toth case, it was up to the U.S. Supreme Court to make the final decision, which it did."

The American Legion meeting in St. Louis, Missouri, adopted a resolution condemning the "illegal and un-American action of the Air Force Military Police" in the Toth case. It expressed opposition to any laws that would make an ex-serviceman liable for return to a foreign country for trial. Senator Duff (R-Pennsylvania) has termed the Air Force's action "high handed." It appeared the Air Force acted "without regard to the rights of the accused." Representative Fullton (R-Pennsylvania), a Pittsburgh lawyer, is working on amendments to the present Military Code of Justice. Fullton says a person in a situation like Toth's should be taken before a U.S. commissioner or judge and given a preliminary hearing before being taken from the country. He favors such cases being tried under federal courts of this country.

In life, Bang Soon Kil was not a man of importance. The military has never been able to find any next of kin. His death may have its place in history as the start of a legal tangle that was ultimately unraveled by the Supreme Court of the United States.

Toth was put aboard a commercial airliner and was greeted by his mother, Mrs. Nattie Mertz, and his sister, Audrey Toth, when he was flown back to Washington, D.C., after the court order by Judge Holtzoff. Toth's freedom was short-lived, however. On March 5, 1954, the U.S. Court of Appeals in Washington, D.C., upheld a law giving the armed services the right to court-martial civilians for serious crimes committed while in service. The Appeals Court reversed Judge Alexander Holtzoff's ruling and directed that Toth be turned over to the Air Force authorities for court-martial.

The three appellate judges who heard the case agreed unanimously that a provision of the UCMJ (Uniform Code of Military Justice) giving the armed services the authority to try former servicemen for serious crimes was constitutional. Both Toth and the government told the press that the case would be carried to the U.S. Supreme Court. The government's account of events previously given by the Air Force went like this:

"Bang Soon Kil, a South Korean civilian, was found in a restricted area by Airman 1st Class Thomas L. Kinder of Cleveland, Tennessee, who was on guard duty. It was an area where an intruder was subject to be shot. Kinder called Toth, who was Sergeant of the Guard, and the Korean was put into a Jeep to be taken to headquarters."

On route, Government lawyers said the Korean grabbed Toth's pistol, and the sergeant stopped the Jeep and pistol-whipped the prisoner. At headquarters, the government account went on, "Lieutenant George C. Schreiber of Hollywood, Illinois, said the men knew their orders and told them to take the Korean back and shoot him. Subsequently, Assistant U.S. Attorney Oliver Gasch told the court, Toth and Kinder drove Bang Soon Kil to a spot in the area and Kinder shot him. Kinder and Schreiber, still in the Air Force when they were arrested, were tried by court-martial, convicted, and sentenced to life imprisonment. Later, Kinder's sentence was cut to two years and Schreiber's to five."

The Appeals Court decision written by Judge E. Barrett Prettyman brushed aside all contentions raised by Toth's attorneys. Those included a contention that Toth, being a civilian at the time charges were placed against him, was entitled to due process of law in the constitutional sense applicable to civilians. This included the right to indictment and trial by jury, and also to preliminary hearing, removal hearing, and all other provisions of the Federal Rules of Criminal Procedure. Judge Prettyman in the decision of the Court of Appeals wrote, "That a man is answerable for a crime as of the time, place, and circumstance of its commission, rather than the time, place and, circumstance of his apprehension, is a familiar concept of law."

Thus he struck down the main contention raised on Toth's behalf, that he was entitled to a preliminary hearing before removal. Prettyman further said, "There is no statutory requirement for a hearing before removal in a military case."

The Appeals Court went on to say that it believed that the statute, which makes a civilian amenable to trial by court-martial, necessarily connotes authority to apprehend him for that purpose and to remove him for trial to the place where the offense was committed. The court went on to state, "We can perceive no constitutional reason why his liability to apprehension and trial according to the rules applicable to him at the time and place of the commission of the crime should not follow him to other places and paths after his discharge into civilian life."

Three judges on the Court of Appeals, which included Judge Prettyman and Judges Henry W. Edgerton and George T. Washington, said it may very well be that Congress should add to the Uniform Code of Military Justice that a civilian apprehended under it should not be removed from the continental United States until he has had a preliminary hearing under either a civilian magistrate or a military tribunal. "Such questions should be of the [sic] of Congress, not the courts," Judge Prettyman said.

Two articles were published on the front page of the *Lowell Sun* on August 22, 1953, in Lowell, Massachusetts. One involved the return of Toth to Washington, D.C., and explained how, upon his alighting from the airliner, his mother stood there with tears streaming down her cheeks. Toth, also in tears, hugged and kissed his mother for a full minute. This was the first time Mrs. Toth had seen her son since he was arrested by the Air Force in Pittsburgh on May 13. The article quoted the 21-year-old former airman as hugging his mother and telling her, "Mom, they can put us down but they cannot put us out."

The *Record-Argist* of Greenville, Pennsylvania, on September 4, 1953, wrote that Toth returned home to a tumultuous welcome where friends staged a block party in front of his Greenville home, kids blew up balloons, men hung lanterns all along the street, women dished out ice cream and sandwiches, and everyone danced to the tunes of Irish fiddlers.

After the Court of Appeals reversed the Habeas Corpus decision of the District Court, Toth was supported by the members of the American Legion. Arthur J. Connell, new national commander of the American Legion, met with Toth and with Pittsburgh Mayor David L. Lawrence in order to have the American Legion intervene in the Supreme Court appeal. Likewise, Pennsylvania State Commander Paul Selecky of Wilkes-Barre and former judge Francis Taptich, the department judge advocate, also met. The American Legion's national and state conventions went on record opposing the Air Force's attempt to court-martial Toth. Likewise, the Veterans of Foreign Wars in Pennsylvania raised funds to support Toth in his appeal.

LATHAM CASTLE
ATTORNEY GENERAL
STATE OF ILLINOIS
160 NORTH LA SALLE ST.
CHICAGO 1

TELEPHONE
FINANCIAL 6-2000

November 6, 1953

Maj. Gen. Reginald C. Harmon,
The Judge Advocate General,
Department of the Air Force,
The Pentagon,
Washington 25, D. C.

My Dear General Harmon:

In view of the wide spread interest which
many people in the State of Illinois have taken in the case of Lieutenant
George C. Schreiber, recently convicted by an Air Force General
Court Martial in Korea of murder and conspiracy to commit murder,
Honorable William G. Stratton, Governor of the State of Illinois,
has directed me on behalf of the State of Illinois to afford additional
legal representation to Lieutenant Schreiber.

Accordingly, I have assigned my First
Assistant in charge of the Chicago Office of the Attorney General,
Mr. Grenville Beardsley, to prepare a brief for this office on be-
half of Lieutenant Schreiber, and to appear before the Board of
Review to make an oral argument on his behalf.

It is therefore requested that before the case
is taken under review by your Board of Review, that time be granted
this office for the preparation of such printed brief, and a date fixed
for oral argument by this office on behalf of the accused.

I am advised by representatives of the
Chicago Newspapers, that the Commanding General of the Fifth Air
Force has approved the finding of guilty and the sentence, but has
reduced the period of confinement to five years, and that the record of
trial and accompanying papers are now enroute by air to your office.

Lieutenant Schreiber has requested his
counsel in Tokyo to forward the copy of the record of trial to Mr.
Beardsley in this office.

11-06-1953 letter L.Castle to Gen. Harmon-pg1

Maj. Gen. Reginald C. Harmon   -2-

          It is requested that I be advised when
the record of trial reaches your office, and that action by the Board
of Review be withheld for a reasonable time to enable preparation
of a brief to be printed and filed for the consideration of the Board
of Review.

Very truly yours,

Latham Castle
Attorney General

LC:ak

LATHAM CASTLE
ATTORNEY GENERAL
ILLINOIS

June 23, 1954

Major General Reginald C. Harmon,
Judge Advocate General,
United States Air Force,
Washington 25, D. C.

Dear General Harmon:

      I would appreciate it very much
if at your convenience you would set a time for my First
Assistant, Grenville Beardsley and myself, to discuss
with you the case of Second Lieutenant George C. Schrieber,
USAF, ACM 7761. I would suggest any hour between 9:00
o'clock in the forenoon, and 4:00 o'clock in the afternoon
on Wednesday, July 14th, if that day would be agreeable to
you.

      If it would be possible for me to have
lunch with you on that day, I would be honored to have you
as my guest.

      Thank you again for your courtesy
when we were in Washington on April 12th, and hoping you
will be able to see us on July 14th.

Sincerely yours,

LATHAM CASTLE
Attorney General
State of Illinois

LC:hl

06-23-1954 letter L.Castle to Gen. Harmon

Gen Kuhfeld/adh/Wrtn 29 Jun 1954

29 JUN 1954

Honorable Latham Castle
The Attorney General
State of Illinois
160 North La Salle Street
Chicago 1, Illinois

Dear Mr. Castle:

Your letter of 23 July addressed to General Harmon has come
to my attention. General Harmon is on leave and he is not expected
back until about 19 July. If you wish to await his return before
you and Mr. Beardsley come to Washington to discuss the case of
Second Lieutenant George C. Schrieber, I will be glad to bring the
matter to General Harmon's attention immediately upon his return.
If you do not wish to await General Harmon's return to the office,
I shall be very glad to discuss the case with you at any time on
Wednesday, 14 July.

Both General Harmon and I enjoyed meeting you and Mr. Beardsley
when you were in Washington last April. I am looking forward to
seeing you both again when you come to Washington.

Sincerely,

Signed

ALBERT M. KUHFELD
Brigadier General, USAF
Acting The Judge Advocate General
United States Air Force

06-29-1954 letter Kuhfeld to L.Castle

8 July 1954
_____
(Date)

Appellate Defense Counsel
AFCJA-32, The Pentagon
Washington 25, D. C.

Dear Sir:

Having been fully advised of my right to petition the
United States Court of Military Appeals for a grant of review in
my court-martial case designated as ACM____**7761**____I hereby
elect and it is my desire to so petition.

I further desire and request that you serve as my appellate defense counsel and as such urge on my behalf before the
Court any and all errors you deem fit and proper.

Very truly yours,

George C. Schreiber

I request that my counsel before the United States Court of Military
Appeals be Honorable Latham Castle, Attorney General of Illinois;
Grenville Beardsley, First Assistant Attorney General of Illinois;
Colonel A. W. Tolen, USAF, Office of the Judge Advocate General of
the Air Force; and Major Norman F. Carroll, USAF, Office of the Judge
Advocate General of the Air Force.

Incl# 5 ³

07-08-1954 letter George to appellate defense counsel

LATHAM CASTLE
ATTORNEY GENERAL
STATE OF ILLINOIS
160 NORTH LA SALLE ST.
CHICAGO 1

TELEPHONE
FINANCIAL 6-2000

July 19, 1954

Brigadier General Albert M. Kuhfeld, USAF,
The Assistant Judge Advocate General,
United States Air Force,
Headquarters United States Air Force,
Washington 25, D. C.

Dear General Kuhfeld:

        Mr. Beardsley is absent from the
office on duty for fifteen days as an Army Reserve Officer,
and his secretary has laid before me your letter of July
14, 1954. I will plan to be in Washington accompanied by
Mr. Beardsley on August 4, 1954. We will come to the
Judge Advocate General's office, if that is agreeable to
General Harmon, at 10:00 o'clock in the forenoon.

        Sincerely yours,

        LATHAM CASTLE
        Attorney General

LC:ak

R: GPM case
2d Lt Geo. C. Schreiber

07-19-1954 letter L.Castle to Kuhfeld

11 MAY 1955

MEMORANDUM FOR SECRETARY OF THE AIR FORCE

SUBJECT: Second Lieutenant George C. Schreiber, AO 2219359 (ACM 7761)

1. The above named officer was tried by general court-martial convened at APO 970 on 17 August 1953. He was convicted of murder and conspiracy to commit murder and was sentenced to a dishonorable discharge, forfeiture of all pay and allowances and confinement at hard labor for the term of his natural life. The findings of guilty and so much of the sentence as provides for dismissal from the service, total forfeitures, and confinement at hard labor for five years were approved by the convening authority and affirmed by the Board of Review. The Judge Advocate General has concurred in the decision of the Board of Review and did not deem it necessary to take action under Article 67(b)(2). A copy of the decision of the Board of Review was served on Lieutenant Schreiber on 8 July 1954, together with an explanation of his right to petition the United States Court of Military Appeals for a grant of review. Lieutenant Schreiber filed such a petition within the time prescribed by law and it was granted by the Court on 4 October 1954. The United States Court of Military Appeals rendered its decision affirming the decision of the Board of Review on 15 April 1955. Accordingly, appellate review in this case has been completed.

2. On the night of the offense, Lieutenant Schreiber was the base Air Police Officer, Airman First Class Kinder was posted as a guard in the ammunition dump, and Airman First Class Toth was Sergeant of the Guard. Kinder detected a prowler in the ammunition dump and apprehended him. Almost immediately thereafter, Toth arrived and put the prowler, an unidentified Korean, into a jeep to transport him to the Air Police Operations office. En route, Toth stopped the vehicle and pistol-whipped the Korean for no apparent reason. Upon arrival at Operations, the Korean was semi-conscious, had a cut on the right cheek and there was blood about his head and face. Lieutenant Schreiber was called to the office and informed of the circumstances surrounding the apprehension of the Korean. At about this time, the guard shift, including Kinder, returned to Operations after completing its tour of duty. Schreiber called Kinder into the Operations building and questioned him concerning the apprehension. Thereafter, Kinder noticed Schreiber and Toth in conversation and heard Schreiber ask Toth where the Korean could be taken, to which Toth replied, "B-14, Sir". Schreiber then turned to Kinder and asked him to take the Korean up on the hill and shoot him. Kinder replied that he could not do it. Thereupon,

Schreiber specifically ordered Kinder to take his carbine and go with Toth.
Kinder asked if that was an order, to which question Schreiber replied, "yes".
Schreiber also assured Kinder that he (Schreiber) was accepting full responsibility for shooting the Korean. Kinder, Toth, and two other airmen transported
the Korean to Revetment B-14 at the bomb dump. The Korean was helped out of
the truck and Kinder was left with him while the others drove away. Thereafter,
Kinder shot the Korean once with his carbine. The bullet entered the body
just below the right shoulder blade. The others returned to the scene when
the shot was heard and shortly thereafter Schreiber arrived with an ambulance.
The Korean was taken to the base dispensary where examination disclosed he
had a gunshot wound on the right side of the chest and lacerations of the
lower right eye and scalp. The victim was suffering from shock. Although
the victim was treated for his wounds and shock, he died shortly after
arrival at the dispensary. The gunshot wound caused or at least materially
contributed to the death of the victim. Schreiber told the Operations NCO
not to make an entry in the log book that the Korean had been brought to
Operations, but instead he personally made the entry that a Korean had been
found in the bomb dump and was shot. In January and February 1953, during
an official investigation by the Office of Special Investigations, Schreiber
notified all the airmen concerned with the incident that under Article 31
of the Code they could not be required to make a statement and that it would
be best for all concerned not to make statements.

Lieutenant Schreiber testified in his own behalf and stated that when
he first saw the Korean he decided to release him and, accordingly, directed
Toth to take the Korean out and told Kinder to take his carbine and assist
Toth. He denied ordering the shooting. He explained that he advised Kinder,
Toth, and the others not to make statements to the OSI, because he was concerned
for "the welfare of these boys" since they were under his command. The
evidence, although in conflict, fully supports the findings of guilty of
murder and conspiracy to commit murder.

2. Lieutenant Schreiber was born on 15 October 1927 at Berwyn,
Illinois. He is a Catholic and is not married. He was graduated from
high school at Riverside, Illinois, in 1945 and from Valparaiso University
in Indiana in 1950 with a Bachelor of Science degree. During his attendance
at high school and college, he actively participated in baseball and basket
ball and majored in physical education at college. Upon graduation from
college, he procured employment as an instructor in physical education with
the Brookfield, Illinois, Junior High School. On 29 June 1951, he enlisted
in the Air Force as a staff sergeant for three years in order to attend Officer
Candidate School. He successfully completed the school on 20 December 1951
and was honorably discharged for the convenience of the Government. The
following day, he accepted an appointment in the United States Air Force
Reserve in the grade of second lieutenant and was ordered to extended active
duty. On 28 March 1952, he completed a twelve-week Air Police School for

05-11-1955 Memo for Sec of AF-pg2

officers. Lieutenant Schreiber was transferred to the Far East in July 1952 and was assigned to Air Police duties in Korea. The offenses of which he stands convicted were committed in September 1952. However, the accused continued in his assignment as Air Police officer until 1 April 1953, at which time he was assigned to administer the education and training programs for base personnel and for Republic of Korea Air Force officers.

Three effectiveness reports have been rendered on Schreiber, all of which reflect that he is a very fine officer of great value to the Air Force. The last of these reports was executed about three weeks after his trial. The reporting officers uniformly described him as capable, intelligent, conscientious, and cooperative. They report that he exercises sound judgment, willingly accepts responsibility, commands the respect of both airmen and officers and performs his duties in an exemplary manner. In addition, since Schreiber's conviction, several of his superior officers have stated they would be willing to have him assigned to their respective organizations again. In fact, one of these officers stated that Schreiber was number one of all the officers that came under his jurisdiction as Provost Marshal of Far East Air Forces. Schreiber has been awarded the United Nations Service Medal and the Korean Service Medal with two bronze service stars. In addition, he was promoted to first lieutenant in December 1952, but the promotion was revoked a few months later when investigation disclosed his commission of the instant offenses.

3. Although Schreiber has been convicted of murder and conspiring to murder, there are circumstances present which extenuate the seriousness of the offenses. Initially, it should be noted that Schreiber had been commissioned for a period of nine months and was only 25 years of age at the time the offenses were committed. He arrived overseas in a combat area only one month prior to the offense and was immediately charged with the security of an ammunition depot, the preservation of which was vital to the combat operations of the Fifth Air Force. In addition, prior to undertaking this responsibility he was thoroughly briefed by his superiors and advised of the difficulties then being encountered in safeguarding such depots. Within two months prior to Schreiber's arrival, two other ammunition dumps had been blown up. The losses from theft in the one to which accused was assigned averaged $150,000 per month. The authorities suspected that the thefts from and destruction of these depots was due to guerilla action. A doctor testified at trial that although accused's sanity was in no way questioned, he did possess at the time of the offense an underlying severe anxiety state evidenced by excessive worry, constant internal tension, startled reactions and irritability related to his duty assignment. In view of accused's youth, lack of military experience, and the grave responsibility confronting him in a combat area, the existence of such

3

a state of mind at the time of the offense is readily understandable and
appreciated. Under such circumstances, I conclude that the murder committed
was due to the momentary exercise of poor judgment under stress in response
to a sense of duty, however perverted it appears now, and not from malice
toward the victim or for any personal gain. I might add that through Schreiber's
diligent and intelligent attention to duty the average monthly losses at the
depot were reduced to approximately $150.00.

4. Lieutenant Schreiber has been confined at the Branch, United States
Disciplinary Barracks, Camp Cooke, California, since November 1953. Schreiber's
records in confinement disclose that he has been quartered in the honor
barracks and assigned duties as a clerk-typist in the Troop Information
and Education Section and as an instructor in the Academic School. In
these assignments, as in his daily adjustment, Schreiber has been an
outstanding example to custodial personnel and prisoners alike, and has
in many respects facilitated the institutional rehabilitation program by
his actions. His work and evaluation reports have been consistently
outstanding and reflect a desire and effort on his part to do more than
he is asked to do. The Classification Board unanimously recommended
remission of a portion of the confinement and also recommended parole.
In this regard, the Chief Psychiatrist noted that parole would serve no
useful purpose as Schreiber is not considered to be in need of the supervision
or continuing control afforded by this type of release.

Numerous letters, telegrams, petitions and resolutions recommending
clemency have been received and are attached to the record of trial. This
correspondence is representative of people from almost every walk of life,
including veterans, labor groups, public officials, the clergy, and professional associations. A great number of these people based their opinions
on inference and innuendo from newspaper reports which can hardly be described
as entirely accurate. Nevertheless, a substantial number were quite intimately
acquainted with Schreiber and personally knew of his ability as a teacher and
of his participation in civic and religious activities. This correspondence
reflects that Schreiber's offenses are not in keeping with his established
character in the civilian community. Accordingly, these people have expressed
disbelief that Schreiber could have committed the offenses of which he has
been convicted.

5. Lieutenant Schreiber has stated to the Classification Board of the
Disciplinary Barracks that he does not want to be restored to duty and in
view of the nature of his crimes, I am of the opinion that restoration is
not feasible. However, Schreiber has already served one year and eight
months of the approved confinement, and as pointed out above has an outstanding
record in the Disciplinary Barracks and is not in need of further supervision
or custodial control. Accordingly, and in view of the circumstances

4

extenuating the commission of the offenses as discussed above, I am of the opinion that no useful purpose will be served, either for the accused or society, by requiring the accused to serve the balance of the confinement remaining. I recommend that the sentence be approved and ordered executed but that the unserved portion of the sentence relating to confinement be remitted. A form of action designed to carry this recommendation into effect if it meets with your approval is appended hereto.

1 Incl
    Action by S/AF

REGINALD C. HARMON
Major General, USAF
The Judge Advocate General, United States Air Force

05-11-1955 Memo for Sec of AF-pg5

DEPARTMENT OF THE AIR FORCE
WASHINGTON

OFFICE OF THE SECRETARY

MAY 1 1 1955

<u>ACTION</u>

by the

<u>SECRETARY OF THE AIR FORCE</u>

In the foregoing case of Second Lieutenant George C. Schreiber,
AO 2 219 359, Headquarters, 75th Supply Group, the sentence is approved
and will be duly executed but the unexecuted portion thereof relating to
confinement at hard labor is remitted.

(ACM 7761)

05-11-1955 Memo for Sec of AF-pg6

R/T 7761

HQ USAF

COMAFFOUR HAMILTON AFB CALIF

COMAFFIVE MAIN NAGOYA HONSHU JAPAN

FROM AFCJA-21

For Staff Judge Advocate. Second Lieutenant George C. Schreiber, AO 2 219 359, tried by general court-martial convened at APO 970 on 17 August 1953 is subject. Notify all concerned that sentence to be dismissed from the service, to forfeit all pay and allowances and to be confined at hard labor for five years was approved and ordered executed but the unexecuted portion thereof relating to confinement at hard labor was remitted by the Secretary of the Air Force on 11 May 1955. Second Lieutenant Schreiber ceases to be an officer of the United States Air Force at 2400 hours, 18 May 1955. Copy of General Court-Martial Order No. 13 dated 11 May 1955 will be forwarded upon publication. Notify this Headquarters, attention AFCJA, date officer is notified of disposition of case and send copy of this message with signature of officer acknowledging receipt thereof to above address. File ACM 7761)

UNCLASSIFIED   1   1

CAPTAIN DANIEL O'LEARY

AFCJA-21   75801   GORDON B. BERG, Colonel, USAF
                                         Acting Dir of Mil Just, OWJAG

05-11-1955 Memo for Sec of AF-pg7

ACM 7761, Second Lieutenant George C. Schreiber, AO 2219359

The following is a breakdown of correspondence received either by the Secretary of the Air Force or the President of the United States in connection with this case and which is attached to the record of trial for review by the Secretary of the Air Force pursuant to the authority vested in him by the Uniform Code of Military Justice, Article 71:

1. Veterans Groups
   a. Grace Frazier Post #773, the American Legion
   b. Kenneth E. Brady Post #7660, Veterans of Foreign Wars
   c. Brookfield Post #2868, Veterans of Foreign Wars
   d. Ladies Auxiliary of Brookfield Post #2868, Veterans of Foreign Wars
   e. Fifth District, the American Legion, Department of Cook County, Illinois
   f. Edward Feely Post #190, the American Legion, Brookfield, Illinois
   g. Cicero Post #96, the American Legion, Cicero, Illinois

2. Labor Groups
   a. Illinois State Federation of Labor

3. Religious Groups
   a. Pastor of Brookfield, Illinois, Catholic Church

4. Public Officials
   a. Mr. Dan Kulie, President, Village of Brookfield, Illinois
   b. Mr. Frank J. Kessel, President of the Board of Education, District #95, Brookfield, Illinois
   c. Mr. Noble J. Puffer, Superintendent of Schools, Cook County, Illinois
   d. Mr. M. W. Hummel, Brookfield Superintendent of Schools
   e. Town Board, Township of Riverside, Illinois

5. Professional Associations
   a. Brookfield Education Association (teachers)

6. In addition, there are attached to the record of trial numerous letters from individual citizens and a resolution containing the names of hundreds of citizens of Brookfield, Illinois.

All of the correspondents express disbelief that Lieutenant Schreiber could be guilty of the crime of murder and request that he be discharged honorably from the Air Force. They state that such an offense would be entirely out of keeping with his character. These citizens point to accused's excellent record as a teacher in the public schools of Brookfield and attest to the respect and admiration that they had for him. Although some of these people were obviously influenced by newspaper publicity, a great number knew him personally and based their recommendations for clemency on personal knowledge of Schreiber's moral character.

05-11-1955 Memo for Sec of AF-pg8

CHAPTER 30

Toth and the Supreme Court

WHAT HAPPENED TO Robert Toth?

As you know, Toth was the sergeant of the guard at the time of the killing. It was Toth who took the Korean to the bomb dump in the hills. It was Toth who pistol-whipped the Korean into senselessness. Remember, Mullins said that the pistol-whipping was, in his view, unprovoked. Mullins didn't interfere because Toth was his superior. It was Toth who was quoted as suggesting, "Do you want us to take him into the hills like we used to do?"

Toth was charged both as an actor and as a co-conspirator along with Kinder and Schreiber. While he tried to help Schreiber with his favorable testimony at Schreiber's trial, I found him to be somewhat of an overly aggressive person. He had a deep hatred of the Air Force because of the apprehension, his virtual kidnapping from his place of employment in Pittsburgh, and his return to Korea as a military prisoner.

With a six-to-three decision, the United States Supreme Court ruled in favor of Toth. Justice Hugo Lafayette Black wrote the majority opinion. Black said that the Constitution gave Congress the power to make rules and regulations for the land and naval forces. The opinion stated that those rules apply only to people who are in the military forces. Once a serviceman leaves the military and becomes a regular citizen, the military has no jurisdiction over the person, and hence has no power to court-martial him. The case was brought by Toth's sister as writ of habeas corpus and was entitled *Toth v. Quarles, Secretary of The Air Force*, 350 U.S., 11 (1955) 76 S. Ct., 1. The case was argued on February 8-9,1955, and was decided on November 7, 1955.

Justice Black ruled, with the concurrence of Justices Tom C. Clark, William O. Douglas, Felix Frankfurter, John Marshall Harlan II, and Earl Warren. This majority was comprised of several of the greatest justices to ever serve on the court. The dissenting opinion was authored by three of the lesser lights to ever serve on the court, namely Harold Burton, Sherman Minton, and Stanley Forman Reed.

Justice Black, writing for the majority, said that allowing the military to court-martial civilians would deprive them of constitutional rights. Article III of the Constitution creates a judicial system run by independent judges. The Fifth Amendment gives citizens the right to be charged by a grand jury before having to stand trial for a crime. The Sixth Amendment says criminal trials at the election of the defendant must be jury trials so that citizens will be judged by their peers in the community. Military courts-martial do not use independent judges, grand juries, or jury trials. To allow the military to court-martial civilians would deprive them of these rights.

Solicitor General Simon E. Sobeloff argued for the United States Air Force. William A. Kehoe Jr. argued for Toth. The solicitor general argued that the majority opinion would allow military criminals to escape justice. The majority countered this by saying that Congress could enact laws to use civilian courts to try civilians for crimes committed in the military. The military was not allowed to make up for the lack of legislation, enabling such trials by hauling regular citizens into a military court. Apropos of this issue is the issue of the Blackwater cases, which arose in Iraq and in which charges have been dropped. Justice Reed wrote for the dissenters. He felt it was unfair for Toth to escape a trial just because he got out of the Air Force before the killing was discovered. He felt that it was proper to allow the military to try former servicemen for military crimes.

As a practical matter, no one was seriously punished for the killing of Bang Soon Kil. Air Force Secretary Harold Talbott dismissed Schreiber from the service after he had served twenty months of his five-year sentence. Talbott suspended Kinder's dishonorable discharge, and allowed him to return to the Air Force. Toth, who insisted he was not present at the killing, escaped trial altogether.

In fact, in speaking with George, I discovered that he was never really in confinement at Lompoc. He worked in an administrative capacity and was always referred to as Lieutenant Schreiber. He was allowed to wear his uniform and insignia of rank. He was, however, restricted to the base and could not use the officers' club.

The Supreme Court wrote the following words, which in my opinion were right on with reality.

"We find nothing in the history or constitutional treatment of military tribunals which entitles them to rank along with Article III courts as adjudicators of the guilt or innocence of people charged with offenses for which they can be deprived of their life, liberty, or property. Unlike courts, it is the primary business of armies and navies to fight or be ready to fight wars should the occasion arise. But trial of soldiers to maintain discipline is merely incidental to an army's primary fighting function. To the extent that those responsible for performance of this primary function are diverted from it by the necessity of trying cases, the basic fighting purpose of armies is not served. And conceding to military personnel that high degree of honesty and sense of justice which all of them undoubtedly have, it still remains true that military tribunals have not been and probably never can be constituted in such a way that they can have the same kind of qualifications that the Constitution has deemed essential to fair trials of civilians in federal courts. For instance, the Constitution does not provide life tenure for those performing judicial functions in military trials. They are appointed by military commanders and may be removed at will. Nor does the Constitution protect their salaries, as it does judicial salaries. Strides have been made toward making courts-martial less subject to the will of the executive department, which appoints, supervises, and ultimately controls them. But from the very nature of things, courts have more independence in passing on the life and liberty of people than do military tribunals."

Stated another way, the highest court in the land and some of the great justices of the court recognized the evil of command influence in the adjudication of military personnel by military courts. The court refused to allow the enactment of the Uniform Code of Military Justice in 1950 to subject well over three million veterans to the imperfect justice of courts-martial for offenses punishable by as much as five years' imprisonment, as the code provided. Congress had the right to legislate that ex-servicemen, once discharged, could be tried for such offenses by the United States district courts, but Congress declined to do so until 2000. Since then, it has enacted such legislation via the Military Extraterritorial Act of 2000, as amended in 2004, to cover all persons accompanying the military, whether military or civilian personnel.

The court further said, "There are dangers lurking in military trials which were sought to be avoided by the Bill of Rights and Article III of the Constitution. Free countries of the world have tried to restrict military tribunals to the narrowest jurisdiction deemed absolutely essential to maintaining discipline among troops in the active service." The court in its opinion gave a history of the trial by courts-martial of those accompanying the military and of the trial of those discharged from the military. The opinion cited the Declaration of Independence as setting forth as one of the grievances by the signers that the king of Great Britain had deprived the colonists of the benefits of trial by jury in many cases, and that had "affected to render the military independent of and superior to the civil power." Another charge was that the crown had transported colonials "beyond the seas to be tried for pretended offenses."

The Toth decision is a landmark case, and it was cited in an opinion of the United States Court of Claims in the case of *Dumas v. United States*, 620 F. 2d. 247 (Ct. Cl. 1980). This opinion held, "The fundamental necessity for obedience, and the consequent necessity for the imposition of discipline, may render permissible within the military that which would be constitutionally impermissible outside it."

The Toth decision was the seminal case in modern times to define the limits of presidential and military power in the trial of civilians by court-martial. On June 10, 1957, the United States Supreme Court in the cases of *Reid v. Covert*, 354 U.S. 1, reversed its decisions in *Kinsella v. Krueger*, 351 U.S. 470, and *Reid v. Covert*, 351 U.S. 487, and, expanding upon the arguments of the majority in the Toth case, ruled that, "When the United States acts against its citizens abroad, it can do so only in accordance with all the limitations imposed by the Constitution, including Article III, 2, and the Fifth and Sixth Amendments." I believe that the decision in the Reid case is important both to military jurisprudence and constitutional law.

Much has been written about the Guantanamo detainees and the authority of the president as commander in chief of the armed forces to establish military commissions to deal with detainees held by the United States around the world, including at Guantanamo. I would note that Professor Arthur Miller formerly of Harvard Law School submitted a brief in the case of *Hamdan v. Rumsfeld*, 548 U.S. 557 (2006), before the U.S. Supreme Court and cited in his brief the Toth decision as having some authority in limiting the president's power to try the detainees by military commission.

This last issue is and shall be the subject of many present and future writings.

My comment is that the issue of trials by military tribunals is not a new one. However, it is becoming increasingly important as the "War on Terror" continues as an undeclared war under our Constitution. But for the rule of law and the interpretation of the constitutional limitations upon the power of the president as commander in chief of the armed forces, liberty as it now exists in the United States could be eroded in favor of a military dictatorship.

An example of the untrammeled extension of military power is a press statement read by Colonel Morris Davis, USAF, who was in charge of prosecuting Guantanamo detainees. Davis was critical of Justice Stephen Breyer of the U.S. Supreme Court during the arguments of the Hamdan case. Justice Breyer was questioning government counsel as to whether the "Global War on Terror" allowed the president to claim almost unlimited presidential war powers. Colonel Davis said, "Towards the end of the argument, Justice Breyer said, in talking about the current conflict, 'This is not a war, at least not an ordinary war.'"

Justice Breyer noted that the principal charge against the defendants was "conspiracy" and that such an offense was not cognizable under international law. He went on to say, "If the president can do this, well then he can set up commissions to go to Toledo, pick up an alien, and not have any trial at all, except by that special commission."

The military in this country has always been subject to civilian control and has honored the rule of law and the defense of the Constitution. The military has heretofore avoided political controversy. Colonel Davis, initiating an attack on Justice Breyer for his questioning the extension of the military powers of the president, is an example of the military repudiating the rule of law in favor of military control. The arguments of Colonel Davis make a mockery of the Constitutional precept that having the president as the commander in chief of the armed forces was a declaration of the military being subordinate to civilian control. It was never intended by the framers of the Constitution to invest in the president dictatorial powers. President George W. Bush declared himself a wartime president. Under the law authorizing the Uniform Code of Military Justice, the commander in chief is given awesome authority to promulgate the rules of military law as executive orders. All of the Manuals for Courts-Martial are published and have the force of law, by virtue of Congress giving that authority to the president. Without the Supreme Court's limiting that power to members of the land and naval forces, it would not take much in any given instance to establish a military dictatorship in this country. Without the checks and balances of constitutional limits of power and our separate but equal branches of government, it would be easy for the unscrupulous to turn the country into one ruled by military law and the courts-martial.

CHAPTER 31
Defense of Following Orders

"I WAS ONLY following orders"

This was the defense mounted by Thomas Kinder at his trial as advanced by his counsel, Major Charlie Y. Weir. This phrase has been used consistently by those accused of crimes involving violations of the laws of war and in killing innocents. There is an excellent article on this defense to war time crimes in the Duke Journal of Comparative and International Law, James B. Insco, 13 Duke J. Of Comp. & Int'l L. 389.

This defense was raised by numerous Nazis prosecuted for war crimes, by Japanese war criminals, and most recently by Serbs and Croats charged and tried before the International Criminal Tribunal for Yugoslavia. This defense will undoubtedly be raised by some of our troops charged with crimes in Iraq and Afghanistan, if has not already. In the aforementioned article, the author asks whether the United States should allow terrorists tried before military commissions to use the defense of obedience to superior orders to escape conviction and punishment.

The military, and indeed the Supreme Court of the United States in the Toth case, recognized the importance of discipline, which includes unqualified obedience to orders by soldiers in combat situations. Does the law require the soldier to recognize and identify which orders are legal and which are not in the heat and stress of combat? For instance, in the Korean War, the 5th Air Force pilots were ordered to bomb and strafe civilian refugee columns, over their protests. The 8th Army was ordered to shell and machine gun the same refugee columns, thereby killing and maiming innocent men, women, and children alike. No one was charged with a war crime nor punished for this action. The orders were considered legal under the aegis of wartime and combat necessity to prevent infiltrating North Korean troops from entering to the rear of the Allied forces.

To enforce absolute liability for following what is later determined to have been an illegal order ignores the tenet that a successful military is built upon the basis of discipline that requires total and unqualified obedience to orders, without hesitation or doubt.

At odds are the supremacy of the law versus the promotion of good order and discipline.

There are those who would adopt the rule of "Respondeat Superior," that is where the one who gives the order is criminally liable for the acts of the subordinate, who is vindicated by following the illegal order. The issue here is that, if the subordinate knows the order to be illegal, shouldn't that person be equally liable for his known illegal act?

There is also the Manifest Illegality Doctrine. This holds one responsible for the acts committed when the illegality of the orders would be manifestly obvious to anyone possessing average intelligence and understanding. Here, it is doubtful that ignorance of the law would constitute a valid defense. The law presumes that orders are legal and punishes the perpetrator only where the act is obviously illegal.

In the notorious case of Major Henry Wirz, the villain in the book *Andersonville* as commander of the prison camp where over twelve-thousand Union prisoners died of disease and starvation, he asserted a superior orders defense. He was convicted by court-martial and executed. Likewise, when Adolph Eichmann asserted a similar defense to his trial in Israel, he too was convicted and hanged.

Compare the British handbook of the *Law of Land Warfare*, published in 1912, which adopted the belief that obedience to orders was a complete defense. Lassa Oppenheim, a British international law scholar, wrote, "If members of the armed forces commit violations by order of their government, they are not war criminals and cannot be punished by the enemy. . . . In case members of forces commit violations ordered by their commanders, the members cannot be punished, for the commanders are alone responsible."

In 1914, the United States adopted the British rule of a complete defense for the subordinate following orders, deemed illegal, but with the proviso that the commanders giving the illegal orders could be tried and punished by the belligerent into whose hands they may fall. This rule governed our military in both world wars.

When the United States decided to try and punish Axis war criminals, it revised the rule. On November 15, 1944, the rule was revised to say, "However the fact that the acts complained of were done pursuant to the order of a superior or government sanction may be taken into consideration in determining culpability either by way of defense or in mitigation of punishment."

The UCMJ adopted in 1950 and effective May 31, 1951, in the Manual for Courts-Martial states, "The acts of a subordinate, done in good-faith compliance with his supposed duties or orders, are justifiable. This justification does not exist, however, when those acts are manifestly beyond the scope of authority, or the order is such that a man of ordinary sense and understanding would know it to be illegal."

Suppose that Lieutenant Schreiber had given a standing order that anyone found in the bomb dumps at night – if, once challenged, failed to stop and be apprehended – be shot on sight. Is there any doubt that such an order would have been legal and Kinder would have had the obligation to shoot the Korean, Bang Soon Kil? Judge Advocate General of the Air Force Major General Reginald C. Harmon, in his recommendation for clemency to Secretary of the Air Force Harold E. Talbott, which is copied in this book, recommended clemency based upon the combat exigencies in which Schreiber and Kinder acted, as well as Schreiber's overall attitude, both prior to his conviction and after his conviction. I am certain that Kinder's defense, that he was obeying orders, coupled with his promise to assist the prosecution against Schreiber, resulted in the complete remission of his sentence and his restoration to active duty in good standing. Hence the giving of the order was used in both cases as a mitigating circumstance. On Kinder's appeal, the Air Force Board of Review held that his carrying out of the alleged order to kill the Korean was so manifestly illegal that it was no defense.

After several pertinent cases arose during the conflict in Vietnam, the Manual for Courts-Martial was changed to read as follows. "Obedience to Orders. It is a defense to any offense that the accused was acting pursuant to orders unless the accused knew the orders to be unlawful or a person of ordinary sense and understanding would have known the orders to be unlawful."

According to the author of the aforementioned Duke law journal article, there appears to be no satisfactory statement of current international law regarding the defense of superior orders. In 1944, the United Nations War Crimes Commission could not reach an agreement on a satisfactory rule of law on the issue due to the varied practice and laws of its member states.

As the military commissions undertake the trials of the so-called terrorists in U.S. military custody, said to number over fifteen-thousand people, will the military judges permit the defense of superior orders, and follow the UCMJ, under whose jurisdiction the president formed the commissions? That story has not yet been written.

In a combat situation, a standing order to kill the enemy combatants is understood by every soldier. Schreiber's duty station was continually described by the witnesses in his trial as being in a combat situation. Had he given a standing order to shoot first and ask questions afterward, would he have been charged?

CHAPTER 32

The War Within the War

TIGER KIM WAS born as Kim Chong-won. He was born on the same mountain as Kim Jong Il, the North Korean dictator and Soviet puppet ruler. Tiger Kim had a reputation as a brutal and violent man. He was born on Mount Paekkdu, a mountain renowned for its Siberian tigers, wolves, and bears. Tiger Kim served in the Japanese army during World War II. He volunteered for the imperial army in 1940. He served in New Guinea and the Philippines during the war. He liked to be known as the Tiger of Mt. Paekkdu, from whence came his nickname. He was a huge man with much bulk and muscle.

For several months after the end of the war with Japan, he served as the bodyguard for the head of the Seoul Metropolitan Police. He then appeared as a leader in the Korean National Police and later the Korean Army. He was described as "ruthless and effective in the American Army's anti-guerrilla campaign. He refused to take orders from the Americans, who were the occupying power following the surrender of Japan. An American in 1948 termed him a rather huge brute of a man and witnessed him and his men mercilessly beating captured rebels, including women and children. By 1949, he commanded a Korean army regiment.

American Lieutenant Colonel Emmerich, an advisor to the South Korean army, was determined to kill Tiger Kim. Tiger Kim had murdered some of his own officers and men for alleged disobedience. He beheaded many POWs and purported guerrillas. When the international Red Cross protested his killing of POWs, he was relieved of his Army command, but then appointed as deputy provost marshal by South Korean President Syngman Rhee, whom he befriended. He bullied the press and was appointed the ruler of Pusan, Korea's largest port, as the head of the martial law regime in Pusan. He was a trusted confidant of the corrupt Rhee. When the south captured Pyongyang, the North Korean capital, in the early part of the war, Tiger Kim named himself deputy provost marshal general.

Most of the foregoing is from an article by Bruce Cummings for *Japanese Focus*, dated July 23, 2008, and the citations contained therein.

Because of the brutality by Koreans, such as that of the national police against a large segment of the population and the mass murders of so-called leftists, a huge resentment existed against the government of South Korea and its American sponsors. One result was that, while the United Nations forces were at war against the communist forces of North Korea, China, and the Soviet Union, there was also a war with the war. In this war, thousands of South Koreans took up arms as guerrillas fighting the government of South Korea, the regime that was responsible for the murder of their families, including the killing of refugees trying to escape the war zones. None of this information was made known to the American troops serving there during the hostilities, and indeed for decades after the armistice.

Among his many crimes, Tiger Kim was noted for his kidnapping of farmers and city boys alike to serve in his national police force. In addition to ruling the city of Pusan, Tiger Kim ruled the wartime capitol of South Korea, Chinhae, where the 75th Air Depot Wing was headquartered. There was a wire fence surrounding the base from the road that ran by it. Guarding the perimeter was a squad of national police under the command of Tiger Kim. These men were

THE WAR WITHIN THE WAR

mostly ignorant farmers with no real training who were conscripted to that duty. Tiger Kim ran the black market in Pusan and Chinhae, which traded in all kinds of property stolen from the American forces, including vehicles, tires, rims, batteries, spare parts, ammunition, and weapons. On one notable occasion, my colonel called me to his office and told me that we'd had some Jeeps taken from our motor pool. He directed me to seek out the local national police chief to protest and to see if we could retrieve them. I ventured into Chinhae to the police station and was ushered into the chief's office. That is where I met Tiger Kim. He was somewhat fluent in English, but we used an interpreter so there would be no misunderstanding. I was cautioned not to accuse the police of wrongdoing. So I went into some detail as to the problems we were encountering with the theft of our motor vehicles and spare parts, mostly from the motor pool but also some items from our warehouses. He ordered tea for me and for himself, and he listened politely. When I finished my story, he asked a subordinate to come to his office. He requested that the subordinate bring to us the guard who had been on duty the night that the Jeeps were stolen. A man came in with a frightened look on his face and bowed to Tiger Kim. He said nothing. Tiger Kim ordered the man outside into the courtyard of the police station and, without a word being said, he withdrew his pistol and shot the man in the head, killing him instantly. He turned to me and asked if I was satisfied with his efforts to curb the thefts. Bewildered and in a state of shock, I said nothing and left. I reported the incident to the colonel, and nothing more was ever mentioned about it.

We knew that Tiger Kim ran the operation and was responsible for much of our theft problems, but we tried to have as little to do with the Korean police as possible. We would put a place, such as a bar or a brothel in town, off limits to our men and, within a week, new ones would open that were not off limits.

In an article in *Japan Focus* dated July 4, 2008, and written by Charles J. Hanley and Jae Soon Chang, writers for the Associated

Press, they tell of the direct and indirect involvement of the United States in the mass murders that took place in South Korea, with U.S. military officers sometimes present. These massacres have been hidden for over fifty years. As they told it, through the years of right-wing dictatorships, "victims' fearful families kept silent. . . . Reports of the South Korean slaughter were stamped 'secret' and filed away in Washington. Communist accounts were dismissed as lies." In 2007, the Truth and Reconciliation teams began excavating the site of what is said to be one hundred fifty mass graves. A State Department cable cited in their article stated that General MacArthur viewed the executions as a Korean "internal matter," even though he controlled the South Korean military.

CHAPTER 33
South Korea

SOUTH KOREA IN the early 1950s was a far different place than the modern South Korea of today. Korea itself was a divided land then as it is now – divided along the 38th parallel into North Korea and South Korea. North Korea shares borders with China, Manchuria, and Russia. Korea in both parts, north and south, is a peninsula attached to the Asian mainland. South Korea is bordered by North Korea, on the west by the Yellow Sea, on the east by the Sea of Japan, and on the south by the Sea of Japan and the Korean Strait.

In the early 1950s, the country was ill defined and divided politically by a strong communist presence on both sides of the 38th parallel. It had a long history of Russian and Chinese influence when it became a Japanese protectorate in the early part of the 20th century. It remained such until the surrender of Japan to the Allied forces in 1945. In the early 1950s, it was not a priority of American foreign policy to reunite the two Koreas or to fend off Russian and Chinese influence on Korean politics. Rather, American foreign policy had been involved in Europe, such as in Greece in defeating the efforts to establish a communist government in that seminal democracy. The United States was also engaged with the Soviet Union in Germany and other parts of Europe and was using its military and diplomatic energy and resources in the west and not the east. It can be clearly stated that, after cessation of hostilities in World War II, the foreign policy of the United States in Asia was in the firm control of the military and was implemented by one man alone, General of the Armies Douglas MacArthur.

After China fell to the communist insurgency under Mao Tse Tung and the efforts of General George C. Marshall as the post-war secretary of state failed to bring about the Chiang Kai- Shek regime in mainland China, all of the diplomacy of the United States seemed to be directed at saving Western Europe from communist influence.

The Marshall Plan designed to rebuild Western Europe from the destruction of the recent war did not extend to Korea, which had been in the service of the Imperial Japanese forces in World War II. Hence, post-war South Korea was mainly agrarian, with little heavy industry. Korea is a bleak and mountainous country. When I was there during the war, it had mostly unpaved roads and a rudimentary and war-damaged rail system. Being surrounded by water on three sides, the country was ocean-dependent both for much of its food and its imports. Korea had little by way of natural resources or even tillable soil. It possesses a bitter climate as well, with long and bitterly cold winters and very hot and steamy summers. One seems to follow the other with short autumns and springs. General MacArthur's efforts as the de facto ruler of the Japanese government were largely directed at the rebuilding of infrastructure and Japanese industry, while keeping the communists from asserting governmental control to any great degree.

While not totally ignored, it is fair to say that Korea was not on the priority list for U.S. foreign policy or foreign aid in 1950. The United States maintained a small military advisory group in South Korea to help that government rebuild an army and navy. At the same time, a Russian-trained activist in North Korea by the name of Kim Il Sung had taken control of the North Korean government with Russian and Chinese assistance, installed a communist regime, and was determined to unite North Korea and South Korea under his rule. It was under these general circumstances of history that what was then referred to by the American government as a "police action" and which now we refer to as the Korean War began. Almost as many Americans died in Korea as in Vietnam. This little-known war has been called "the Forgotten War." It is a war with little known to the American public of today, having been overshadowed by the Vietnam War and the most recent wars in Iraq and Afghanistan. This bloody war and its participants came as close as ever to igniting a nuclear holocaust between China, the United States, and the Soviet Union. This was due to severe miscalculations on the parts of all involved as to the intentions and the willingness of both China and the United States to commit its military forces on the ground and the Soviet Union to commit its air forces on behalf of its communist allies. (As a footnote to this history, the author spent several years in Russia working with the U.S. Department of Defense and the Russian Ministry of Defense Industries and met numerous Russians who participated in the air battles over the Korean peninsula during the Korean War and served as advisors to the Chinese and North Korean armies.)

The surprise assault by the forces of North Korea was a brilliant military success, and it allowed those forces to take control of almost ninety percent of the South Korean mainland, driving the defenders into what was known as "The Pusan Perimeter." It was against this background that available U.S. land, sea, and air forces were committed to the battle, later to be augmented by other forces supplied by other members of the fledgling United Nations. The UN was allowed to become involved because, during this critical period, the Soviet Union was boycotting the UN Security Council, of which it was a permanent member and over which it could have exercised veto power. After the entry of the U.S. and UN forces, the North Korean Army was driven back close to the Chinese and Manchurian borders. General MacArthur was about to declare victory when China and Russia entered the battle with their own resources. The south was forced to retreat below the 38th parallel, and the ground war was stalemated for the next two years, with the loss of countless lives on all sides.

It was against this background of history that this story unfolded.

EPILOGUE

SEVERAL YEARS AFTER the end of the trial, I was practicing law in Portsmouth, New Hampshire, at 62 Congress Street in a suite that I had built out in 1956. I was establishing a private practice at the time and, out of nowhere, my secretary said there was a man named "Billy" who was asking to see me. To my amazement, it was Major Billy S. Holland. He looked wan and drawn. He told me that he had long wanted to see me to apologize for his conduct both before and during the Schreiber trial. He said he knew Schreiber was innocent, and that he believed Schreiber's story. He said that he did not believe Kinder, and felt that Toth and Kinder set out to cover themselves by implicating Schreiber. He said that he was aware of the pressure that the OSI agents put on certain witnesses, such as Addleman and Penabaker by giving them the Hobson's choice of being charged as defendants or testifying against Schreiber. He went on to say that he believed that his JAG career was at risk if he did not get a conviction and, hence, this led to his no-holds-barred style in the presentation of the case. He told me of his deep belief in God and in the Catholic religion. He explained that all of this had manifested itself in his having nightmares and, eventually, to his having a nervous breakdown. He told me of how he was hospitalized for a period of time because of his feelings after the trial. He told me that it took him several years to accumulate the courage to face me. He wanted to clear his conscience and square things with his God by seeking me out and extending his sincere plea and request for my forgiveness. I didn't know what to say as I listened to a tortured soul beg me to give him solace and peace. I could not, and I did not. He left, first shaking my hand and telling me that George Schreiber was one of the finest people that he ever knew, a person of extreme good conscience, and a practitioner of their mutual religion with all of the belief and ethics that he now possessed. He told me of how he could not reconcile his religious beliefs with what he had done in the Schreiber trial. He said that, until he made his confession to me and, I believe, to Jesse, God would not let him enter his cathedrals in peace. I never knew if he sought out George for his expiation, but I think he must have, as I was a minor player in this theater. I had long since put this case away in my waking memory, or so I thought. If that was true, I would not now be telling this story all of these years later.

Does anyone really expiate such sins by confession? I really don't know that answer. Millions try, but do they ever really succeed, or is there that torment during the waking hours of the night when they cannot sleep and be at peace with themselves?

Just as the publisher was ready to print the galleys of this book, an astonishing thing happened. I received an email from a young lady who lives in Marietta, Georgia by the name of Paula Rotondo. She introduced herself as George Schreiber's granddaughter. She said he died before she was born and so she never knew him. She told me that he died quite young when her mother, Nancy, was 18 years old. I quickly responded to Paula and she sent me a photo of herself and her grandmother. Paula aspires to be a writer and a journalist. In searching the web she came across a news article in the *Portsmouth Herald* Newspaper about the impending publication of this book. I next heard from Paula's mom, Nancy. She wrote about her relations with her father, George Schreiber. The next person whom I had the pleasure of hearing from was George's wife of 26 years, Judy Schreiber. I spoke with Judy in an extended call and learned that George died of lung cancer in 1982, at 55 years of age. He and Judy had a very loving relationship and raised four children, Gary, Sue, Nancy and Gregg. At the time of his death, Gregg was 17, Nancy was 18, Sue was 22 and in her last year of college, and Gary was 23, newly graduated and in his first job. Judy lives in Mount Prospect, Illinois in the same house that George and she occupied during their married years. She has nine grandchildren.

She told me of how she met George. He resumed his career of coaching sports and teaching at the school where he taught in Brookfield, before he enlisted in the Air Force. She was a primary school teacher and their paths crossed. They courted and married.

She told me a little vignette about how she first met George. Her mother was a school secretary at the same school as George and she had gone there to give her mother a ride home. While waiting for her mother, George entered the room where she was waiting; he was dressed in his sweaty gym clothes with a whistle around his neck. He looked at Judy and said, "you look like you could use a little exercise." He convinced her to go home and change and come back to the gym to "exercise." She thought that he was going to have an adult exercise class, but it was only her. They ran up and back on the gym floor shooting hoops for an hour, when he said, "you had better go and take a shower as the American Legion team is coming shortly." She said that she was in the same locker room that she used as a grammar school kid. He gave her a ride home in an old convertible that had a hole in the floorboard, so he very gentleman-like wrapped her legs in a blanket.

George went to work for the Illinois Bell Telephone Company and was a District Manager when he passed on, having worked there for over twenty-five years in Chicago. She didn't meet George until some years after his release and knew only what she learned from her mother and some news articles about his trial. George rarely said anything about his trial. She told me that George was not pardoned by the President, but that his dishonorable discharge was reduced to a dismissal. She said that upon his being released from confinement at Lompoc he was given the opportunity to reenlist in the Air Force with the rank of Sergeant, which he declined to do.

Judy told me of when George returned from Lompoc, before being rehired as a teacher, he had to appear before the Gross School Board of Education to tell his story and answer questions. The Board unanimously reinstated him. At the first PTA meeting of the year, when all the teachers were introduced, all the parents and staff spontaneously arose and applauded as George's name was called. She was so happy for him and joined in the applause.

George was an avid fisherman and would take the family on fishing trips to a place near International Falls, Minnesota; and that her children all liked to fish. Since our contact Judy has made me an honorary member of the Schreib Tribe, an honor which I accept with deep appreciation.

While I was talking to Judy about the injustices which took place in the case of *The United States v. Lieutenant George C. Schreiber*, I was explaining to her some of the events which made the trial a mockery of justice in my opinion. I began to choke up with emotion in recalling to George's wife the sheer injustices to which I bore witness in 1953. After ending our phone conversation it struck me that if nothing else, I could be proud and happy about bringing to his family the true facts about his being charged, tried and convicted, and the ensuing outcries in the press and by those of us who were participants in that case because of the many inequities imposed on a loyal and dedicated teacher and Air Force officer. If nothing else, we all can be proud of George C. Schreiber who led an exemplary life without complaint. He left the complaining to us who still survive and remember. It is with pride that I have told this story.

George's Unit at attention

George in his late 40s

George with Family

Grandkids with Judy

LaVergne, TN USA
23 December 2010

209798LV00008B/7/P